The Ship
of the Line

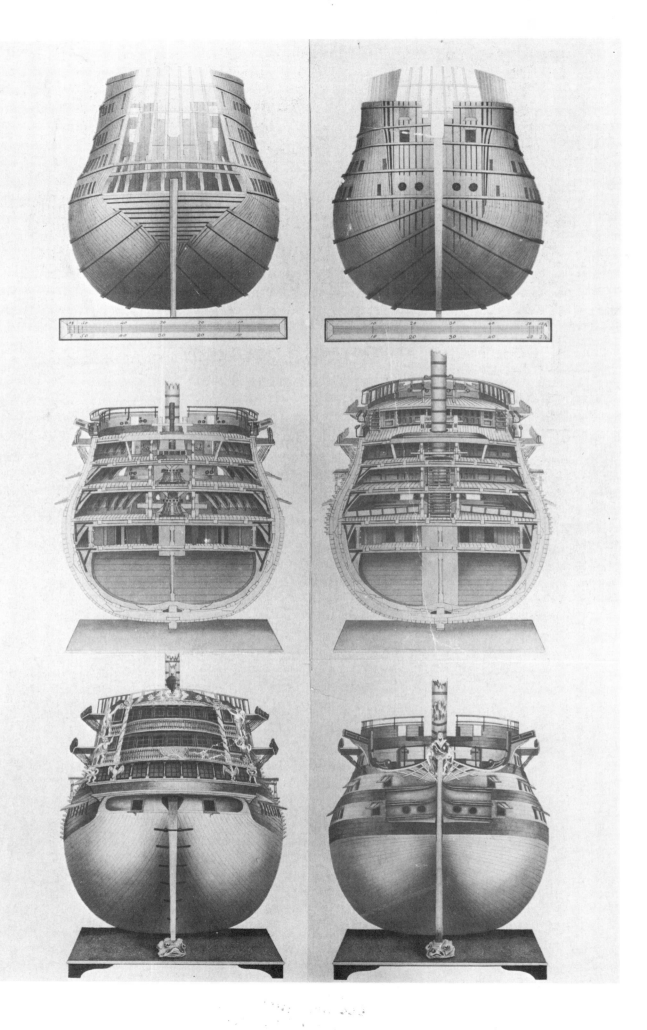

The Ship of the Line

VOLUME II:
Design, construction and fittings

Brian Lavery

With illustrations from the collection of the
National Maritime Museum, Greenwich

NAVAL INSTITUTE PRESS

© Brian Lavery 1984

First published in Great Britain 1984 by
Conway Maritime Press Ltd,
24 Bride Lane, Fleet Street
London EC4Y 8DR

Published and distributed in the United States of
America and Canada by the Naval Institute Press,
Annapolis, Maryland 21402

ISBN 0-87021-953-7

Library of Congress Catalog Card No: 83-43279

This edition is authorized for sale only in the
United States and its territories and possessions,
and Canada

Manufactured in the United Kingdom

Contents

1. Hull Design

THE UNDERWATER HULL OF A SHIP IS BY NECESSITY A VERY complex shape, if it is to combine in suitable fashion the advantages of speed, weatherliness, and stability, to allow for good steering, and to be effective in all likely conditions of wind and weather. Yet the men who designed and built this underwater hull were mostly ill-educated, and often illiterate. In the second half of the seventeenth century it was still possible to find a master shipwright in one of the royal dockyards who was unable to write his name, or to measure a piece of timber properly.[1] Yet he was expected to draw the plans of very large, expensive, and complicated ships, and the evidence is that he did so with a fair degree of success. The working shipwright, who had the job of interpreting the plans and translating them into solid form, was even less likely (until the end of the eighteenth century) to be well educated, and it is not surprising that, throughout the age of the ship of the line, the draught of a ship, though complex as a whole, was based on very simple premises – for the ship designer based his work on two shapes, the straight line and the circle, which are very easy to reproduce. Anyone with two nails and a piece of string can mark out either on a piece of timber.

The medieval shipwright, building only very small ships, had relied on his hand and eye to produce a suitable form, as craftsmen in some primitive cultures still do today. He had used clinker building, and had assembled the planks first and then fitted the internal framing. This had begun to change in the fifteenth century, for larger ships, and the use of carvel instead of clinker building, had demanded that the frame be much stronger, and be built first. With a previously constructed frame it was extremely difficult to make adjustments as construction proceeded so it became necessary to design the frame first on paper, and from approximately this time we can date the first use of ship's draughts. They probably originated in Venice, and eventually reached England via Portugal and Holland.

For centuries the design of a ship was seen as an integral part of her building, and the shipwright who cut out and assembled her timbers was, in theory at least, equally capable of drawing her plan. In Britain there was no serious attempt to separate the craft of shipwright from the profession of naval architect until the nineteenth century, though in practice the division was noted much earlier. In 1664 it was complained that only the most favoured apprentices were trained in the design of ships, and those of the humbler sort could expect to spend their days as, literally, hewers of wood.[2] At the same time, there were many at the top of the profession who did not fully understand the use of draughts, and tended to cling to the older methods of hand and eye. In 1665 the overseer of a ship being built by contract in Bristol apologised for the poor quality of the draughts he was sending to the Navy Board: 'Would have presented it in a better form, but there are no workmen about there who understand the manner of doing it.'[3]

Until at least the 1740s the detailed design of the ship was the prerogative of the master shipwright concerned, whether he was in a royal dockyard or the owner of a merchant yard, whether he was skilled in the modern methods of construction, or rooted in tradition and ignorance. From the 1650s there was an increasing supervision of design by the central administration, and draughts were usually sent to the Admiralty and Navy Board for inspection. In 1716 this was regularised, and an order was issued that when a ship was built or rebuilt 'the master shipwright of the yard where the same is to be performed to transmit to this board not only a draught or model of such a ship, as to their dimensions, but how they propose to finish them, as well inboard as out.'[4] However, the effectiveness of this supervision depended much on the individuals concerned. Dummer, during his period as Surveyor, had carefully examined the draughts of the 1691 programme, and had gone as far as to substitute his own if he thought that those proposed by the master shipwrights were unsuitable;[5] but Dummer was an unusual shipwright, and it is likely that undue interference with the rights of the master shipwrights contributed to the friction which led to his dismissal. Ackworth, on the other hand, was a much more traditional character, and he actually complained about being given the job of supervising design, and resented the amount of work involved.[6]

In view of all this, the drawing of a ship's draught was a relatively simple process by the standards of modern design. The first task was to draw the line of the keel, 'the only line whereon all the rest depend.'[7] The depth of the keel was then drawn, and the draughtsman proceeded to the stern- and stemposts. The sternpost was relatively simple, being a straight piece of wood on which the rudder was hung. English shipwrights tended to favour an angle of around ten degrees for the sternpost, whereas those of France preferred it to be more upright. The stem was more complex, and the principles guiding its design changed more through the years. The shape of the bow, as shown on the profile plan, was usually circular, though ellipses were occasionally used. In early times the stem had a great rake, sometimes half the length of the keel, but this was unsuitable for a ship intended to carry a full deck of guns, and it soon began to be reduced.

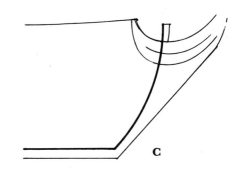

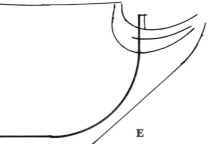

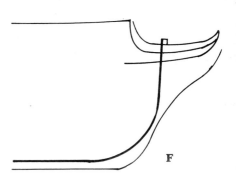

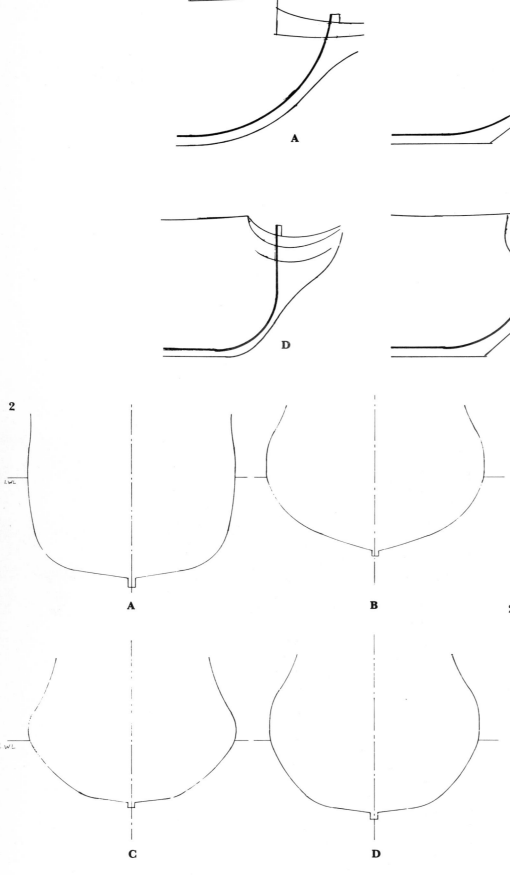

1 VARIATIONS IN THE RAKE OF THE STEM

A. About 1625: the diameter of the sweep is greater than the rake, so that it continues to be angled forward at its end.

B. 1670, Deane's *Doctrine*: the diameter of the sweep is equal to the rake.

C. Keltridge, 1685: large diameter sweep, no longer tangential to the keel.

D. 1677, short rake: the sweep is of small diameter, and is continued upwards by a straight line.

E. Early eighteenth century: rake has increased again, and is somewhat greater than in the late seventeenth century.

F. Late eighteenth century: rake has increased again, and is similar to that of 1677, except that the straight portion is angled slightly forward.

2 TYPES OF MIDSHIP SECTION

A. Square – typical large merchant ship.

B. Wedge-shaped – as used by Symonds.

C. Hexagonal – typical of fast French ships.

D. Rounded – typical British ship of the line.

In the 1620s the fore rake was about one-third of the length of the keel, and equal to the breadth. By Deane's time in 1670, it had been reduced to three-quarters of the breadth, and less than a quarter of the keel length. It was drawn as a circle, tangential to the keel, and, in the case of Deane's design, vertical at its upper end, level with the upper gun deck; but this soon began to change, for during the 1677 programme it was recognised that the rake had to be still further reduced, or, to put it more aptly, the keel had to be made longer in proportion to the total length of the ship. From this point the gun deck length was taken as the standard for measurement, and shipbuilders were sometimes given permission to vary the length of the keel above a certain minimum, if they thought it would contribute to the sailing qualities of the ship.[8] The shape of the bow remained circular, but it was no longer tangential to the keel, perpendicular at its upper end, and taking up the whole shape of the bow. In the Keltridge draughts of 1684 the line of the bow rises sharply out of the keel. In other ships the circle was of much smaller diameter, and carried to its full height by a straight line. In some, several circles were used to make up the full shape. The rake of the bow tended to increase again in the first half of the eighteenth century, and was reduced in the second half.

Appended to the bow were the knee and its head, and various other fittings, but these had more to do with the structure and decoration of a ship than with its hull lines. The shipwright would next go on to completing the profile plan, marking in the wales, gunports, decks, and top of the sides. The main change in these features over the years was in the reduction of sheer. In the seventeenth century the decks of most ships curved sharply upwards towards the bow and the stern, partly to allow the water to drain away towards the midships, but largely because this arrangement created a high and imposing stern. By nature the wales had even more sheer than the decks, for it was intended that they should cross from one deck to another, thus giving some form of diagonal bracing before Seppings' time. The war of 1689-97 showed the faults of such great sheer, and there was a gradual process of reducing it, until it was almost abolished in the early years of the nineteenth century.

Having completed his profile plan, the shipwright now went on to the more complex task of drawing the underwater lines of the ship. First he had to choose his midship section. In the abstract there were many possibilities here: several basic forms were possible, and within these there was an infinite number of variations; but in practice he was limited, by experience and the nature of his tools and materials, to four basic shapes. A completely rectangular section was ruled out by the difficulty of finding suitably shaped wood for the internal structure, and the impossibility of planking it; but something approaching a rectangle was used for most merchant ships of the seventeenth century, though the corners were rounded. This had the advantage of allowing a large displacement on a relatively small hull, and was essentially stable, but it tended to produce a slow ship. It was occasionally used for ships of the line, as with the *Courageux* and *Plantagenet* in the 1790s,[9] and of course with the ships taken over from the East India Company at the same time, but in general it was considered

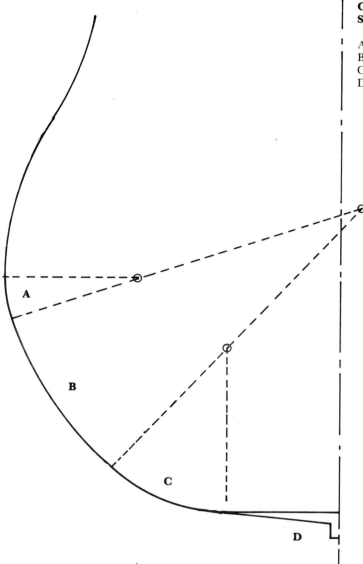

CURVES IN A MIDSHIP SECTION

A. Breadth sweep
B. Reconciling sweep
C. Floor sweep
D. Floor deadrise

suitable only for sluggish merchant ships. At the other extreme was the wedge-shaped section, as favoured by Symonds in the 1830s. This moved easily through the water, and its relatively flat sides produced a resistance against lateral movement, so that it was suitable for fast and weatherly ships. Unfortunately it was basically unstable, producing deep and rapid rolling and hence was unsuitable for a ship intended to carry a heavy gun armament. It was successful with yachts and despatch boats, but Symonds' attempt to extend it throughout the navy was ultimately a failure.

Between these two extremes, there were two possible compromises. One, much favoured by eighteenth century French designers, was the double-bilged type, roughly hexagonal in shape. This too had relatively flat sides, which tended towards weatherliness. It produced a lower centre of gravity than the wedge, and so was more stable, but allowed for finer lines than the square section, and so was faster. However, it was used in Britain only in direct imitations of French design, and usually in frigates and sloops rather than ships of the line, for the sharp curves demanded peculiar shapes of timber, and so it was an expensive form of construction. The French ships most copied in Britain, the *Invincible* and the *Courageux*, had it in a less than extreme form.

The British battleship designer, then, tended to favour the second compromise: a midship section which, at first sight, appears to be almost round, but in fact was made up of three curves and one or two straight lines, as were most midship sections during the age of sail. At the bottom of the section was a relatively flat part, known as the floor. In the earlier days it was often literally flat, but by the second half of the seventeenth century it tended to rise at an angle of four or five degrees, and to be joined to the keel by a slight curve known as the deadrise curve. Typically, a ship of the line had a floor of about a third of the total breadth, whereas merchant ships had more, and smaller, faster ships had less. Tangential to the floor was a curve known as the floor sweep, and another curve, the breadth sweep, passed through the point of maximum breadth. These two curves were joined by another of rather greater diameter, known

as the reconciling sweep, which was tangential to both. Above the waterline was another series of curves, which will be discussed later. The term 'midship section' was in itself a misnomer, for it was usually situated, not in the middle of the ship, but slightly forward. It represented the section of the hull with the greatest breadth and area.

Now the rest of the underwater hull had to be drawn, based on the midship section and the rakes of bow and stern. In the early days, the process was simple. The shape of the midship section was simply repeated along the length of the ship, being moved upwards and inwards towards the bow and stern, and joined to the keel where necessary with a straight line or reverse curve, known as the deadrising. This system was called whole moulding, presumably because the same mould, or template, could be used for every frame in the ship. On the draught, only two lines were needed to show the basic form of the hull. One was the rising line, shown on the profile, or sheer plan. At the

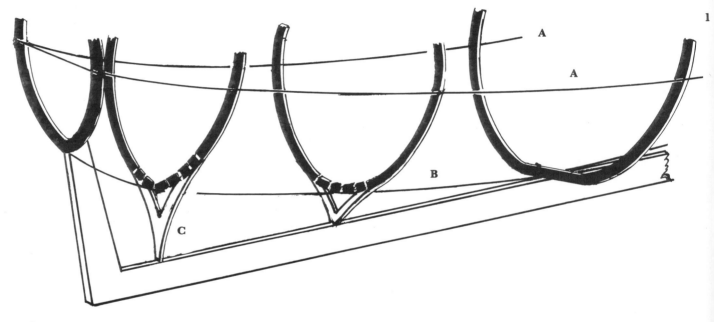

1 WHOLE MOULDING

The solid black parts are the midship section, as repeated throughout the length. The white parts are the deadrising, which joins the moulded section to the keel in each individual frame.
A. Narrowing lines
B. Rising line
C. Deadrising

TWO VERSIONS OF WHOLE MOULDING

2 From a Spanish book first published in 1587. Note the enormous sheer, caused by the need to keep the maximum breadth parallel to the rising line of the floor.

3 As used for a boat in the late eighteenth century.
The Science Museum

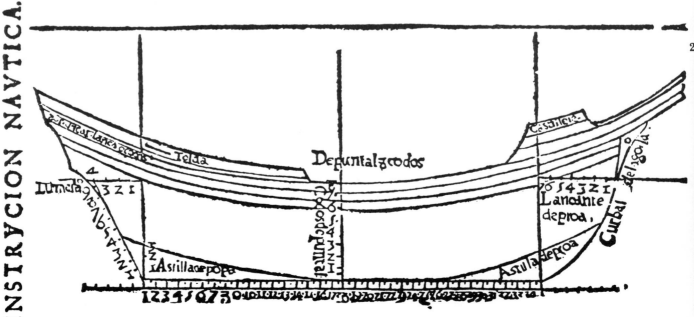

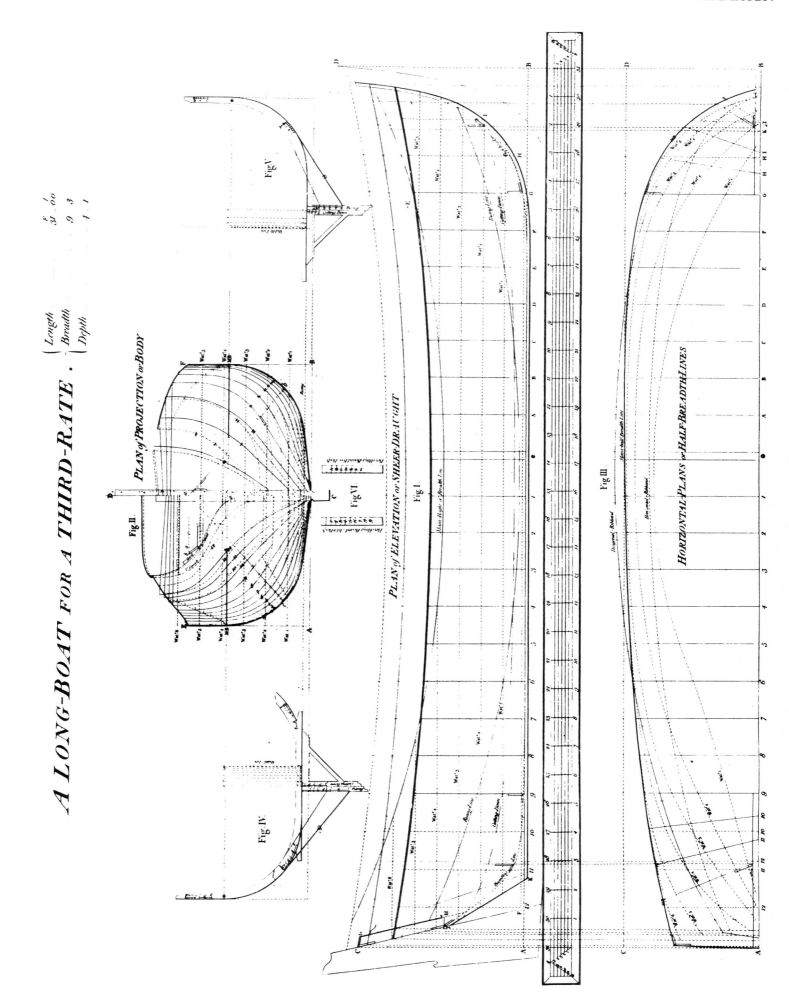

A LONG-BOAT FOR A THIRD-RATE.

Length — — — F. 1
Breadth — — 9 3
Depth — — 1 1

PLAN of PROJECTION or BODY

Fig.II.

Fig.VI.

Fig.V.

Fig.IV.

PLAN of ELEVATION or SHEER-DRAUGHT

Fig.I.

FigIII.

HORIZONTAL PLANS or HALF-BREADTH LINES

The Matthew Baker draught: the rising line of floor and the narrowing line of maximum breadth can be clearly seen, as can the narrowing line of floor for the forward part. The rising line of breadth is not shown.
The Science Museum

midships it was on, or close to, the top of the keel, and it rose in a regular curve towards the bow and stern. It represented the line of the floor, which was a purely theoretical concept except in midships, for towards the ends the shape of the lower part of the timbers was actually formed by the deadrise. Nevertheless it was essential, for it showed the designer where to position his moulds. The second curve, the line of maximum breadth, was shown in the plan view. This gave the second co-ordinate for the position of each mould on the frame. This line, as its name suggests, represented a series of real points along the side of the ship.

Whole moulding was to survive into the nineteenth century for small boat design, but for large ships it was already obsolete well before the period of the ship of the line, though it was to have some residual influence on the method of drawing ships' lines throughout the age of sail. It had several grave disadvantages. Firstly, it gave very little guidance on the complex shapes of the bow and stern, and these still had to be interpreted by the builder. Secondly, it tended to produce local 'bumps' along the hull, especially towards the ends of the ship. Thirdly, it was unsuitable for the heavy gun armaments coming into use in the sixteenth century. To give a reasonably sharp entry and run, it was necessary that the rising line should curve up rather steeply. The line of maximum breadth would rise in direct relation to this. It would be impossible to use a deck with as much sheer as the rising line, and so the deck often had to be broken, and raised at the bow and stern. This provided a practical solution throughout the sixteenth century.

It is clear that by the time of the Armada campaign this system had been superseded. In the new system the three sweeps, floor, reconciling and breadth, still retained the same diameter along the length of the ship, but the relationship between them varied. Instead of relying solely on the rising line of the floor, the height of the maximum breadth was now fixed by its own rising line, independent of the floor, and much flatter, so that the maximum breadth was kept much lower. Similarly the floor was given its own guiding line on the plan view, the 'narrowing line' of the floor. The consequences were twofold: ships were made much more suitable for a heavy gun armament, and the shipwright was given much more flexibility in the design of his ship, for the shape of the hull above water no longer depended so closely on the underwater lines. It is impossible to date precisely the beginning of this new system in England. It was clearly in use by the time of the Matthew Baker draughts of 1586, and there we are told of a 'new rule' recently introduced.[10] Probably it began with Hawkins' naval reforms on the eve of the Armada campaign.

Nevertheless this system too had its disadvantages. It offered no answer to the problem of shaping the bow and the stern, and it could still produce a poorly faired hull. In practice a shipwright would probably fair the hull after the construction of the frame, by fixing battens to it and trimming off any bumps; but this was a haphazard method, and increasingly risky as ships became larger. Furthermore, the constant diameters of the breadth sweeps could cause problems, especially towards the ends of the ship. There was less difficulty at the bow, which was expected to be relatively full, but it had long been recognised that the underwater hull must taper almost to nothing at the stern,

or the rudder would be ineffective. If the reconciling sweep was to meet the large breadth sweep, then the maximum breadth towards the stern would have to be kept small. This helps to explain why the ships of the early seventeenth century had such narrow sterns, and why heavy broadside guns were rarely mounted on the aftermost extremities. The obvious answer was to reduce the diameter of the breadth sweeps towards the stern. Again it is difficult to find a precise date for the introduction of the new system. The first indisputable evidence of its use is in Deane's *Doctrine of Naval Architecture* of 1670, but the sterns of large ships began to become wider in the 1640s, and it soon became common to carry heavy guns right up to the extremities.

A further refinement is to be seen in Deane's *Doctrine*. In his completed draught of a Third Rate the floor sweeps, as well as the breadth sweeps, can be seen to vary, though to a lesser extent. The text of the *Doctrine* gives us no clue as to how or why this was done – indeed it implies that both the breadth sweeps and floor sweeps should remain constant throughout the length of the ship – but perhaps the answer is to be found in the use of waterlines. These are not shown in any of Deane's draughts, but in the text he suggests drawing waterlines at 15-feet intervals, with a view to 'finding those lines to go fair, making neither swell nor cling'.[11] This was an important step, for the use of waterlines allowed the designer to fair the hull on paper rather than after construction, and to consider the shape of the ship, not merely as an abstract geometrical solid, but as something which was intended for moving through the water. It might be necessary to vary the sweeps to help with the fairing.

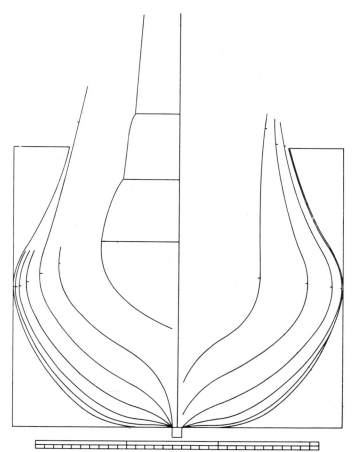

An early seventeenth century body plan, showing the narrow stern produced by the second version of whole moulding. *By courtesy of the Society for Nautical Research*

Yet again we are faced with identifying the date and source of the changes, and again we are forced to speculate. We know that Peter Pett produced unusually fair lines for the *Constant Warwick* and the other early frigates, and that Deane, despite his professional rivalry, was in many ways influenced by his early training under the Pett family. Moreover, we know that Pett based his designs on captured Dunkirk frigates. Waterlines would obviously be of some use to him in taking off the lines from the ship he intended to copy, and this may have helped inspire the new system. In any case, the use of waterlines became common in the years after Deane wrote his *Doctrine*. A draught of a Sixth Rate of around the same time shows them actually drawn, and the Keltridge draughts of 1684 also have them. In future years diagonal and vertical fairing lines were to join the horizontal ones, and the shape of the hull was to be fully faired before construction began.

Throughout the seventeenth century there was controversy among shipwrights about the best form for the rising and narrowing lines, and particularly about the rising line of the floor. An anonymous shipwright of the early part of the century favoured an ellipse, drawn by a mathematical method using trigonometry.[12] Pett, a few

years later, preferred to keep his methods secret. Deane was probably unusual in favouring a circle for all his rising and narrowing lines, and he castigated those who disagreed with him, 'having myself tried both elliptical and diminishing'. He refers, rather mysteriously, to those who 'will say they can make a ship's body fuller or leaner, good or bad, without the rising line'. He considered that, if their advice were taken, 'then the King may have his ships want quality as these pretenders do sound judgement'.[13] Other shipwrights appear to have simply used a fair and regular line, drawn according to their experiences or prejudices, and this seems to have been the most common method in the early eighteenth century.

The system of drawing the underwater lines of a ship had made many rapid advances in the century between 1580 and 1680, but there were many who were still not satisfied. For all the changes, shipwrights were still a closed and secretive group, with notable exceptions like Anthony Deane. Phineas Pett had attempted to conceal the rising and narrowing lines of the *Sovereign of the Seas* from the view of anyone but the King.[14] His son Peter had caused laughter at the inquiry into the Medway disaster by claiming that it was better that the Dutch should capture the actual ships than his models, as the latter would reveal the secrets of his design.[15] Despite progress the ship designer still had one foot in the world of medieval craftmanship. He relied on the elementary shapes of the straight line and circle, and the proportions of his ships were decided from his own experiences, or prejudices. He might have learned his trade fifty years before, and have seen little reason to change his ideas since.

In opposition to this breed of shipwright was a new scientific school, led by Pepys himself. The Secretary of the Admiralty was also a Fellow of the Royal Society, and its president from 1684, and this brought him into contact with the leading scientific minds of his time, from Isaac Newton downwards. In an age of scientific revolution, and with an energetic administration at the Admiralty, it would have been surprising had much attention not been devoted to new methods for the design of ships. Sir William Petty, perhaps the founder of the science of statistics, engaged in discussions with Pepys and Deane, tried to work out a system of naval architecture from first principles, and devoted much of his energy to a proposal for a 'double bottomed' or twin-hulled vessel.[16] Sir Henry Sheeres, the greatest English engineer of his day, and the builder of the great mole at Tangier, conducted rather crude test tank experiments, and proved, not surprisingly, that a Mediterranean galley had the fastest hull form, that an 'English sharp frigate' was faster than a 'full bodied English ship', and that all were faster than a Dutch merchant ship.[17] Pepys asked his expert advice on 'whether there are no considerable deficiencies in the doctrine and practice of shipbuilding remaining yet to be supplied.'[18]

Practical shipwrights were sometimes involved in this scientific enquiry. Edward Dummer, when Assistant Surveyor of the Navy, suggested a refinement of Sheeres' experiments, by making models of all known ship types and testing them.[19] Deane, a Fellow of the Royal Society, was involved in scientific discussions at all levels. Pepys gave him credit for the most important of all the improvements

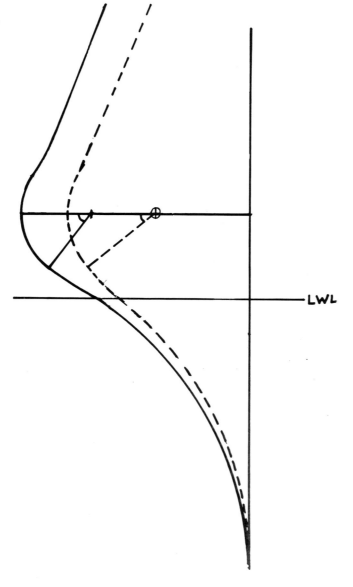

Section near stern, showing the effect of the reduction of breadth sweeps. The dotted line shows the old system, with constant breadth sweeps throughout the length. The relatively large breadth sweep, and the need to keep the underwater hull narrow, causes a narrow maximum breadth above the waterline. The solid line shows the later system. The smaller breadth sweep makes a larger maximum breadth possible, without a corresponding increase in underwater breadth.

LWL

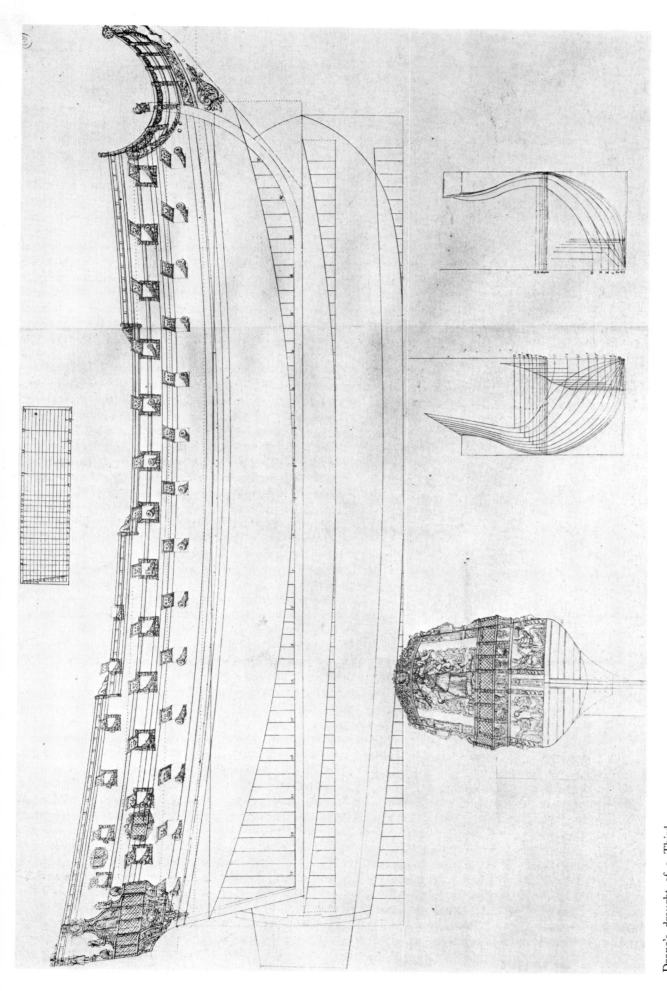

Deane's draught of a Third
Rate, 1670.
The Science Museum

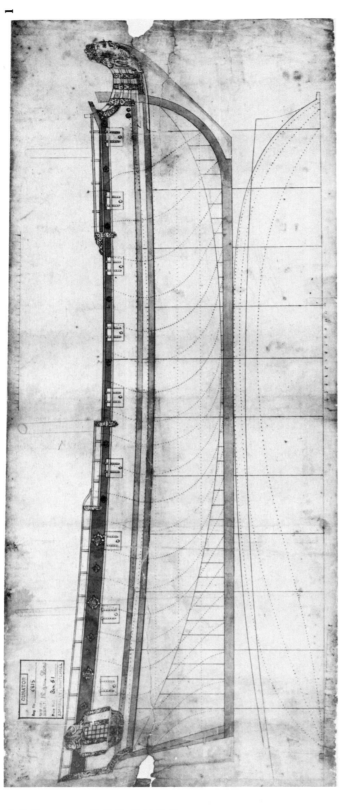

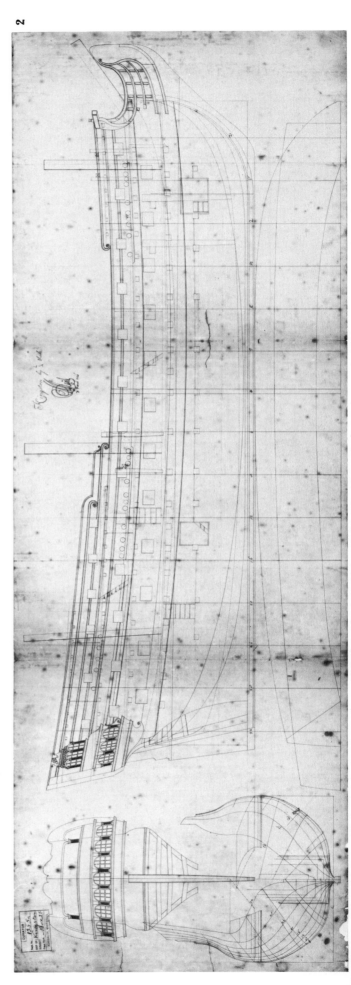

1 The draught of a Sixth Rate, c1670, possibly the earliest example of the use of waterlines for fairing. *National Maritime Museum*

2 A typical early eighteenth century draught: note the large fore rake as compared with the later seventeenth century, the constant diameters of the floor sweeps, and the great reduction of the breadth sweeps in the after body. *National Maritime Museum*

of this period, the method of calculating the displacement of a ship before she was launched. Though it seems unlikely that Deane himself was responsible for this invention, it was certainly a great advance, and the first scientific innovation of real value.[20]

Mathematicians and pure scientists also took part. John Wallis, professor of geometry at Oxford, co-operated with Phineas Pett jnr in attempting to find a mathematical formula for the complex shape of the underwater stern.[21] Newton himself attempted to find the 'solid of least resistance', and this had much influence on Sutherland, one of the most important writers on naval architecture of the early eighteenth century.[22]

Yet in the medium term this had virtually no effect. The average shipbuilder would have been far too ignorant to understand a mathematical formula, and the solid of least resistance, while it might have been useful in occasional circumstances, took no account of the lateral forces imposed on a ship by wind and water. Abstract experiment could not comprehend all the factors involved, and ship design remained rooted in the builder's experience. A ship of the line was too large and expensive an object for rash experimentation, and the scientific theories remained on paper. By the end of the century, men less imaginative than Pepys, Deane and Charles II were in control of naval affairs, and the weak link between the scientist and the ship designer was broken.

The failure of the scientific experiment, and the new age of conservatism in the eighteenth century, restored the shipwright to his old place in society. Men like Pett and Deane had had direct access to kings, had enjoyed international reputations, and moved in the highest levels of society; their successors in the eighteenth century were reduced to the role of the humble artisan, 'judged at once to be social inferiors and experts'.[23] From 1706 they were bound by the establishments, and while it is true that the shipwrights had a considerable role in forming the establishments, they were not the sole voice, for they could often be dominated by their superiors, as by Churchill in 1706, or the Norris Committee in 1745 (see Volume I). Moreover, once the dimensions were fixed, the role of the individual master shipwright was almost a menial one. Faith was placed in proportions as the key to a good ship;

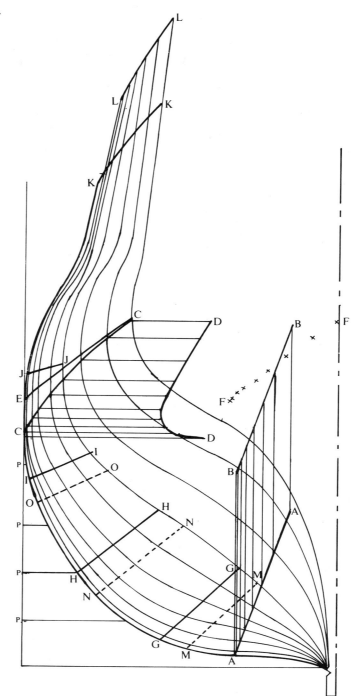

LINES ON A TYPICAL DRAUGHT OF THE EARLY EIGHTEENTH CENTURY

AA. Floor line: represented by the narrowing of floors line on the horizontal plan, and the rising line of floors on the sheer.
BB. Centres of floor sweeps: parallel to the floor line, since the floor sweeps are of equal diameter.
CC. Line of maximum breadth (lower).
DD. Centres of lower breadth sweeps.
EC. Line of maximum breadth (upper).
FF. Centres of upper breadth sweeps (marked by X): the sweeps are of constant diameter.
GG. Floor head: purely structural, like HH, II and JJ, showing the limits of the floor timbers in the framing of the ship.
HH. First futtock head: showing the limits of the first futtocks on the structure.

II, JJ. Second and third futtock heads.
KK. Toptimber line: showing the limits of the main structure. Above this the framing was of lighter construction.
LL. Topside: the final limit of the height of the structure.
MM. Diagonal of floor ribband: the position of this was marked on each individual frame, and known as the surmark (or sirmark). To these were attached a ribband, along the length of the hull, which was used for fairing. The line was also drawn on the horizontal plan, similarly for fairing. In later years it was to be used as the basis for drawing the floor sweeps
NN. Diagonal of the first futtock ribband: served a similar function to the floor ribband.
OO. Diagonal of second futtock.
P. Waterlines: often drawn across the lines plan, but here left to one side to avoid confusion. Sometimes drawn on the horizontal plan, to help with fairing.

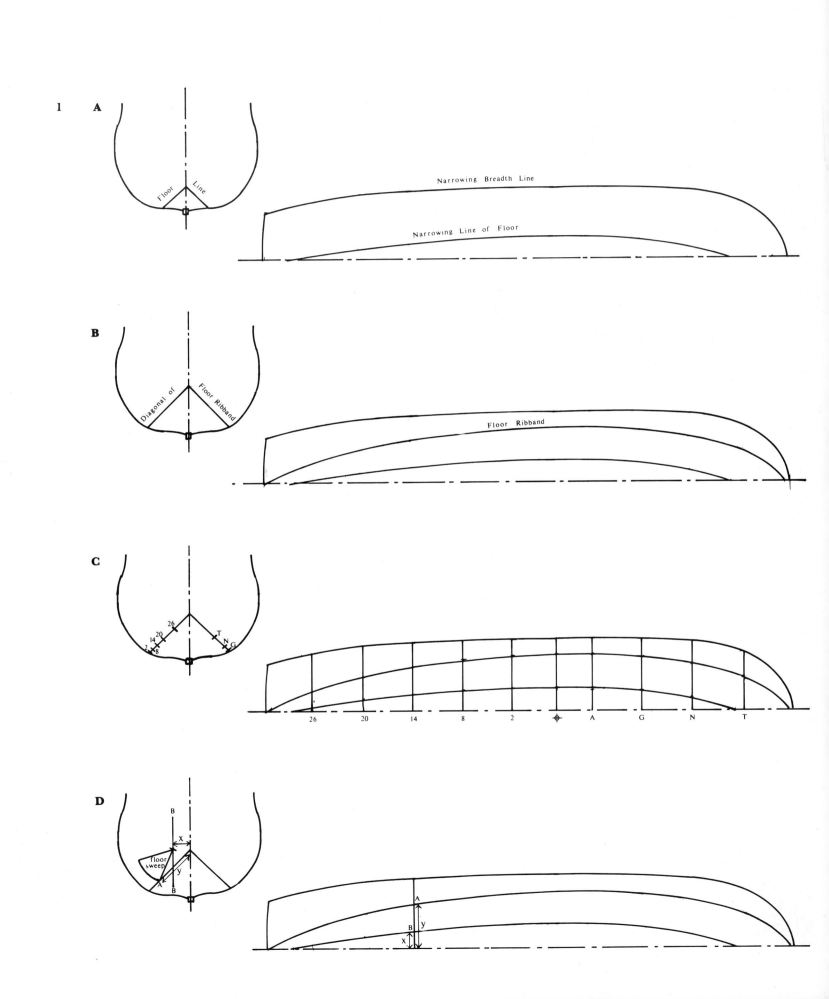

the actual drawing of the lines was secondary, and the designer merely had to ensure that 'the bodies were shaped to lines of as little resistance as is consistent with the nature of the service expected'.[24] Preparing the lines remained the prerogative of the master shipwright – but just as one would give measurements to a tailor and expect him to produce a suitable costume without further interference, and a master shipwright was in a similar social position.

Certainly there was some improvement in the actual drawing of draughts in the early eighteenth century. The crudities of seventeenth century drawing were abolished, and draughts were executed neatly and efficiently. From 1716 the system of central supervision was regularised, and the basis was laid for the Admiralty collection, which allows us to study ship design more systematically than in any previous period; but design in itself, as practiced in the first half of the eighteenth century, was unoriginal, if not reactionary. There was some increase in the use of fairing lines, and the breadth sweeps continued to be reduced towards the ends of the ship, especially towards the stern; but the floor sweeps, forming the main basis of the underwater lines, continued to be of fixed length. 'It is usual for all the floor sweeps to be of one radius,'[25] it was written in 1750. The body plan had become increasingly complex,

1 DEVELOPMENT OF THE METHOD OF DRAUGHTING THE LOWER HULL

A. The old system, using the narrowing lines of floor and breadth.
B. Diagonal of floor ribband added.
C. Frame stations marked on the horizontal plan, and transferred to the diagonal line of floor on the body plan.
D. Drawing the floor sweep for one frame. The point where it crosses the diagonal can be found from the horizontal plan (y) as can the distance of the centre of the floor sweep (B) from the middle line (x). The length of the floor sweep is fixed. Its centre on this frame can be found by drawing a circle of diameter equal to the floor sweep, centred on point A, and finding where it crosses the line BB.

2 The draught of the *Bellona* class, 1757: a typical Slade design, in that the floor sweeps are reduced in diameter towards the bow and stern, and the rising line is a curve rather than a straight line in the body plan. This suggests the use of the diagonal of floor ribbands system. *National Maritime Museum*

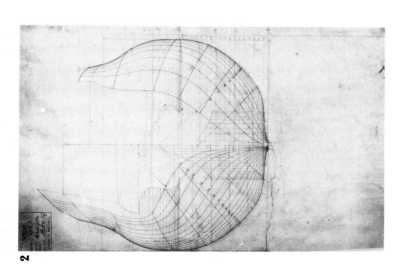

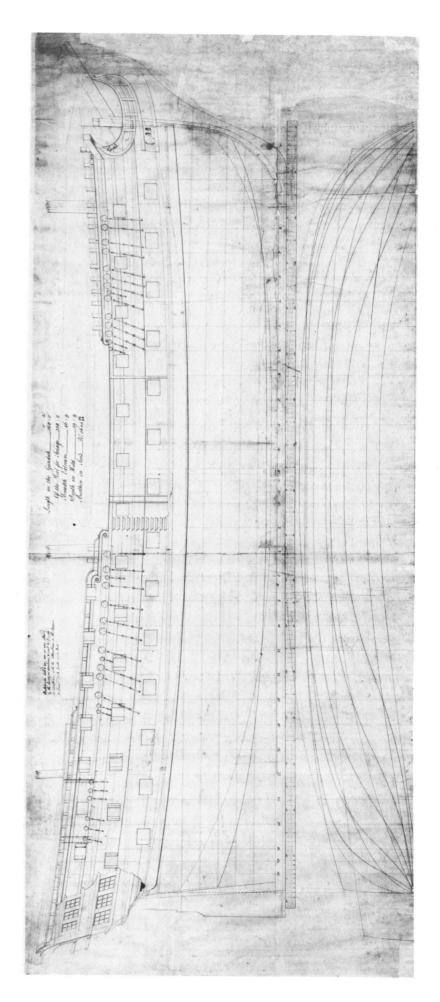

but in principle little had changed since the mid-seventeenth century.

Moreover, the rising and narrowing lines of the floor, which guided the floor sweeps and therefore were crucial to the underwater form of the hull, were a poor basis on which to design a ship. They were purely theoretical lines, and only in the extreme midships did they coincide with the shape of the hull. They were of no use at all in the fairing of the ship, and indeed if they were not very well placed they could sometimes inhibit it. Most draughts of this period show the rising line on the body plan as a diagonal, with another diagonal parallel to it, representing the centres of the floor sweeps. This system produced a very stereotyped hull form, little advanced from that of a century earlier.

Around 1750 there are signs of a move to abandon the old rising line. Murray's treatise of 1750 mentions that instead of the rising line 'some make use of a diagonal in the body plane, to limit the half breadth of the floor in every rising line.'[26] Thus the designer would begin the underwater lines with a new diagonal, above and outboard of the old rising line on the body plan. It would also be represented in the horizontal plane by a line outboard of the rising line, but roughly equidistant from it, and continuing to the ends of the ship. Both these lines were arbitrary. What they represented, in their separate planes, was a line which would pass through some point on the floor sweeps throughout most of the length of the ship. The lines representing the positions of the timbers had already been drawn on the horizontal plan, and from these could be found an exact position on the body plan, through which the floor sweep would pass. From the narrowing line of the floor could be found the distance of the centre of the floor sweep from the centreline, and in most cases the diameter of the floor sweep was already determined from the midship section. Therefore it was possible to draw the floor sweep on each individual frame.

The new line, known as the diagonal of the floor ribband, can be seen clearly on some of Slade's draughts of the 1750s, for example the *Bellona*. Apart from making for better fairing, it allowed more flexibility in forming the hull, and the line of the centres of the floor sweeps in the body plan was now curved upwards, causing the hull to be slightly

THE CENTRES OF FLOOR SWEEP LINE

The top drawing shows the earlier convention, and the other the system applied after about 1765.
1. The rising height of breadth line.
2. The narrowing breadth of floors line.
3. The constructional line of stemson-kelson-sternson.
4. The rising of floors line.
5. The conventional position of the rising line of the centre of floor sweeps.
6. The position that the rising line should actually occupy.
7. Line of the centres of the floor sweeps.

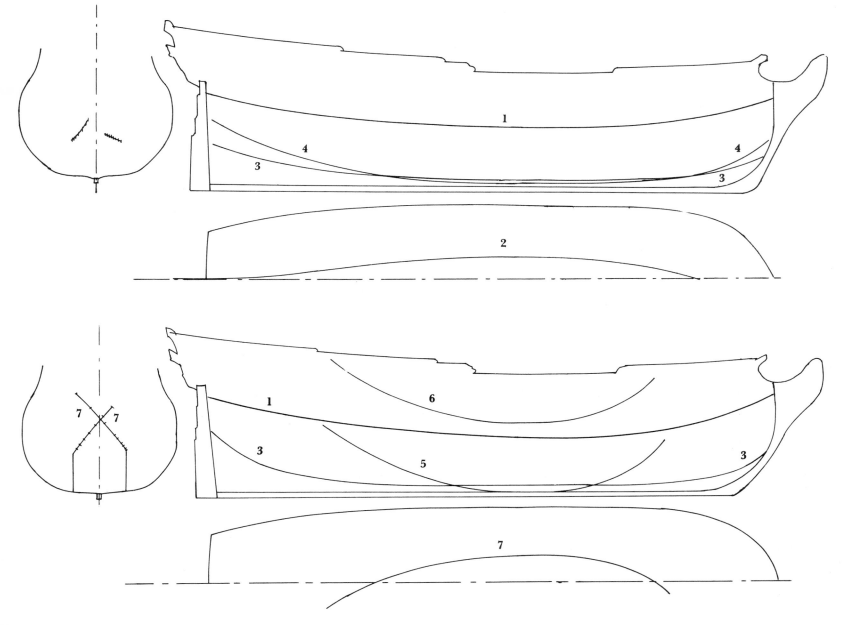

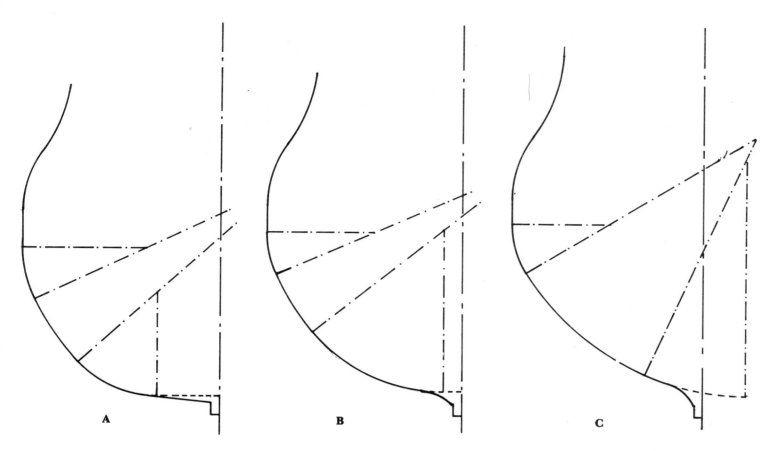

USE OF THE CENTRES OF FLOOR SWEEPS

A. Midship section, virtually the same as in the old system.
B. Several stations aft of midships, the floor sweep has greatly increased in diameter and makes up most of the underwater shape of the frame.
C. The last station to use the centres of floor sweeps: the centre has now moved across the middle line of the ship, but the floor sweep is still 'real', and forms part of the shape of the frame. There is still only a small amount of deadrise.

sharper. This probably goes some way towards explaining the success of Slade's designs.

Yet ship design had not completely broken from the old system of whole moulding, for the theoretical concept of the floor still remained the basis of the underwater shape, and it was still normal to have constant floor sweeps throughout the length. Nevertheless, the diagonal of the floor ribband provided a lead into further development, for it was possible to eliminate the old form of rising line altogether, and move straight onto the centres of the floor sweeps, instead of their bases on the floor. Around 1765 a new line, known as the centres of the floor sweeps, begins to appear on draughts. It is rather confusing in some ways, because it took over the position formerly occupied by the rising line of the floors, though it should actually have been several feet higher, 'and the reason for not keeping the said curve line or heights in the sheer plan as in the body plan is because it would interfere with the curve lines above'[27] – that is, with the lines of wales, decks and gunports. Further confusion was caused by the fact that the new line was still known as the rising line, though it served a rather different function from the old rising line of the floors.

The line of the centres of the floor sweeps was drawn on the sheer draught first. Like the old rising line it began just above the top of the keel in midships, but it curved upwards much more steeply, ending well away from the bows and stern, so that only the midships section, from a half to about two-thirds of the length of the ship, was covered by it. It was also shown in the horizontal plan, by a line which similarly began in midships in the same position as the old narrowing line of the floors, but curved more sharply and eventually crossed over the middle line and continued for some distance past it.

Directly on the midship section, where the floor was 'real', the centre of floor sweeps served the same function as the rising line in the old system, except of course that it defined the centre rather than the limit of the circle; but as it moved away from the midships its function began to change. For, in consequence of the sharp upward curve of the line, the floor sweeps increased greatly in diameter, to such an extent that most of them could not form a tangent with a horizontal line above the floor in midships. In other words, they were not floor sweeps at all in the original sense of the term. The old floor sweep, which away from midships had merely served to guide the foot of the reconciling sweep, was in effect abolished.

There were several consequences. The new type of 'floor sweep' reached well down below the level of the old sweep, and took over some of the room formerly occupied by the deadrising. Thus it gave the designer much more guidance in forming the lower parts of the hull, where the old floor sweep would have been of little help. It helped to reduce the sharp reverse curve which had often been necessary in the old system.

1

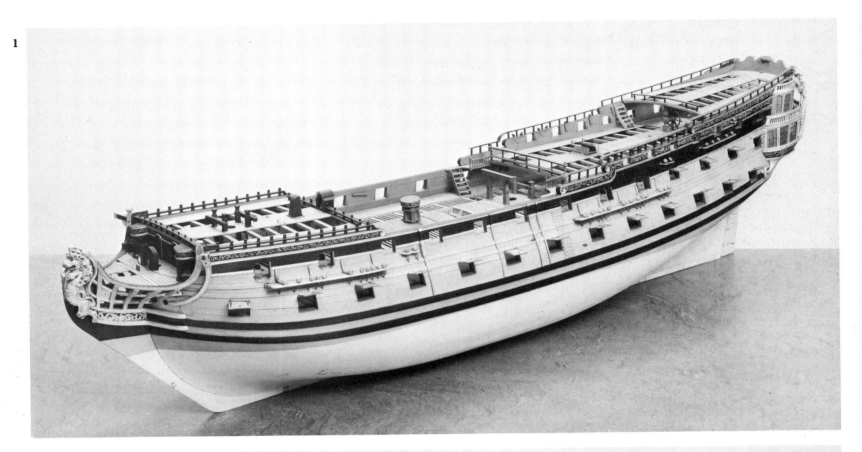

2

Furthermore, the new form of rising line no longer attempted to dictate the form of the bows and stern, for it ended long before reaching these extremities. These crucial and complex shapes were therefore left to the discretion of the shipwright. Having completed drawing the body sections in the area covered by the rising line, he would draw fairing lines on the horizontal plan, and then extend them outwards towards the bow and stern. Having done this, he would transfer the points thus indicated to the body plan, and join them together with segments of a circle.

At the bows, he would probably use segments of a circle to form the waterlines, for the bows were intended to be full and round, and about this time it is noticeable how the shape of the bow changes: the characteristic hollow of the early years of the century begins to disappear. At the stern, he might experience some difficulties. As usual there was the problem of having a sharp run, which would bring the water easily to the rudder, while keeping a large breadth above the waterline to allow room for the guns and cabins, and also a large breadth on the load waterline itself to give stability. Williams was apparently the first to use the new system, on the *Royal Oak* of 1765 and it seems that he fell into the temptation to make the waterline too narrow. As Kempenfelt wrote in criticism of the *Alexander* class,

> the after body is too clean near the water's edge, by which, when by the wind, the quarter is not supported; which also tends to make her crank, and prevents the ballast being stowed near the centre...I am told it is the practice of the French and of our best builders to make the afterbody clean underwater; but at the water's edge to give a fullness to support or resist the pressure of the sail.[28]

Nevertheless, provided the designer was not too ambitious to gain speed at the expense of stability, the new system offered him much greater scope. Many successful ships, such as Rule's *Caledonia*, were designed by it.

The new system went a long way towards breaking the old dependence on the midship section to form the lines throughout the length of the ship, and in that sense it represented great progress; but much remained of the old system. Above the floor sweep, the breadth and reconciling sweeps continued to serve the same functions. In practice there appears to have been a gradual transition between the different systems, and some draughts, originally executed by the rising line of floor system, were later redrawn using the centres of floor sweeps without any apparent change in form. This suggests that the centre of floor sweeps system may have been in use before it was actually shown on the finalised draught.

The introduction of the new methods of drawing largely coincided with the new attitudes of the Admiralty towards ship design, and contributed greatly to the relative success of British warships in the Seven Years War and after. They also coincided with an increasing specialisation among shipwrights, for, from this time onwards, design was almost entirely concentrated in the hands of the Surveyors and their assistants. They had an increasingly large staff of draughtsmen and clerks to help them, and in the 1780s the Surveyors Office began to develop as a separate department within the Navy Board.[29] As a result, we can again see an improvement in the standard of draughting, and many of the later eighteenth century products show a very high standard of skill.

Like previous innovations in the system of drawing lines, the new methods were purely geometrical. They made it easier for a designer to produce a suitable form for his ship, but he still relied on his own experience, and on the criticism of others, to estimate how that form would behave in service. In other countries progress was moving in a different direction, and again science was being applied to shipbuilding. Scientific theory had virtually no impact on British design after the failure of the seventeenth century experiments, but in France, and in several other countries, attempts were still being made to find theoretical principles to guide ship design. From the 1680s onwards French scientists and mathematicians, encouraged by the government, had considered and disputed over the forces acting on a ship. Men like Hoste, Bernouilli and Euler had produced elaborate theories about the behaviour of a fluid penetrated by a solid, about the stability of a floating body, and about the effect of wind and waves. However, the scientists disagreed among themselves, and their theories, even if they could have been understood by the men in the dockyards, contained too many fundamental errors to be of any real value. The design of a ship on purely theoretical principles was well beyond the reach of the eighteenth century, for it demanded a knowledge of hydrodynamics which was not to be attained for over a century, and the reconciliation of a variety of factors which would give problems to a modern computer.

Far more effective were those who approached the problem from the other side, with more limited ambitions, and attempted to find means of assessing a design before building. Such a man was Bouguer, who discovered the means of calculating the metacentre, which could be used to calculate the stability of a design. His work was taken up by Chapman of Sweden, who elaborated and publicised the system. Chapman's drawings of ships, showing the metacentre, were published in Britain soon after their first publication in Sweden, but the text of his work was not translated into English until 1811, and in this respect the British still lagged behind in the application of scientific principles. Nevertheless there were some Britons who made a real contribution. In 1743, for example, Thomas Simpson set out a better method for calculating the displacement of a ship.[30]

Scientific interest began to revive in Britain in the 1790s, due to the widespread belief that British ships were inferior to French, which led to the foundation of the Society for the Improvement of Naval Architecture. In the mid-1790s Thomas Attwood discoursed before the Royal Society on the stability of ships, and interpreted the work of the foreign authors to the British scientific public. Colonel Beaufoy conducted a far reaching series of experiments with models, and these were to have some effect on future design, including that of Symonds in the 1830s.[31]

This revival eventually had its effect on the government, and in 1811 the School of Naval Architecture was opened at Portsmouth, to train the 'superior class of shipwright apprentices' in ship design. For the first time, there was in Britain a formal separation between the intellectual work of designing a ship and the manual work of building her: the

1 The effects of the new system of **2** drawing: the *Edinburgh* (top), a 70 on the 1719 establishment, is drawn by the old rising line system, and has a distinctive hollow in the bows; the *Warrior*, a 74 of 1783, was drawn by Slade to the diagonal of floor ribband system, and has a much fuller bow. *The Science Museum*

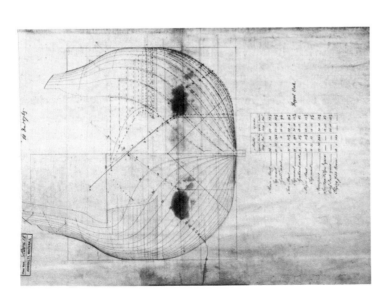

The draught of *Royal Oak*, 1765: the first Williams design for a ship of the line, and the first to use the centres of floor sweeps system.
National Maritime Museum

new 'scientific school' was officially established. Despite the statements of their critics to the effect that the new shipwrights were immersed in theory to the neglect of practice, the products of the School of Naval Architecture did not indulge greatly in obscure mathematical theory, as the French theorists had done. Instead, they tended to concentrate on the calculation of displacement, weight, and stability, and the more immediately useful applications of mathematics. They produced no spectacular results in the short term, and the elaborate calculations involved in any rational assessment of ship design took a very long time to do – it was said that it took two people one year to calculate accurately the centre of gravity of a ship of the line.[32] Perhaps this is why the Admiralty eventually lost patience with the School, and abolished it in 1832, yielding to the criticisms of the amateur ship designers among the sea officers.

Until the very end of the age of sail, science was merely an aid to the design of a ship. It could not displace the practical experience of the designer and his predecessors, and it could only be useful in assessing the design, not in helping to form it. Even this limited value was not always made use of, and the ship designers of the early nineteenth century were still capable of error. Despite several centuries of experience, the system of designing the underwater lines of the hull of a ship of the line had much in common with that used in the days of Deane and the Petts.

Above water, the problems of designing a ship were different. Hydrodynamics still had some importance in the area just above the waterline, which might be immersed from time to time, but the main considerations lay elsewhere. Wind resistance had some effect, and a high superstructure could catch the wind and reduce weatherliness, and this problem came to be recognised by the end of the seventeenth century, though there is no sign that it was ever systematically considered. In some ways, the problem had more in common with one of land architecture, for the designer had to consider how to provide suitable accommodation for guns and men, and in some periods grandiose decoration was of primary importance.

It was of course necessary that the maximum breadth should be some distance above the waterline, or the stability of the ship would be gravely impaired. In midships it was placed a few feet above the load waterline, but it rose upwards towards the bow and stern, in curves of varying steepness according to the times. In the early days great sheer had been necessary, because the early system of whole moulding caused the maximum breadth to rise sharply. It continued long afterwards because it was believed necessary to allow water on the decks to drain away towards the pumps at the centre, and because it helped create a high and imposing stern. Throughout the eighteenth century it was progressively reduced, and it was cut down to a bare minimum early in the nineteenth. Some rise in the maximum breadth line was necessary however, for the ends of the ship tended to be more immersed than the midships during pitching motions. Thus as the bow or stern sank deeper into the sea, it would tend to displace more water, and thus to right itself.

In the seventeenth century the maximum breadth was merely a single point on each frame, but subsequently it was extended upwards for a few feet in midships, so that part of the midship frame was completely vertical. This vertical section, known as the deadflat, was progressively reduced in the frames towards the bow and stern, and reduced to nothing at the extremities of the ship. It contributed to stability, for in effect it raised the height of maximum breadth, and allowed a ship to heel further to one side without danger.

Above the maximum breadth, the hull 'tumbled home', or tapered inwards, for it was believed that the keeping of the weight of the upper deck guns near the centre line helped to increase stability. In the first half of the seventeenth century the breadth sweep was simply continued upwards above the maximum breadth, and a line tangential to it carried the shape of the frame up to the topside. By the time of the true ship of the line, however, several changes had been made in this practice. The upper

Curves in the midship frame above the maximum breadth:
A. Toptimber sweep. B. Above breadth sweep. C. Deadflat.

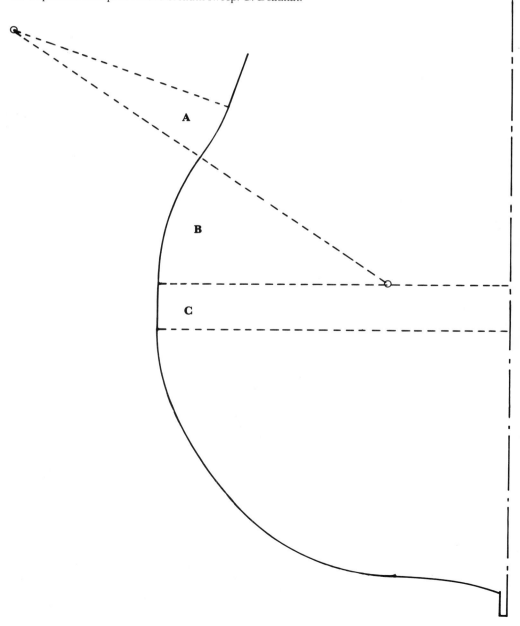

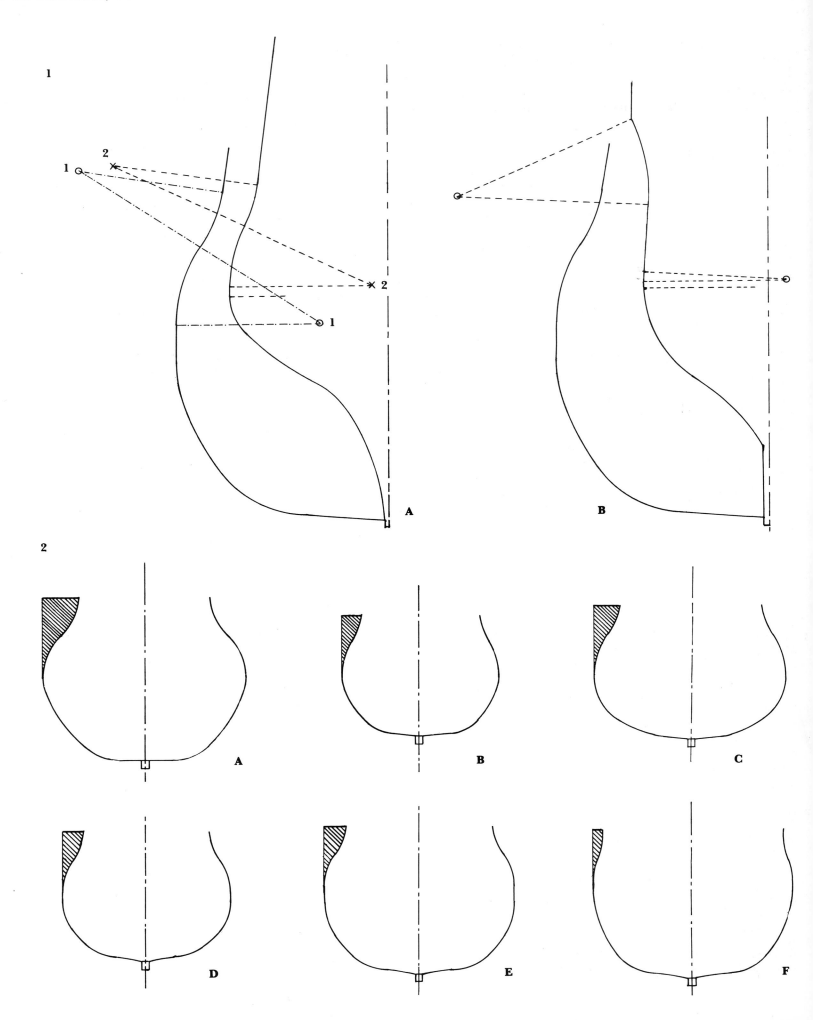

shape of the frame was no longer a straight line but a reverse curve, tangential to the breadth sweep. The sweep below the breadth now tended to reduce in diameter towards the ends of the ship, but this was not necessary above the breadth, so that the upper breadth sweep usually began in midships at around the same diameter as the under breadth sweep, but unlike the latter retained the same diameter throughout the ship. The toptimber curve above it also retained the same diameter, so that, as in the second version of whole moulding, all the frames above the maximum breadth were composed of the same circles, but their relationship varied, and they moved upwards and inwards towards the ends of the ship. Tumblehome, like sheer, was progressively reduced over the years. In the proposed establishment of 1733, for example, the breadth at the topsides was increased more than the maximum breadth. In the early years of the nineteenth century it was further reduced, and ships became, in the parlance of the times, 'wall sided'.

Every designer of a ship of the line had to face an essential contradiction in fixing the height of his main gun deck. He needed to keep it well above the waterline, or it would be impossible to open the gunports when the ship was heeling, or in a rough sea. On the other hand, he could not afford to place it too high, for the great weight of the main guns would cause grave instability. In the seventeenth century Pepys had admired the French and Dutch ships because they carried their guns 4 feet from the water when fully loaded. In later years, as ships became much larger, administrators aimed much higher, and in 1745 the Admiralty wanted the Norris Committee to design ships which could carry their guns 6 feet out of the water. The committee failed to achieve this, but it was revived with the planning of the 'Surveyors' class' in 1806, and this time, because there had been further increases in size since 1745, the designers were apparently successful.

One factor which, of necessity, remained almost constant throughout the years was the height between the decks, for human beings remained of approximately constant size, and it was necessary to give them room to live and to work the guns. In the seventeenth century there was apparently some temptation to make the decks a little higher than the absolute minimum, to give grandeur to the ship and comfort to her officers – even Deane, not generally a man to sacrifice performance for the sake of appearance, agreed that the deck which covered the captain's cabin should be a little higher than the others[33] – but in general a height of from 6 to 7 feet was allowed from plank to plank. Since this did not include the deck beams, it would have been difficult to allow much less, and it verged on a serious discomfort for any tall seaman. The necessity to keep within certain limits when fixing the height between decks was of course a major factor in ship design. It contributed largely to the failure of the three-decker 80, and the two-decker 44.

The completed draught of a ship of the line was the result of decades of collective experience, and years of training in the designer responsible for it, as well as several weeks of work for the draughtsman who did the actual drawing. Having been completed, and approved by the necessary authorities, it passed into the hands of the men responsible for the actual construction of the ship.

1 CHANGES IN THE SHAPE ABOVE THE MAXIMUM BREADTH ALONG THE LENGTH OF THE HULL

A. Aft, the sweeps retain the same diameter as in the midship section, but the relationship between them varies, as in the second version of whole moulding: the centres and limits of the sweeps are shown, for the midship frame (1) and the stern frame (2).
B. Forward, the same procedure is followed, except in the bows, where a large breadth is retained at the level of the forecastle deck, despite the narrowing of the maximum breadth. In this case, the above breadth sweep is very short and an almost vertical line is drawn tangential to it. This is carried outwards by means of a reverse curve.

2 REDUCTION OF TUMBLEHOME, 1637–1800

A. *Sovereign of the Seas*, 1636: large tumblehome, typical of the early seventeenth century.
B. Third Rate from Deane's *Doctrine*, 1670: greatly reduced tumblehome. Deane may have used less tumblehome than the typical designer of the period.
C. 70-gun ship, 1690s: tumblehome slightly increased over Deane's *Doctrine*.
D. 60-gun ship. *c*1730: considerable reduction of tumblehome since 1690.
E. 64-gun ship, *c*1770: tumblehome similar to that of 1730.
F. Large 74, *c*1795: great reduction of tumblehome.

2. Hull Construction

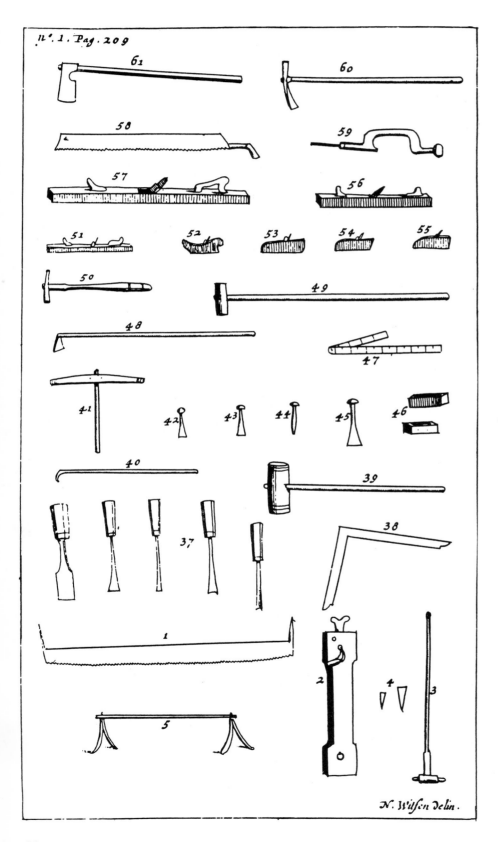

A seventeenth century Dutch shipwright's tools, from Witsen's *Architectura Navalis*, 1690.

OFFICIALLY THE FIRST STAGE IN THE BUILDING OF A NEW ship was the laying of the keel, but much preliminary work had to be done before that stage was reached. First the Admiralty, in co-operation with the Navy Board, had to decide the most suitable place to build it. In peacetime, with plenty of space and labour to spare in the royal dockyards, there was usually no problem. In wartime, when the majority of new ships were started, contract builders had to be employed. Contracts were awarded on a strictly competitive basis, to the builders who offered the lowest prices per ton, but the Navy Board had already carried out a preliminary screening, and only invited tenders from shipbuilders who were considered suitable. Those with little experience, poor facilities, or a record of bad workmanship, were likely to be excluded from the competition, though standards tended to be lowered during an extreme emergency.[1]

The fixed capital required by a shipbuilder was remarkably small. In 1681 the Blackwall yard, the largest private shipyard in the country, had a total stock valued at £860.[2] A few buildings were needed, for administration and the storage of the more valuable components, but timber was stored in the open, and most of the work was also done in the open air. The main requirement was a suitable site, which a private shipbuilder usually rented from a local landlord. It had to be on a river which was wide enough to allow room for launching, and close to the supplies of timber and other raw materials. A further requirement for naval shipbuilding was that the yard should be near one of the naval dockyards. There were occasional experiments with building ships away from the main areas of naval construction, and Bristol was used for two ships of the line in Charles II's time, while several of the ships of the 1691 programme were built at Hull. However, these exceptions simply proved the rule – the failure of the 1691 programme was largely blamed on the contractors, and the Navy Board advised against the building of any more 'out of our view'. The construction of a contract-built ship was supervised by a naval overseer, usually a dockyard foreman, but far from a dockyard there was a danger that he would become lazy or corrupt, and ignore the use of defective timber, or poor workmanship. The vast majority of ships of the line were built in certain specific areas: on the Thames and Medway, in or around the dockyards at Deptford, Woolwich and

Chatham; in Hampshire, centred on Portsmouth dockyard; and to a lesser extent in the area around Plymouth dockyard. In the nineteenth century Pembroke and Bombay were added to the yards under government control. Three-deckers were sometimes built in dry-docks, but most ships of the line were built on slips, or 'launches' as they were once known.

The number of men required to build a ship was also small by modern standards. In 1675 Deane estimated that there were only 1922 shipwrights in the whole country.[3] In 1804 there were only 35 in Adams' yard at Bucklers Hard, though two 74s were building there. Around the same time it was said that a Second Rate could be built in one year by 46 men.[4] Yet the supply was never adequate to meet the wartime crises. Entry to the trade was strictly controlled, and the only means was by a seven-year apprenticeship. Unless he was lucky enough to be apprenticed to a master shipwright or a senior official in a dockyard, where he might be initiated into some of the secrets of ship design, an entrant to the trade would spend his time working with an individual craftsman, learning how to cut wood to shape, fit it into position and fix it with wooden trenails or metal bolts. He would gradually acquire his own tools, which included adzes, saws, hammers, drills, and other woodworking instruments. Neither employers nor workmen had any wish to allow unskilled labour on the actual building of the ship, and any man who attempted to enter the trade by an irregular route would find himself in severe danger from his own workmates.[5] As a result, the supply of trained shipwrights could be expanded only very slowly, and there was strenuous competition for their services during a large building programme. Merchant yards could lure men with large pay, but dockyard wages were fixed by the government. In the seventeenth century it had been possible to impress shipwrights into the dockyards in the same way as seamen were impressed for the fleet, but this custom died out in the eighteenth century, leaving the dockyards with a labour problem. They did, however, offer secure and relatively permanent employment, whereas private builders took on workers for one contract only.

The other essential commodity for shipbuilding was of course timber, and that too was often in short supply. Apart from the keel and sternpost, which were long and straight and therefore made of elm, shipwrights invariably favoured

Parts of a First Rate, c1700.
National Maritime Museum

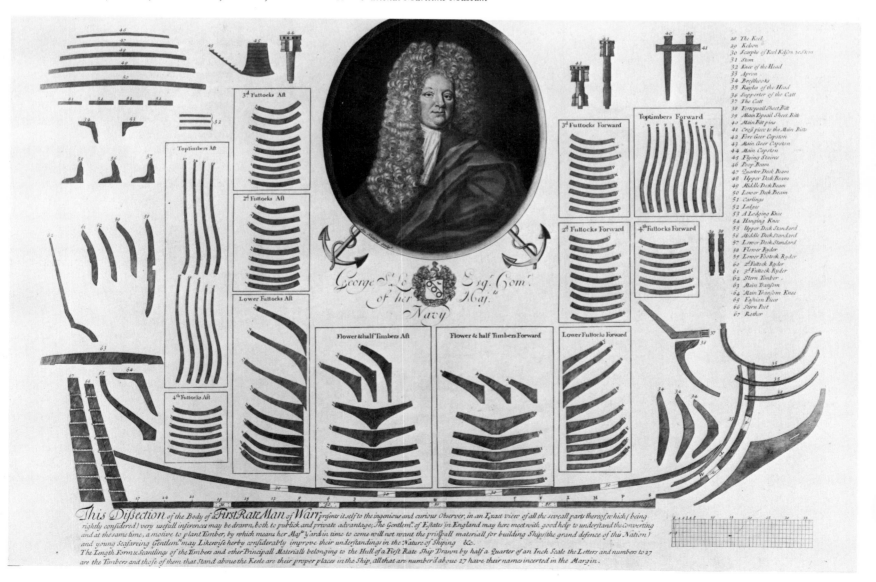

English oak for all the main parts of a ship's structure, and had a severe prejudice against any foreign variety; but this position could not be long maintained, and during the timber crisis of 1677 agents collected 'East Country Plank' from the Baltic to supplement native supplies. The use of foreign timber, including Dantzig oak, increased over the years, and the maintenance of the supply line to the Baltic became an important factor in British foreign policy.[6]

Nevertheless native supplies were preferred, and efforts were made to utilise the resources of the homeland. Numerous works, beginning with John Evelyn's *Sylva* of 1661, tried to explain to landowners the importance of planting trees, but it was a difficult task. Timbers large enough for a ship of the line took a century to grow to full maturity, and the landowner's investment was a long-term one. The curved pieces for knees and futtocks had to have the grain running in a suitable way, and these were often difficult to find. The timber had to be sited near a coast or suitable waterway, for it was very difficult to transport a large piece for more than a few miles overland, although the canal building of the later eighteenth century may have helped solve this problem. In 1771 the Admiralty ordered that three years' future supply should be kept in the dockyards, but this was impossible to maintain, especially as ships were to become larger and more numerous in future years. In 1787 it was decided that woods other than oak could be used for some of the less vital parts.[7] Nevertheless the timber problem continued to increase into the nineteenth century. Indian timber was widely used, both for ships built in that country and for those in the home dockyards.

The scope allowed to a builder in the construction of a ship declined over the years. In the seventeenth century a dockyard master shipwright had almost complete discretion. Apart from a brief statement of the dimensions and the number of guns, which need not be strictly adhered to, his powers to decide the design and scantlings were virtually unlimited, except that he would of course be held responsible if the ship failed. The private builder was more restricted, for he had greater temptation to 'build slight', and complete details of dimensions and scantlings were included in his contract.[8] The 1719 establishment gave a detailed list of scantlings which was binding on the dockyard builder, and from this time on most of the structural detail was laid down by the central administration. After 1745 the builder, whether dockyard or private, was normally confined to a draught provided by the Navy Board, and this, as well as defining the lines of the ship, also gave much information on the structure. The deck beams, transoms, and other constructional features were usually shown. The earliest ships' draughts consisted of a single sheet, and still left much unsaid about the arrangement of the structure, but from the 1750s the number of sheets began to increase, and deck plans, framing plans and sometimes planking diagrams were included so that every part of any importance was pre-ordained for the builder.

Having prepared his draught, or received it from the Navy Board, the builder would begin cutting timber for his ship as soon as possible, for, if he was a private builder, much of his payment depended on prompt delivery. The rough trees were squared and cut into planks by sawyers, working in pairs in a sawpit. In the mould loft templates known as moulds were cut to the actual size of the individual timbers, from thin board. These would guide the manual workers in cutting the timbers. The timbers were then 'converted', that is, cut roughly to shape by shipwrights with saws. Blocks were laid on the slip to take the keel, and that vital piece was cut to shape.

The keel was long and straight, and even the largest elm tree could not yield a large enough piece of timber for it. It was therefore made in several parts – usually four or five for

The keel and stem of a ship of the line, early nineteenth century (from Fincham's *Outline of Shipbuilding*). The false keel (a) has its scarphs in the vertical plane. The scarphs of the main keel are horizontal, and marked x. The floor timbers are butted into the keel, and are shown in cross section. Above these is the kelson, marked g, with its scarphs at o. The large piece shown in cross section above the forward end of the kelson is the step of the mizzen mast. The stempost (d) leads directly up from the keel and has several scarphs. Behind it is the false stempost, and forward of it are various irregularly shaped pieces of timber which make up the knee of the head. The whole structure is held together by long bolts, marked with dotted lines. The breast hooks and deck hooks, marked n, are shown in cross section aft of the false stempost.

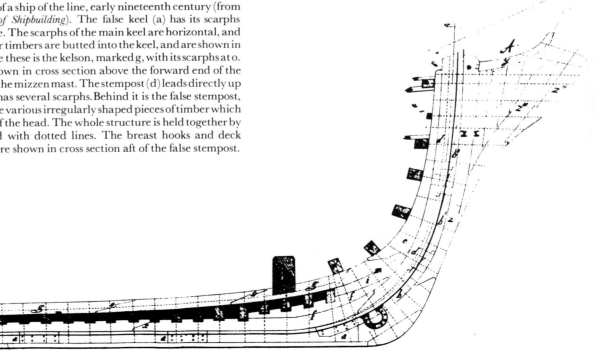

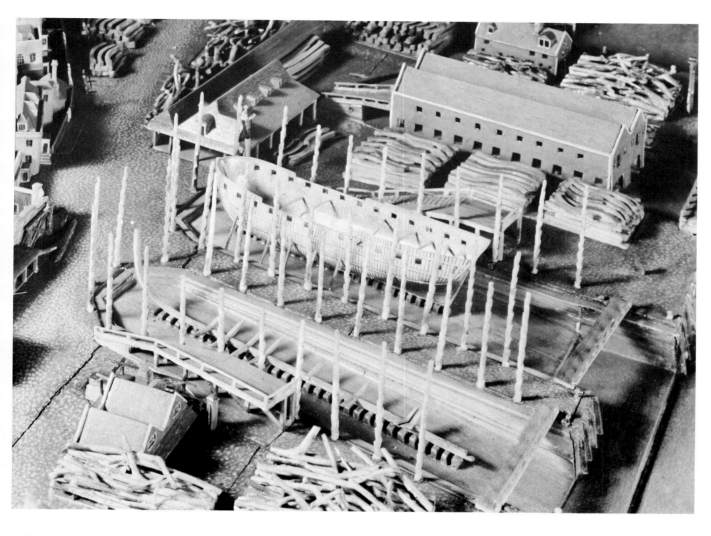

A model of Woolwich Dockyard in 1774. In the foreground, the keel of a large ship has been laid on blocks, and some of the floor timbers have been crossed. Behind, a frigate is in frame. Around both ships are placed posts to help in raising the frames, and support them during construction. In the background can be seen piles of timber stored in the open, some cut approximately to shape, the others left rough.
The Science Museum

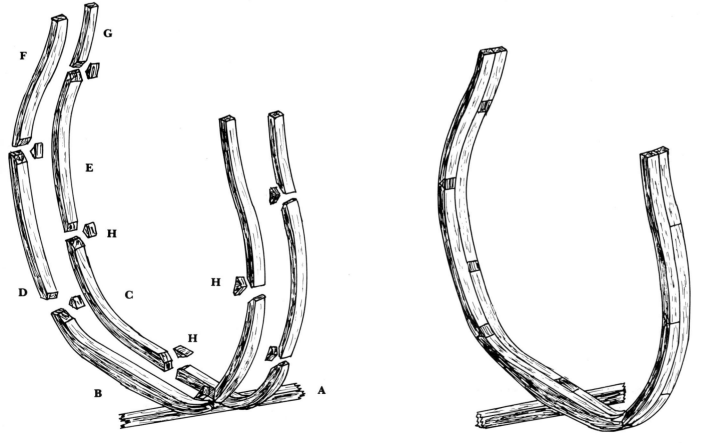

THE PARTS OF A MID-SHIP FRAME
A. Keel.
B. Floor timber.
C. First futtock.
D. Second futtock.
E. Third futtock.
F. Fourth futtock.
G. Toptimber.
H. Chocks.

a ship of the line. The keel pieces were joined together by means of scarphs. In the simplest form of scarph the ends of the two pieces to be joined were simply cut at an angle to form an overlapping joint, but there were many variations, with 'tabling', 'coaking' and the 'flemish scarph with hook and butt' to produce a stronger link. The keel itself was approximately square in midships. It maintained the same height throughout its length, but the width was reduced slightly towards the ends. Under it was the false keel, of the same width, but much shallower. It served to protect the main keel from damage if the ship ran aground, and also from shipworm, being sheathed before it was fitted, for it was difficult to work on the underside of the main keel when the ship was in a dock.[9] It also helped to add some strength to the main keel. The scarphs in the main keel were made in the vertical plane, while those in the false keel were horizontal, and did not overlap with those of the main keel. For a time around 1800, two false keels were fitted, partly to improve the ships' weatherliness.

The sternpost was fitted to the end of the keel. This was made of a single straight piece of elm, before the introduction of the round stern, for it was an important part, having to support the rudder, and much of the weight of the stern. Forward of it was the inner post, to give extra strength, and sometimes a false sternpost was fitted aft. The stempost, in the bows, was of different construction, for it was of course curved. It was therefore made from several pieces of oak, scarphed together. All these pieces, the keel, stempost and sternpost, had a triangular groove running along them. This was the rabbett, which was intended to take the ends of the planking, and provide a secure, leak-proof join.

A single frame for a ship of the line was large in size and complex in shape, and there was no possibility of cutting it from a single piece of timber. It too had to be divided into sections. The lowermost portion of each frame was the floor timber, which was placed across the keel and bolted into place. At the head of the floor timber would be joined the second futtock, and above that the fourth futtock. Alongside this structure would be another, of similar shape but different construction, so that the joints of the two frames did not overlap. This second frame consisted of the first futtock, third futtock and toptimber. Where possible it was bolted directly to the first frame, so as to form a single assembly with no serious point of weakness. In the seventeenth century each futtock was fitted separately to the main structure, and the different frames were not always bolted directly one against the other.[10] In the eighteenth century the futtocks and toptimbers for each set of frames were joined together away from the slip, and then the whole structure was raised and joined to the keel and floor timber. In the early eighteenth century the first futtocks stopped short of the keel, leaving a space which formed a gutter for the bilge water. After 1715 strength took priority and the first futtocks were brought down to meet over the keel. The ends of the timbers were cut at an angle, and a wedge was fitted between them in the hope of strengthening the join.

It was necessary to pierce the sides of the ship for gunports, and this inevitably caused some weakness in the structure, and problems for the shipwright. Contracts often enjoined the builder that 'great care be taken to dispose of the frame so justly that as few timbers as possible be cut by ports.'[11] In practice this could be achieved if the ports were properly staggered. Between each gunport and its counterpart on the deck above, there should be room for one pair of frames, which could therefore reach the top of the sides uncut. This meant that half the frames would be complete, and these were fitted first, and small pieces of timber placed between them to form the sills of the gunports. This usually left room for a further set of partial frames directly above and under the gunports.

Towards the bow and stern the floor was non-existent and the timbers rose steeply from the keel. There a different system had to be adopted, for it was not possible to find pieces of oak with grain at such a sharp angle. Half frames which terminated above the keel instead of being carried across were substituted for floor timbers. The angle

METHOD OF CONSTRUCTING THE FLOOR TIMBER, c1800

A. The floor timber.
B. Chock to complete the formation of the floor.
C. Kelson.
D. Deadwood 'with scores taken out as shown by the ticked lines for the reception of the floors'.
E. Keel 'which may be dislodged by the ship striking the ground with violence, and would endanger her safety'.
F. False keel.
G. Plank of the bottom.
H. Limber strakes.
I. Limber boards.

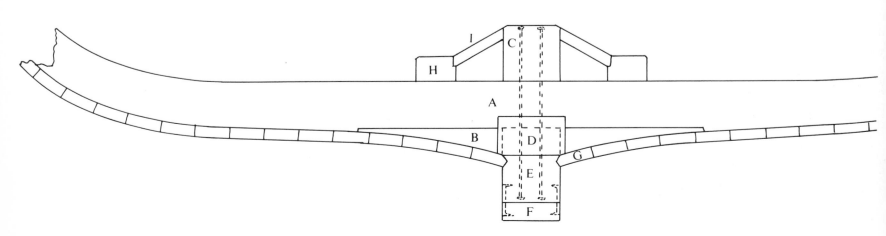

D   B   C   F   A   E

between the sternpost and the keel, and the similar space between the stempost and the keel, was filled in with an assembly of irregularly shaped pieces of timber known as the deadwood, and the ends of the half timbers were butted into these. To lock this whole structure into position the kelson, made up of several pieces of timber scarphed together, was brought on above the half timbers and floor timbers, over the line of the keel, and bolted into position.

When they were fitted into position the frame timbers had already been 'converted', that is roughly cut to shape by sawing. After the frame had been assembled, it was time to cut them more accurately to shape, to produce fair lines. This process, known as trimming, was done with an adze, and was one of the most skilled parts of a shipwright's work. To aid this trimming, and to hold the frames in position until the planking was to be fitted, ribbands were fitted to the sides. These were simply long strips of timber, bolted temporarily to each frame. In the eighteenth century their position was shown on the draught of the ship, and it was marked on each frame during conversion, when it was known as the sirmark. In midships the ribbands were flexible, but at the bows and stern, where curves were sharper and the shape more crucial and complex, they were replaced with harpins. These were cut to shape in advance, so that the curves could be formed more accurately. The shape of the harpin had to be 'laid off' from the draught by complex geometrical means, and was one of the more difficult tasks demanded of the mould loft draughtsmen at the beginning of the eighteenth century.

At the extremities of the bow and stern, frames perpendicular to the keel would have been of little help in forming the shape of the hull, and would have contributed little to its strength. Viewed from above, the bow was almost circular at the waterline, and the first few frames

STAGES IN THE FRAMING OF A 74-GUN SHIP

A. The floor timbers crossed.
B. The frames raised between the gunports, and the gunport sills fitted.
C. The framing completed amidships.
D. The bow framing completed, showing cant frames and hawse pieces. The model shows the round bow which became standard after 1804.
E. The stern and quarter framing. The relative weakness of the extreme stern is clearly shown.
F. The external planking completed.
The Science Museum

were fitted parallel to the line of the keel, so that they could face the flow of the water. These were known as the hawse pieces, because they were bored for the hawse holes of the anchor cables. They made no direct contact with the keel, but ended against the side of the most forward of the more normal frames. In the seventeenth century the frames immediately aft of the hawse pieces were perpendicular to the keel, like the midship frames. In 1715 it was ordered that the frames near the bow and stern should be fitted at an angle, to make them 'more supportive to the body and circular to the movement of the water.'[12] The aftermost of these frames, known as cant frames, was angled only at a few degrees from the midship frames, but the angle slowly increased with each frame, keeping them roughly perpendicular to the line of the planking at each individual station. The cant frames usually coincided with the half frames, joined to the deadwood.

Until Seppings' reforms, the main structure of the bows ended at least one deck below that of the sides of the ship. Above this, the forecastle was closed in by a flat structure known as the beakhead bulkhead, of relatively light construction. On either side of the stempost, two stout

The framing plan of an 80-gun ship of about 1800, from Steel's *Naval Architecture*.

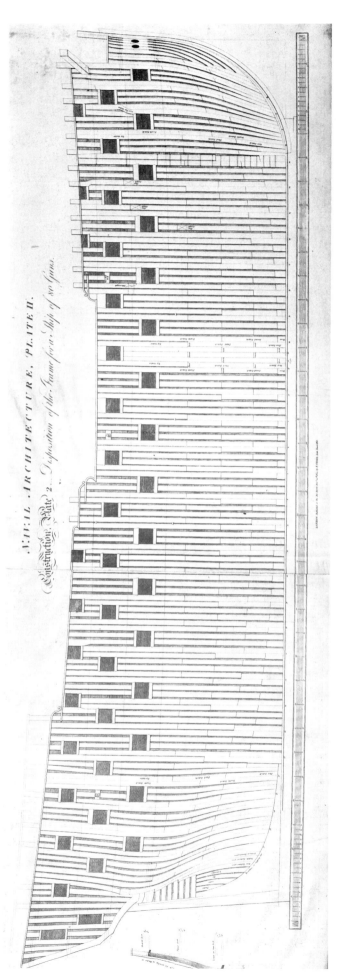

pieces of timber jutted upwards. These were the knightheads, which would prevent the bowsprit from being forced to one side or the other.

Forward of the stempost was the structure which would support the head of the ship, and its appendages. It was made of several pieces of timber, scarphed and butted together, all in the same vertical plane as the keel and stempost. The part directly under the head was the knee of the head. The lowest portion, directly ahead of the keel, was the gripe, believed to be of importance in keeping the ship on a steady course. Between was the cutwater, so called because it would be the first part of the ship to penetrate the water in its forward motion.

Towards the stern the structure resembled that of the bows, with half timbers, deadwood and cant frames; but in the extreme stern yet another form of construction was used. Instead of the hawse pieces, rising vertically and parallel to the line of the keel, horizontal timbers known as transoms were the main feature. Clearly they had originated in the fifteenth and sixteenth centuries when flat sterns were in fashion, and this probably explains their name. Since the early years of the seventeenth century English ships, in advance of continental construction, had been built with rounded sterns underwater, but the old structural form was to survive into the nineteenth century. The transoms were shaped according to the lines of the hull. The uppermost one, the wing transom, had only a slight curve on its aftermost edge, but this increased with each of the lower transoms. The lowermost one was shaped rather like an isoceles triangle, with the long edges forming the sides of the ship, thus giving a sharp run to the rudder. In the seventeenth century it had been the custom to use two half transoms in the lower positions; by the orders of 1715, all were to be made of a single piece, fitted across the sternpost. Below the transoms were a few short vertical timbers, known as filling pieces. As well as joining with the sternpost, the transoms linked with the last of the complete frames, known as the fashion pieces. By careful arrangement it was possible to have two or three fashion pieces, each supporting several transoms; but the individual transoms had no direct connection with one another, and each was supported at only three points, by the sternpost and a fashion piece on each side.

This would not have been a grave source of weakness, except that the wing transom had an unduly heavy workload for a single timber, in that it had to support the whole structure of the stern above it. The corners of the upper stern were formed by the side counter timbers, shaped to form the two counters which helped cover the rudder head and form much of the basis for the decoration which was regarded as so important for so long. Above the counters, they were straight, rising at an angle of about 30 degrees from the vertical for the open stern, less for the closed stern. They had a rather tenuous join with the fashion pieces, but in essence they were supported by the ends of the wing transom, and they in turn formed the base for all the side timbers aft of the fashion piece. Other timbers, of similar shape to the side counter timbers, arose out of the wing transom to help form the almost flat surface of the upper stern. They were of light construction, neither as strong or as closely spaced as the heavy futtocks and

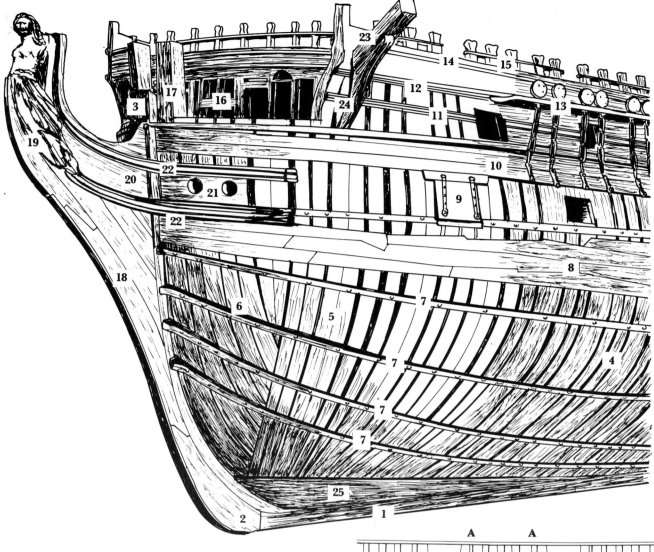

1. Keel.
2. Gripe.
3. Top of stempost.
4. Square frames.
5. Cant frames.
6. Hawse pieces.
7. Harpins.
8. Main wale.
9. Gunport.
10. Upper wale.
11. Decorative moulding.
12. Channel wale.
13. Fore channels.
14. Gunwale.
15. Timberheads.
16. Beakhead bulkhead.
17. Knighthead.
18. Knee of the head.
19. Figurehead.
20. Trailboard.
21. Hawse holes.
22. Cheeks of the head.
23. Cathead.
24. Cathead knee.
25. Deadwood.
*Based on a model in the National
Maritime Museum*

toptimbers of the sides. It is not surprising that the stern of a ship was its weakest point in action, unable either to bear heavy guns or resist enemy shot. Furthermore, this light structure was covered only with flimsy boards, and large spaces were left for glass windows. The other features of the stern, the stern and quarter galleries, were merely light appendages, which did not form part of the main structure.

After the main structure of the hull, from the stern timbers to the knee of the head, had been assembled, trimmed and faired, the ship was often allowed to 'stand to season' – to be left for a number of months or years to allow the sap to drain from the timber. This procedure was regularised by the orders of 1773, in the wake of the hasty construction programme of the Seven Years War[13]; but it was not unknown before that time. In 1677 a government speaker asked Parliament for more time to build the thirty ships, on the grounds that 'No merchant will put one plank on the outside of a ship that has not lain 12 months,'[14] but most of the ships of that programme were built far too quickly to allow time for seasoning. The *London* of 1706 was allowed to stand for three years, but 'in 12 months time she wanted to be rebuilt though she had never been at sea.'[15] In 1715 it was ordered that 'all ships' frames, after they are

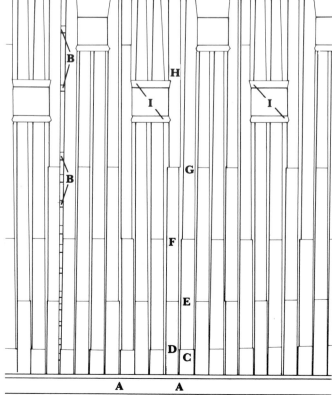

**THE FRAMING OF THE
ELEPHANT OF 1786**
The system used here differs from that shown in most of the illustrations in this chapter, in that the pair of frames between the gunports (A) are not contiguous except at floor level, but are kept apart by lines of small chocks (B). On the draught these are shown in only one place, but were used throughout the frame in practice.
C. Floor timberheads.
D. First futtock.
E. Second futtock.
F. Third futtock.
G. Fourth futtock.
H. Toptimber.
I. Gunport sills.
This and the remaining uncredited drawings are based on originals in the Draught Room of the National Maritime Museum

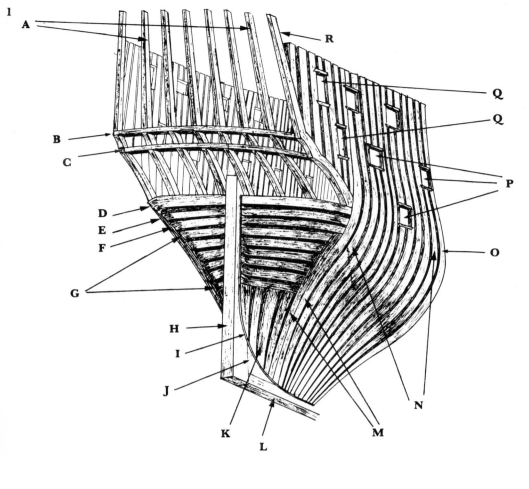

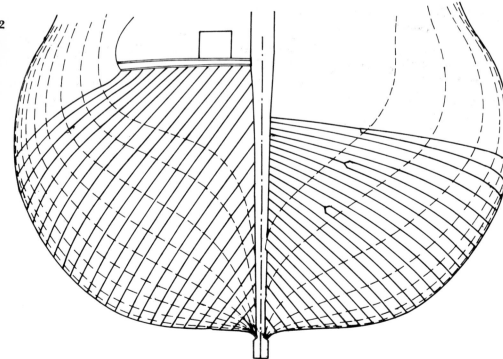

converted, stand some time to season, at least (if possible) one whole winter, and that upon the advance of the next spring to plank and work them up,'[16] and this would seem to have remained the practice throughout the long peace. It fell into disuse during the mid-century wars, and was revived in a stronger form in 1771, when ships were ordered to stand in frame for a full year. Again the practice fell into disuse during the American War, only to be revived as soon as peace was established. Its utility was doubtful, and the custom of allowing the frame to stand in the rain for such a time was of dubious value. Various remedies were attempted to reduce the damage by rainwater, such as leaving out certain parts which might trap the water, and building roofs over other parts[17]; but there were still complaints that some hulls were rotting before the seasoning was finished. The only fully effective method was to build within a ship-house, as the French and Americans were to do in the nineteenth century. But this practice was not often adopted in Britain.

It was now time to begin the planking. The first stage was to fit the wales – thick pieces of timber which would help to strengthen certain crucial parts of the ship. Their immediate purpose seems to have varied a little over the years. Anthony Deane believed that they should have much greater sheer than the decks, so that they help to link two decks together and give a primitive form of diagonal bracing.[18] By the early nineteenth century they almost followed the line of the decks, for they were intended to provide a secure anchorage for the bolts which helped support the latter. Normally there was one set of wales for each deck: a two-decker had main or lower wales level with the gun deck, and channel, or upper, wales at the height of the upper deck; a three-decker had middle wales in addition. In early times, double wales were used. Two long

1 THE SQUARE STERN, c1810
Note the weakness of the structure above the wing transom, and the fact that the whole stern is supported by the wing transom and the counter timbers. This shows the closed stern; the open stern was even weaker.
A. Stern timbers.
B. Upper counter.
C. Lower counter.
D. Wing transom.
E. Filling transom.
F. Deck transom.
G. Filling transoms.
H. Sternpost.
I. Rabbet.
J. Deadwood.
K. Filling pieces.
L. Keel.
M. Fashion pieces.
N. Cant frames.
O. Last square frame.
P. Gunports.
Q. Doors to quarter galleries.
R. Side counter timber.

2 The underwater planking of a 60-gun ship, c1730: the forward part, shown on the right, has three planks, known as stealers, which end before reaching the stempost, while the others taper gradually as they approach the bows. The reduction of planking is less necessary at the stern, shown on the left, for some of the planks end at the lower counter, others at the sternpost.

strips of timber, approximately square in cross section, were fitted along each side in the appropriate positions, and the timber between them was thicker than normal. By the orders of 1715 it was decreed that 'The main wales and strakes between them wrought in narrower strakes, all of a thickness, by lessening the thickness of the wales and increasing that of the stuff between,'[19] so making a single thick portion along the ship's side. For a time the wales continued to be made out of long strips of timber, but by mid-century they were formed out of shorter, wider pieces, tapering towards their ends so that they could be joined together at an angle.

As well as helping to support the upper deck, the channel wales originally had another function in that they gave strength to the channels (or 'chain-wales'). These were flat pieces of timber jutting out from the sides, and intended to spread the shrouds and backstays which supported the masts. In the seventeenth century ships usually had considerable tumblehome, and this meant that the channels had to be fitted low down on the hull, where the breadth was greater. On two-deckers the channels of the fore and main mast were fitted at the level of the upper deck, on three-deckers at the middle deck; while the channels of the mizzen mast were carried one deck higher. The channels of three-deckers were raised to the upper deck experimentally in 1702, and regularly in 1706. Partly as a result of Anson's experience during his circumnavigation, it was found that the channels of two-deckers were too close to

the water to avoid damage, and in 1745, soon after Anson's appointment to the Admiralty, they were raised to the level of the quarterdeck and forecastle. Those of three-deckers reached the same position from 1787 onwards.

For a few strakes under the wales the plank was thicker than normal, slowly reducing until it reached equality with the rest of the planking. The planking of a ship's bottom was a complex process, as the ship narrowed drastically at the bow and stern. At the stern the planks ended against the sternpost, where they fitted into the rabbet, or were carried up to the lower counter. Naturally they had to be reduced gradually in width as they approached the end. At the bow, the problem was more severe, for all the planking had to be brought to an end against the stempost. Shorter planks, known as stealers, were therefore introduced, terminating slightly before the end of the hull, so that the extremities of the other planks would not be made too narrow. Occasionally planking diagrams were used to aid this process, but it seems that throughout most of our period the shipwright relied on his eye and judgement to plank the ship effectively. The bottom piece of planking, known as the garboard strake, fitted into the rabbet of the keel. Above water, planking was simpler, since the sides of the hull were relatively flat, though spaces had to be left for the gunports.

It was of course impossible to make each strake of planking from a single piece of timber, so several were used along the length of the ship. The joints were carefully arranged so that each should be sited over a frame, to which

PARTS OF THE PLANKING OF THE BOWS AND STERN OF THE *MONTAGUE* OF 1779
1. Rabbet.
2. Stealer.
3. Wale.
4. Lower counter.

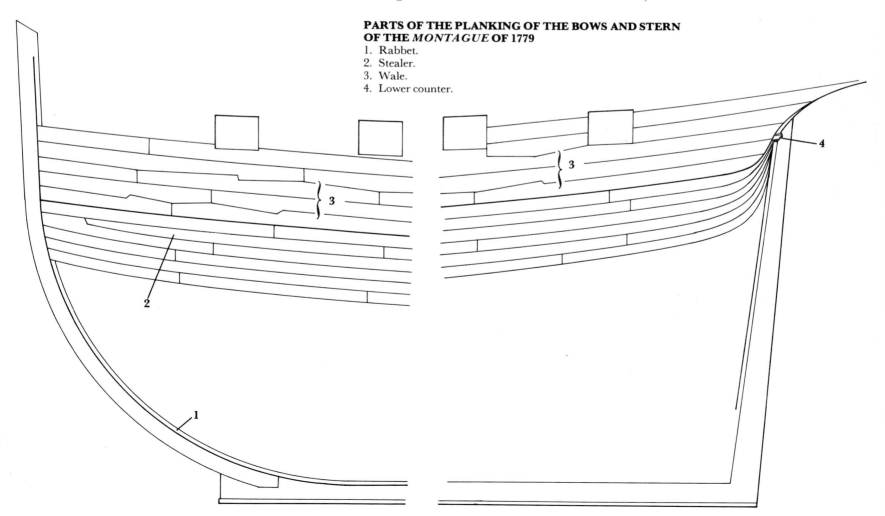

THE MIDSHIP SECTION OF A 74-GUN SHIP, *c*1760, FROM FALCONER'S *MARINE DICTIONARY*.

The original key is as follows:
A. The keel.
a. The false keel.
U. The floor timbers.
V. The futtocks.
W. The toptimbers.
X. The kelson.
Q. The lower wales.
R. The channel wales.
B. The chocks over the kelson. Outboard of them are the riders.
(Internal planking of the hold: I, K and L, the thick stuff, placed over the joins of the futtocks; O, the ceiling, which fills the spaces between; G, the clamps, which support some of the weight of the deck beams).
E. The hanging knees.
F. The standards, which support the deck beams from above.
C, D, d. The deck beams.
N. The waterways.
P. The spirketting.

the ends could be securely bolted, and it was essential that the ends of adjacent strakes should not coincide. On completion all the planking was trimmed with adzes, so that it formed a single smooth surface, even in places such as under the wales where the planks were of different thicknesses. The wales however were left to stand out prominently from the sides until the early nineteenth century when their corners were trimmed. At this stage the hull was caulked – pieces of oakum were hammered into the spaces between the planks to make the joints as near watertight as possible.

Most of the hull was also planked internally. In the hold, heavy pieces of planking known as thick stuff were placed over the joins of the futtocks. Between were strakes of lighter timber, known as footwaling and middlebands. At the centre, the limber boards were fitted at an angle between the first strake of planking and the kelson. At the uppermost part of the sides of the hold was another thick strake, the clamp, which provided support for the beams of the orlop deck. The internal planking of the hold was known collectively as the ceiling. The other decks were also supported by clamps, and the space between the decks was filled by lighter pieces known as spirketting. It was customary to leave out one strake in the upper hold and

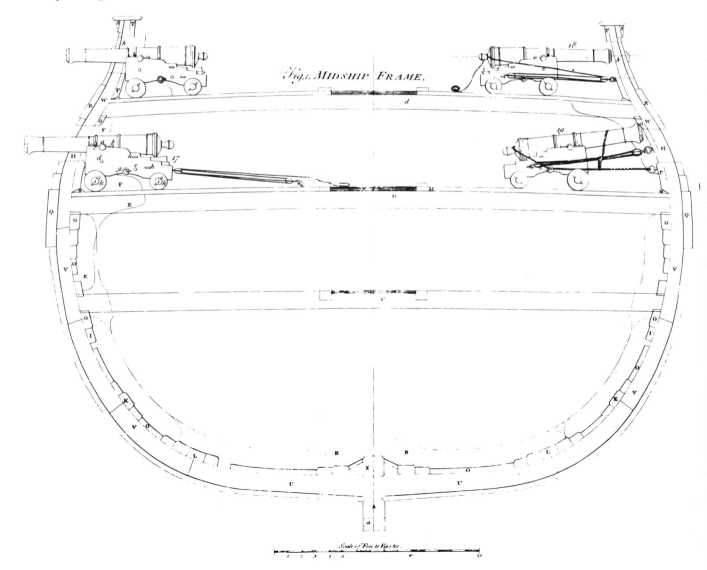

Fig.1. MIDSHIP FRAME.

Scale of Feet to Fig.1 &c.

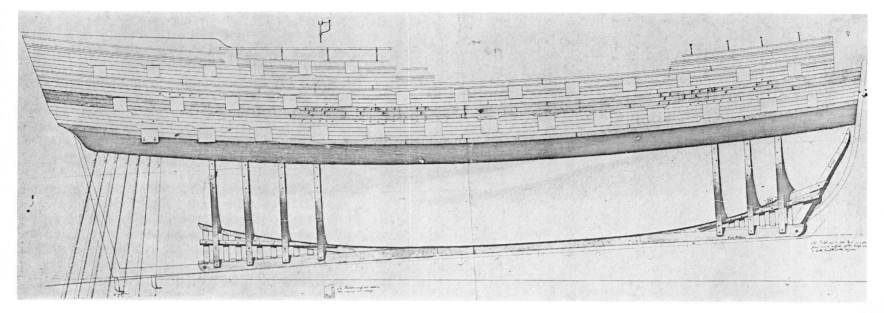

between the orlop and the gun deck, to allow some of the bilge water to drain away.

Over all this was an internal structure of riders, which were heavier but less numerous than the frames of the main structure. Across the centreline at the bottom of the hold were placed 'chocks', which extended outwards slightly beyond the ends of the floor timbers. They curved upwards in the middle, to carry them over the kelson. Alongside them were the riders of the hold, which began just outboard of the kelson and ended just below the orlop deck. Other riders, angled slightly from the vertical, were often placed against the sides of the upper works; they began just above one deck, passed through another deck, and ended just under the beams of a third. In the bows this internal structure was particularly important, for it helped compensate for the inherent flaws in the main structure; heavy riders, known as breast hooks, also strengthened the bow against the pressure of the water. At the stern, where much of the structure was horizontal, longitudinal riders were placed as a counter-balance, and the transoms were fixed against the sides with strong knees. Thus the shipbuilders attempted to remedy the defects of the main structure, and to give extra strength to any potential source of weakness. In doing so, they added a certain amount of extra weight to the ship, and sacrificed some of the space in the hold and between decks.

So far during its construction the frames of the ship would have been held in place by shores, stretching horizontally across each frame, and sometimes diagonally for extra strength, and by external props, which lay at an angle against the sides and were based on the floor of the dock or slip. It was now time to fit the deck beams, which as well as supporting her guns and men, would form an essential part of her structural strength, bracing her sides against the pressure of the water. The lowest deck was the orlop, which, being situated below the waterline, carried no guns and could therefore be made lighter than the others. In early ships, and in smaller ones of the later period, the orlop was not a full deck, but merely a series of platforms in the hold. Even in the largest ships it rarely reached the extremity of the stern, partly because the hull at that point was too narrow to be of any use for human habitation, and

partly because it was allocated as part of a storage space which reached down into the hold. Its beams were rather flimsier than those of the decks above it, but even so it was not usually possible to construct each beam from a single piece of timber. Usually, as with the decks above, two pieces were used, with a long scarph in the middle. The orlop deck was often flat, but the other decks usually rounded upwards towards the middle, to allow the water to drain away, and possibly to help reduce the recoil of the guns. This rounding, like the longitudinal sheer of the wales and of the deck, was progressively reduced over the years.

Beams alone, of relatively light scantling, sufficed to support the orlop deck, for it only had to bear the weight of the anchor cables when stowed, of some light stores, and a few of the middle ranking members of the ship's company. The gun deck, immediately above, was very different, for it had to support the full weight of the ship's main battery, perhaps 32-pounder guns weighing many hundredweight each. The beams themselves were of course much heavier. Builders usually tried to place one beam under each port, where it could support the weight of a gun and join against one of the frame timbers. Other beams were placed between each pair of ports. Pieces known as carlines were placed lengthwise to join the beams together, and between the carlines were placed ledges, relatively light pieces which ran parallel to the deck beams. All this was necessary, because the guns might be moved over any part of the deck, and it would be dangerous to trust their weight solely to a deck plank a few inches thick. Often it was found that a main hatchway or a mast interfered with the run of the deck beams. This was remedied by using curved half beams, which began at the normal position on the sides, but curved backwards to meet the adjacent beam before the centreline.

The other main decks, the upper deck, and the middle deck on a three-decker, were constructed on similar principles to the gun deck, though the scantlings were lighter in proportion to the weight they had to carry. The forecastle and quarterdeck were often similar to the orlop, in that they lacked carlines and ledges. Presumably their guns were light enough to be supported by the planking alone. The poop deck was lighter still: it had originated

A 60-gun ship of the 1745 establishment ready for launching, showing the arrangement of the planking, and the launching cradles.
Sjöhistoriska Museum, Stockholm

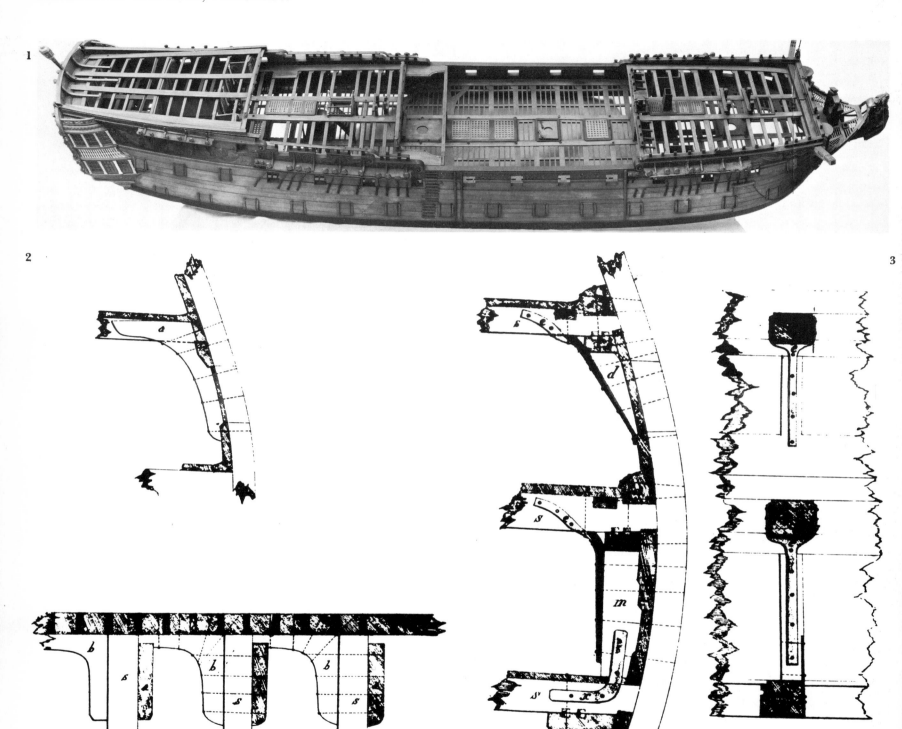

1 The model of the *Ajax* of 1767 shows the differences in construction between the main gun decks and the decks of the upper works. The upper deck, visible through the waist, has heavy deck beams, linked by carlines, which are in turn linked by lighter pieces parallel to the deck beams, known as ledges. At the after end of the waist can be seen a spur, a curved deck beam which is so shaped to avoid interfering with the main hatchway. The forecastle and quarterdeck have lighter beams and no carlines or ledges, for they carried lighter guns. The poop deck is of even lighter construction, for at that stage it carried no guns at all.
The Science Museum

2 The traditional type of hanging knee (above) was secured alongside the deck beam, and bolted to the side of the hull through the timber and planking. In the lower drawing it can be seen from above, marked a. Beside it is the deck beam (s). Forward of that, marked b, is the lodging knee, which holds the deck beam secure in the horizontal plane. One arm of the lodging knee is bolted against the side of the ship. Long bolts hold the other arm to the deck beam, and also pass through the hanging knee. This and the following drawing are from Fincham's *Outline of Shipbuilding*.

3 A slightly later form of hanging knee, from the early nineteenth century, with a different form of iron bracket.

merely as a roof for the cabin, not expected to bear any significant weight at all. In the late seventeenth century it carried a few very light guns, but these were abolished in 1702. From then until the introduction of the carronade, the poop deck was kept clear of armament. The poop-royal, or 'topgallant roundhouse', where it existed, was of even flimsier construction, and was never expected to bear weaponry.

As well as being bolted securely to the frames, and supported by the wales, the deck beams were also braced by knees of various types. These knees were stout pieces of timber, roughly L-shaped, but varying according to the shapes of the surfaces to which they were joined. Because of this shape they required timber of a peculiar grain, and were therefore expensive and hard to find. The hanging knees supported the deck from below. One arm was bolted against the side of the ship, for the stagger of the gunports ensured that the knee of the beam under an upper deck port did not coincide with a lower deck port. The other arm of the knee was fitted alongside the deck beam, and was bolted to it, so that its upper surface was level with the deck planking. Towards the end of the eighteenth century, as the timber problem again began to become serious, a different type of hanging knee was developed. It was roughly triangular in shape, and was placed under the beam instead of alongside it. It was strengthened by iron frames bolted to each side, covering the join with the beam.

As the hanging knees prevented the deck beams from moving in the vertical plane, the lodging knees secured them in the horizontal: one end of the knee was fixed against the beam on the opposite side from the hanging knee, the other against the side of the ship. Similar in shape to the knees were the standards, which supported the beams from above as the hanging knees did from below. Naturally they could not be distributed in the same way as the hanging knees, or they would have blocked off the gunports – normally every second beam had one. The standards and knees did more than support the weight of the decks; they were an essential part of the bracing system which was

intended to prevent the hull being twisted out of shape by the forces of the sea. In the seventeenth century there had been an additional system of bracing, and pillars were placed diagonally across the hold to keep the hull in shape. It was objected that they made it much more difficult to stow the hold well, and they fell into disuse. Nevertheless vertical pillars were continued, both in the hold and between decks, in order to give the deck beams some support near their centres. At the bow the deck was supported by one of the breast hooks, known as the deck hook, and at the stern by one of the transoms, usually the second one below the wing transom, which was known as the deck transom.

The deck was covered with strakes of oak plank, usually 3 inches thick and 9 inches wide. As with the planking of the side, care had to be taken that the joins of each individual strake did not coincide with those of an adjacent one, and that they occurred over a deck beam. A system known as 'four step butt planking' was commonly used. This meant that joins occurred on each individual beam only in one strake in five. Around the edges of the deck, the waterways were placed over the planking. These were long strips of timber, triangular in cross section and a few inches deep, which joined against the sides of the hull. They were intended to keep any water which might find its way onto the deck away from the sides, and to direct it to the scuppers, which were cut through the deck under the waterways. Large spaces were left along the middle of the deck, to allow room for hatchways and ladderways. Around the edge of these holes were raised ledges of timber, known as coamings, which prevented water from falling to the deck below, and warned anyone passing in the dark that he was approaching danger.

Over a period of more than two hundred years, from the time of the Spanish Armada to the time of Napoleon, the changes in ship construction were few – less than the changes in design, in decoration, in armament, in fitting or in rigging. Much was based on long-dead tradition; the transoms, for example, were more relevant to the 1500s than the 1800s, but they still survived. One hundred and fifty years of the line of battle, of sending strong squadrons on long cruises and to foreign stations, had some effect, and some minor changes were made in the system, particularly in 1715, after the experience of Britain's first two European wars; but most of the structure of a ship remained the same as it had been in the time of Matthew Baker, and before.

Against this background, the achievement of Sir Robert Seppings was considerable, though he was aided by the fact that he was living at the beginning of an age of technological revolution. His contribution was a subtle one: the basic form of the ship of the line remained the same, and almost all of its features survived in one form or another; but each was carefully rearranged, altered, or had its purpose changed. The essential structure of the frame, with its floor timbers, futtocks and toptimbers, was superficially unchanged, but Seppings found ways of making the futtocks shorter and more numerous, which was less wasteful of timber. The riders in the hold, previously a series of unconnected pieces which supported individual parts of the ship, were transformed into a structure of interlinked diagonals, with great strength of its own. Even before the

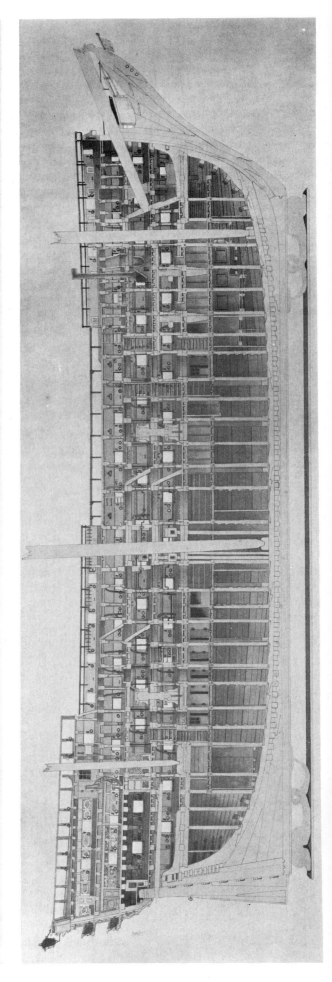

Over 130 years separate these two longitudinal sections of First Rate ships, but the differences in basic structure are small. The ship of 1680 (above) has diagonal braces across the hold, that of 1814 has not. The knees of the *Nelson* of 1814 are of the newer form, with iron brackets. The *Nelson* has the round bow, recently introduced. Otherwise little has changed as regards basic structure.
First Rate – The Science Museum; Nelson – National Maritime Museum

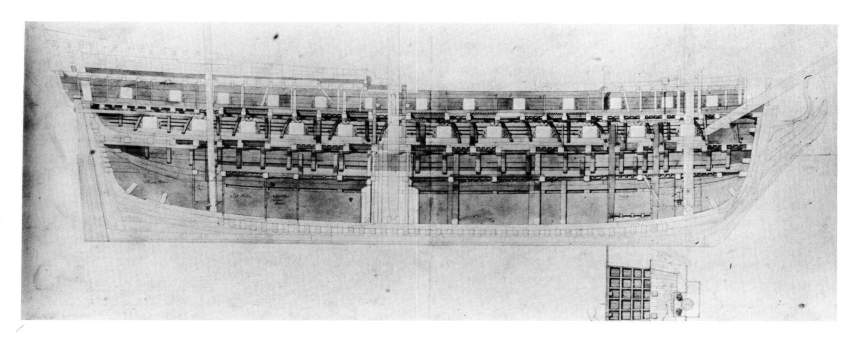

The longitudinal section of a 60-gun ship of the 1745 establishment. *Sjöhistoriska Museum, Stockholm*

This model shows some details of the Seppings system: the lattice-work of diagonal framing figures prominently in the lower part; diagonal beams are fitted between the gunports to give extra strength against hogging. In the lower part of the hull, the spaces between the frames are filled in with scraps of timber, to give extra solidity. The fourth feature of the system, the diagonal planking of the decks, cannot be discerned on the model. *The Science Museum*

circular stern was introduced, the horizontal transoms were replaced with vertical frames, as in the rest of the ship. The decks were planked diagonally, and the ceiling of the hold was abolished.

Seppings' reforms were carried out in several stages. The first, and simplest, was the round bow, by which the beakhead bulkhead was done away with and the hawse pieces and cant frames simply carried upwards to the level of the forecastle deck. The second, and most important, stage, was a package of reforms which became known collectively as the 'Seppings System'. Traditionally this is associated with diagonal bracing, but it must be emphasised that this was only one part of the system, which was designed to make ships much more rigid than in the past. Another aspect was the filling in of the spaces between the lower frames. This was not a new idea – seventeenth century contracts had asked for 'the lower futtocks to fill up the room' between the timbers, though towards the end of the century the saving clause 'whenever possible'[20] had been added, and the custom apparently fell into disuse. Instead of using large and expensive pieces to fill the space, Seppings used small scraps of timber, of 'slab and offal now sold as fathom wood.'[21] As well as making the whole structure more rigid, it was claimed that this prevented the lowest part of the ship becoming a sewer for bilge water, and thus enhanced the health of the crew. The internal planking was left out, to aid inspection of the timbers, to save space in the hold, and because the extra strength which it had once given was no longer necessary. The decks were framed diagonally, because Seppings was well aware that in the old system 'all the materials composing the fabric of a ship are disposed nearly at right angles to each other,'[22] and his total aim was to give diagonal rigidity. His successors were to find that the latter method contributed little to the strength of the ship, and was inconvenient. Longitudinal planking was restored after Seppings' retirement. Cross pieces were fitted between each pair of gunports, with a similar aim, for the sides of the ship, being almost vertical, were better sited to resist a hogging movement than the timbers of the hold.

Nevertheless the diagonal framing was the most important single feature. It was:

composed of a series of triangles, aided by diagonal trussing between the ports, [which] prevents the fabric from being acted upon transversely by the fibres of the materials horizontally placed, so the wales, the planking, the shelf pieces, the improved waterways, and the decks systematically secured, become the tie pieces of the structure. In a word, the system of triangles is so constructed, in conjunction with the planking of the ship, as conjointly to possess that property of a triangle already explained, *viz* that its figure is unalterable as the compression or extension of the fibre of timber will admit it to be.[23]

The internal frame itself was made up of relatively short pieces of timber, to save expense, and it in turn allowed the use of shorter futtocks on the main structure, so that a ship

built on the Seppings system was not vastly more expensive than one built on the old method, though it gained much in strength and performance.

The Seppings system had its critics. There were those who said that the diagonal bracing was weaker at the bow and stern than the old system of riders and breast hooks, and it was in these areas that strength was most needed. More common was the complaint that the braces took up much of the limited space in the hold. Seppings countered this by claiming that the new riders took up less room than the old ones, which were fewer but much larger, and were combined with internal planking, but the majority of sea officers remained unconvinced. The final answer was to use iron riders instead of wooden ones, and these were fitted to frigates in Seppings' time, though not to ships of the line until after his retirement. In fact Seppings contributed little to the use of iron in shipbuilding. His concern, in his own words, was with 'the disposition of the materials which compose the fabric of a ship', rather than with altering the nature of the materials. In a previous generation Snodgrass had done much to bring forward the use of iron knees, and later Symonds was to advance the use of iron riders; in that respect both were more far-sighted than Seppings.

The final, and most obvious, of Seppings' changes was in the stern. The round stern did much to increase the rearward-firing gun power of a ship, but that was not Seppings' main argument for it. He published a long list of captains who had complained about structural weakness in the sterns of the ships, caused not by enemy action but by

The old system of construction (above) constrasted with the Seppings system: the heavy riders of the old system can be clearly seen. The riders of the new system are more numerous, but lighter, and placed to give greater rigidity.

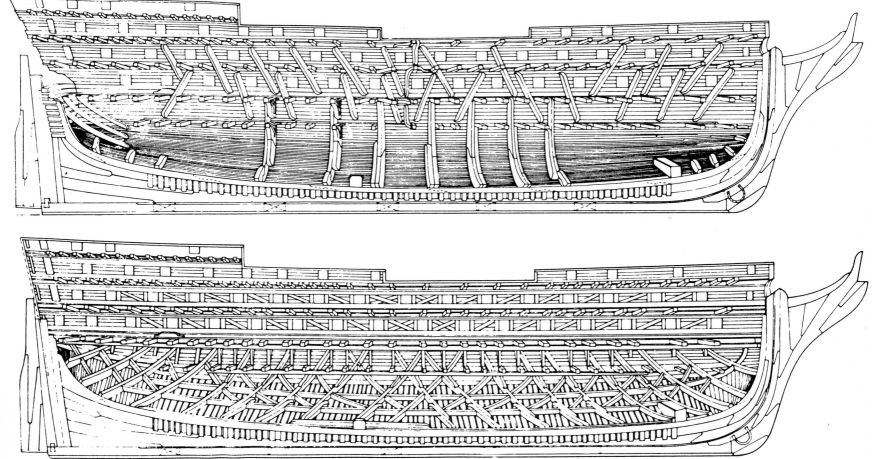

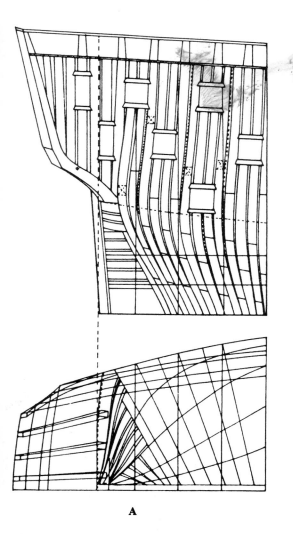

A

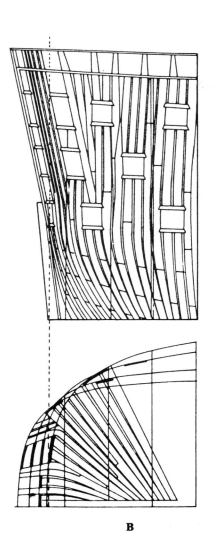

B

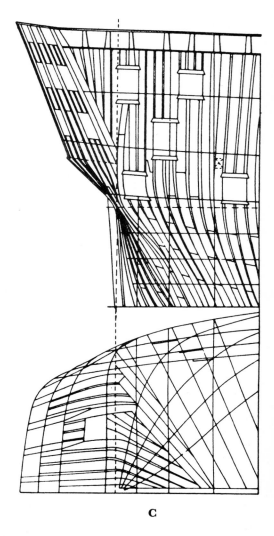

C

the normal wear and tear of a voyage, and showed how his new stern would remedy this.[24] Certainly the old form of stern, with the wing transom supporting almost everything above it, had been the weakest point of a ship, both against the effects of the sea and against enemy shot. Seppings' first attempt at remedy had been to replace the lower transoms with short vertical frames. The wing transom was retained, and continued to bear the weight of the upper stern; but it was now supported by many more pieces of timber than previously. Soon after the Napoleonic wars he took the process much further, and extended the vertical timbers right up to the top of the side. This of course incurred the wrath of the sea officer corps, who loved their old sterns for a variety of reasons, good and bad.

The 'elliptical' stern, introduced during Symonds' term as Surveyor, was a compromise, and a partial return to the old system. The counter was partially restored, though in a simpler form. With it returned the side counter timber, which again bore most of the weight of the frame timbers aft of the fashion piece; but the structure of the rearmost face remained vertical. Instead of the light stern timbers of the old system, widely spaced and joined only with glass and light boards, the elliptical stern had a solid structure of frames, comparable in strength to that of the sides. Below the counter they were supported by a similar structure, so that most of the strength of the circular stern was retained, while appearance and gun power were much improved.

THE EVOLUTION OF THE STERN IN THE NINETEENTH CENTURY.

A. The traditional square stern, with transoms, counters, and vertical stern pieces.
B. The Seppings round stern, composed entirely of vertical timbers, and with no counter.
C. The elliptical stern: the timbers still run vertically, but the counter has been partly restored to help protect the rudder head, and the extreme rear has been flattened slightly to give a more attractive appearance, and more comfort for the officers.

British ships, unlike those of Holland and of other European nations, were invariably launched into the water stern first, for it was found that the slightly bluffer lines of the stern helped to reduce the travel of the ship after she hit the water, and the counter and the outward curve of the hull near the stern prevented her from submerging too far on impact. Launching cradles were built under the bow and stern. These would move with the hull as it entered the water, supporting it and preventing it from rolling as it slid into the water. The cradles were placed on planks running along the floor of the slip, on each side of the ship. Once the cradles were in position, the blocks which had hitherto supported the keel were removed, and the weight borne by the cradles. Props were placed under the wales near the stern, with their lower ends resting on the ground beside the slip. When these were knocked away, the ship would slide into the water. Strong ropes arrested her movement across the water after launch.

The ship as launched was an empty shell, strongly constructed of immense timbers, but unpainted, unsheathed, unrigged, lacking masts, guns, and most of the necessities for survival at sea. If she was built in a merchant yard, she would be towed by boat to the nearest dockyard, usually only a short distance away along a river or across a bay, and there she would be fitted out. If built in a dockyard, she would probably be put into a dry-dock as soon as possible if she were to be sheathed, and after refloating she would be rigged and fitted for sea service. If she happened to be launched in time of peace, she might be laid up 'in ordinary', under the care of a few shipkeepers, often negligent, and run the risk of rotting at her moorings, even before she put to sea.

The *Victory* ready for launching in 1765: rails have been built on the floor of the slip on each side of the keel, and these support the launching cradles, which in turn support the hull under the bows and stern. Props are erected under the aftermost part of the wales. When these are knocked away, the ship will slide into the water.
National Maritime Museum

3. Decoration

ANYONE FAMILIAR WITH MODERN WARSHIPS, WITH THEIR sparse ornaments and sombre paint schemes, must inevitably wonder at the extensive and lavish carvings, and garish colourings which flourished during the age of the ship of the line, especially in its earlier part. Why, the modern mind asks, were governments prepared to spend vast sums of money – up to a tenth of the cost of the hull – on decorations which served no practical purpose, made no contribution to the sailing or fighting qualities of the ship, and added nothing to the material comfort of the crew? Why should governments which were often hard pressed to find the money for more essential tasks, such as feeding their sailors and repairing their ships, be ready to pay for quantities of timber, skilled labour and gold paint, which added nothing to their real military power?

The short answer is, of course, prestige. In the middle decades of the seventeenth century, when expensive decorations first began to spread throughout the fleet, governments were insecure, and needed to display the symbols of their authority. Wars with foreign powers were less than total, and still retained an element of medieval pageantry, useful in preserving the morale of the combatants. Lavish decoration was initiated by the early Stuarts, with the *Prince Royal* and the *Sovereign of the Seas*, but the Puritans who ruled after the Civil War did nothing to restrict it, and in fact helped it to spread throughout the generality of the fleet. The government of Charles II, in an authoritative modern judgement, 'lacked confidence, a sense of grandeur, all belief in its own inevitable destiny.'[1] Yet during this reign the decorations of ships reached almost legendary proportions. William III was an austere man, but during his reign the amount spent on decorations reached even greater heights.

However, the attitude of the central government is only partly relevant to the growth of decorations. Even Charles II, self-indulgent though he was, made several attempts to cut back on the waste of money.[2] At a lower level, the officials of the Navy Board often urged greater economy, but with little success in the seventeenth century; for decorations were not fully under the control of the central administration, and largely remained, like other matters, within the prerogative of the master shipwright – and the shipwrights, almost without exception, had an urge to make their ships as attractive and ostentatious as possible. By contrast with the situation in France, where a grandiose and centralised monarchy encouraged the use of decorations and employed artists and sculptors to increase the beauty and prestige of the fleet, the officials in London, from the King down to the Navy Board, had little real

control over the quality and quantity of ships' decorations. True, a model was usually sent to the Navy Board for inspection before a ship was built, but the official correspondence shows little sign that this led to many amendments, and there is some evidence that the master shipwrights made changes after the model had been approved. As early as 1638 complaints were made of the 'captain, master builder, or the like, whose ambition it is to have "their" ships, as they call them, richest and gayest, to waste the King's treasure in a vain expense, either in point of quality of painting, carving of joining, or in point of curiosity of workmanship.'[3]

In England, then, ships' carvings were done to the design of untutored master shipwrights, and executed by vernacular craftsmen. Kings sometimes influenced the decorations of their great prestige ships, but there was no systematic attempt to impose any standards or uniformity. Yet by the second half of the seventeenth century a distinctive English style had evolved, and the different ships of the fleet had a surprising amount in common. By that time there had evolved what we might call a 'Charles II' style; familiar to many from the model of the *Prince* of 1670, and from Van de Velde drawings. To find the origins of this style, with its circular wreathed gunports and black topsides, its heavily carved figurehead and rails, its elaborate stern with a strong vertical emphasis, we have to look many years earlier.

The beakhead may have originated with the rams of the galleys, but it could never have served such a purpose on a purely sailing warship. Instead, we can see on some of the early galleons a structure rather like a boarding bridge, which could have projected over the waist of the ship under attack, allowed the attackers to enter, and perhaps carried some light guns of its own. It had clearly lost such a function by the later sixteenth century, but it survived in a decorative rather than a functional form. That of the *Prince Royal* was typical – projecting almost horizontally and low over the water, with its flat sides boarded up and embellished with carvings. It still had some practical functions, such as an anchorage for the bowsprit and a base for handling the running rigging of the spritsail – and, traditionally, as the toilet accommodation for the crew – but it was weak, vulnerable and exposed, and most of its length was unnecessary. Over the next few decades, there was a gradual modification. The head of the *Sovereign of the Seas* was not unlike that of the *Prince Royal*, except that its fore part was raised a little further from the water by a slight upward curve, and it tended to taper forward. In the 1640s the pace of change appears to have accelerated: the rails of

1 The head of the *Prince* of 1610, extending well forward, and low above the water.
The Science Museum

2 The *Dunbar* (re-named *Henry*) of 1656 shows many of the typical features of Commonwealth decoration: the head now rises much more steeply; the quarter galleries are of the three-part form which had become normal by then. Square carved port wreaths can be seen on the gunports of the quarterdeck.
National Maritime Museum

the head began to curve upwards more and more, the taper was increased, and the solid sides were abandoned in favour of an open framework. Decoration was transferred from the boards between the rails to the rails themselves, particularly the verticals, which were usually carved in the shape of figures. Thus the head became lighter and more compact, while still being able to perform its more useful functions, and allowing more room for decorations. The old type of head had been supported by a heavy knee in the angle between the head and the stem. In the newer type of head this space was filled in with what amounted to a cutwater, though the term 'knee of the head' was retained for many years. In the 1640s the fore edge of the cutwater was slightly concave; by about 1660 it was generally straight.

In this situation the figurehead first came into prominence. Older ships had usually carried some kind of figure on the extreme fore part of the ship, placed on the end of the head itself, and usually arranged horizontally. With the new head, the figurehead became much larger, and its position was much closer to the vertical. Lion figureheads were used for the majority of ships, though some individuality was retained, and the lions were carved in a wide variety of styles. They often had little resemblance to the beast of that name, but had an almost human face, with long hair, and often a rather emaciated body. The large three-deckers normally had a figurehead of a man on horseback, usually trampling his enemies underfoot. This was a tradition which dated back at least to the time of the *Prince Royal*, but the need to make the figure almost vertical

imposed severe restrictions on the carver, and forced both animal and man into some strange contortions.

By around 1650 the basic form of the head was fixed, and after that the rate of change slowed down again. The main tendency of the next few years was to increase the angle between the cutwater and the waterline, thus making the head yet more compact, the figurehead more vertical, and the curve of the rails yet greater. This was made easier by the gradual abandonment of forward-firing armament. On three-deckers it had been common to make provision for guns to fire forward from both the middle and upper deck, and while this custom prevailed there was a limit beyond which the head could not be raised, without danger of interrupting the field of fire. As late as 1669, the *St Michael* was built with forward-firing guns on the middle deck, and correspondingly low rails on the head. Only a year later, the *Prince* abandoned all attempt at such guns on the middle deck. The angle of the cutwater was raised to about 45 degrees, and the head was thus shortened and gained an appearance, and perhaps a reality, of greater strength. After this it was to be nearly eighty years before any changes were made in its position and basic shape, though the vertical pieces supporting the rails, known as the head timbers, began to curve inwards in the early eighteenth century, whereas in the seventeenth century they had curved outwards.

The decoration of the bow was enhanced by the knighthead. For most of the seventeenth century the bowsprit was placed to one side, and partly held in place by

2

Heads of three-deckers, c1670: the drawing of the *St Michael* of 1669 shows the older form of head, low cut so that the chase guns mounted on the upper deck can fire over it; the model of the *Prince* (which was launched in the following year) displays a much more advanced head, with a much steeper rise and higher rails, so that chase guns can no longer be mounted on the upper deck. The figurehead of the *St Michael* is untypical, being neither the equestrian figure of the First Rates nor the lion of the Third Rates and below. She was originally classed as a First Rate, and these ships sometimes had individual figureheads in Caroline times – in this case a figure of Neptune being drawn in a chariot by a bird.
Drawing – National Maritime Museum; Model – The Science Museum

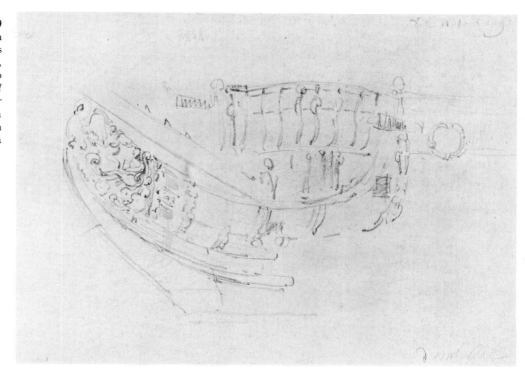

the upper end of the stempost. This was carved in the shape of a human head, hence its name. In the 1680s bowsprits began to be placed centrally, and the term knighthead was retained to describe the two pieces of timber which rose on either side of it, though these tended to be much less decorated than their predecessor.

The head of a ship was a purely maritime feature, having no resemblance to any structure on shore. The stern, on the other hand, was flatter, squarer, and more angular, and could, if the designer so wished, emulate the great palaces, cathedrals and public buildings on shore. French designers often availed themselves of this, and strong architectural influences can be seen, both in the way in which the straight lines and flat surfaces of the stern were accentuated, and in the use of the baroque forms then in vogue in France. In England there were few signs of such a relationship between the artist and the ship designer, where the design was in the hands of the master shipwrights, who had no knowledge of artistic movements ashore. The early quarter galleries did indeed have some resemblance to oriel windows, but in the 1670s these were at least fifty years out of date. The baroque style, with its florid decorations, could be adapted to seagoing use, but it was never common among English architects, and the angular and well proportioned classical designs favoured by Wren and Inigo Jones could not be well adapted to the shape of a ship. A ship designer used wood as a basic material, and this was much easier to carve and bend into curves than stone, which was then gaining increasing prominence as a building material on land.

The stern itself was a relatively flat surface, above the counters, with a curved taffrail at the top. In the early seventeenth century it was very narrow above, but it began to widen in the 1640s, partly as a result of new methods of design. From early in the century, a row of windows was fitted across it at the level of the upper deck, and also across the middle deck on three-deckers. This was for the

convenience of the officers, who were traditionally accommodated there.

These windows offered some opportunity for architectural styling. Before 1640 they usually had plain vertical supporters between them, with arches above, thus giving the appearance of a great house, or public building. This style was replaced during the Commonwealth period, when the arches were abandoned, and the plain pillars replaced with carved figures. This style was extended down through the counters, which had similar carved figures to divide them into segments. The spaces between the figures were decorated with either paintings or bas-relief carvings, usually of heraldic, classical, or astrological figures. Even during the rule of the Puritans, there is no sign of any attempt to introduce a religious theme. The horizontal sub-division of the stern was achieved by comparatively simple mouldings, plain and light in comparison with the carved figures. Thus it gained its vertical emphasis, which was so characteristic of the third quarter of the seventeenth century.

Early Stuart taffrails were usually plain, with only a simple rail to prevent the occupants of the quarterdeck from falling overboard. The *Sovereign of the Seas* had a slightly more elaborate version, and this seems to have drawn attention to the possibilities, for the taffrail became more complicated over the next few years. By 1660 it was formed by a complex series of carvings, which completely obscured the rail on which it was based. The carvings usually incorporated carved figures such as serpents, and various other emblems.

The edges of the stern, which formed corners with the sides of the hull, gained light carved figures in the early 1640s, and these became larger in the 1660s. Usually there were two on each corner: one on the flat of the stern itself; the other, slightly larger, round the corner on the extremity of the sides of the hull. Below the counters, the stern decorations were rather less elaborate. In the 1660s there

The stern of the *Sovereign of the Seas* was unique, in that none of her contemporaries was so heavily embellished, but it nevertheless shows some features typical of the times – the top of the stern is still narrow, and a certain amount of architectural influence can be seen, especially in the shape of the windows.
National Maritime Museum

was usually a painting or carving of a seated figure, apparently in classical dress, with light abstract carvings between. The rudder head was usually carved, commonly with the head of a lion.

Quarter galleries were to become a prominent feature of ships in the mid-seventeenth century. They originated in the open balconies which Elizabethan galleons had carried on their sterns and quarters. By 1600 they were often covered over, and sometimes flanked with turrets, which may originally have been intended to serve as a shelter for musketeers, but soon became devoted entirely to the comfort of the officers. These tended to become rather larger in the 1630s, when there was often a single large turret, with a short open gallery.

The *Sovereign of the Seas* had three turrets joined together, of approximately equal height. All military function had evidently been lost, for they were dominated by large windows on both the lower and middle deck; up to the level of the upper deck the three turrets formed virtually a single structure, but above that each had a separate curved roof, thus giving each the appearance of a lantern. The old open gallery remained forward of the main structure, but this was soon to be abandoned in the vast majority of later ships.

This three-part arrangement was to remain the basis over the next thirty years, though it was to undergo some important changes. The centre dome tended to become larger, and to predominate over the other two. The curves of the dome became large, and gave a much more ornate impression, in contrast to the very angular galleries of the *Sovereign*. By 1670 the two outside domes had almost disappeared on some ships, so that the gallery almost assumed the 'half bottle' shape that was to become characteristic of the later part of the seventeenth century. At the level of the windows the three parts remained virtually indistinguishable: the windows followed the pattern of those on the stern, and in many cases had the appearance of a single row, though other ships accentuated those under the centre dome, and perhaps curved them outwards. Above the three pointed domes were placed more carvings. In post-Restoration times this usually meant a lion on one of the smaller domes, a unicorn on the other, both acting as heraldic bearers to a royal emblem at the top of the largest one. Occasionally this was replaced by a different symbol, as in the *Prince* of 1670, which had the three feathers of the Prince of Wales at the top of a very large central dome. Many ships had a recess on the side of the central dome, with a carved figure placed within it.

Below the level of the windows, the sides and ends of the quarter galleries were angled inwards, and came to an end a few feet below the windows. The surfaces of this area were divided into panels by carved figures, and the panels were filled with paintings or bas-relief carvings. Below that, on the side of the hull itself, was another carving, usually of a winged figure. At the very top of the stern, above the taffrail, were placed three stern lanterns. These had some practical purpose, in that they could be useful in guiding a following ship in a fleet sailing by night, but their size and number suggests their purpose was largely decorative. In the seventeenth century they were spherical in shape.

In the sixteenth century it had not been usual to place carvings on the sides of ships. Instead, they were normally

painted in bright and contrasting colours. The earliest ships built by the Stuarts, such as the *Prince Royal*, had some slight carving and gilding along their topsides, but the *Sovereign of the Seas* broke new ground in this respect, as in many others. Her sides, from the level of the upper deck upwards, were almost completely covered with gilded bas-relief carvings. There was a complex frieze between each pair of gunports, with slightly plainer pillars against the sides of the gunports themselves. This method was clearly too expensive to be used on the generality of ships, but it may have helped inspire the next stage.

This was the square port wreath, which appears to have become common in the 1640s and 1650s. The upper deck ports of the *Sovereign* had in effect been wreathed, in that they had been flanked by pillars, and bounded at the top and bottom by the wales, which were themselves gilded. In later pictures of the *Sovereign*, showing her as she was in the 1670s, we can see that these have developed into wreaths, whereas the more elaborate decorations between the ports look rather less prominent, perhaps because their gilding has not been kept up. In any case, most ships of the Civil War and Commonwealth period acquired a floral decoration around the edges of each of the square gunports on the upper deck, forecastle, and quarterdeck.

Even by this time, we can see the inspiration for the next step. The ports in the waist usually carried no lids at this time, and they were often small and circular, merely allowing room for the gun to project, with little space for elevation or traversing – so they were surrounded by a small circular wreath on many ships. This system had some disadvantages: the small circular gunports must have been

inconvenient in action; and the circular wreaths, in the middle of a line of square ones, broke up the symmetry of the design. Around 1660 there was a trend to replace the old port wreaths, both the full-sized square ones and the small circular ones, with large circular wreaths, which were rather larger than the ports themselves, and only came into contact with the ports at their corners, if at all. Soon they were being fitted to all new ships, and the old square ports fell into total eclipse.

The word 'wreath' tends to imply a floral design, and indeed this was the most common; but occasionally ships had a design consisting of a curved figure on each side, with other carvings joining them above and below. Some ships had two different designs, which alternated along the length. On larger ships the bulkheads of the quarterdeck, poop and forecastle were also decorated with carvings, though on two-deckers they seem to have been much simpler, with only plain wood carving, at least until the 1677 programme. The forward bulkhead, aft of the beakhead, was particularly elaborate, especially on First Rates. It usually had a row of vertical figures, with gilded figures between, often over the surfaces of the gunports.

Much of the beauty of ships of this period comes not from the detail of the carvings but from the general proportions, and also from the style of painting, which was rather restrained in contrast with the ornateness of the decorations themselves. The lower parts were left in their natural wood colour; the topsides were painted black or very dark blue; the decorations themselves, according to the evidence of models, were painted in gold leaf, and thus contrasted strongly with the plainness of the rest of the hull. However,

The *Mary Rose* (ex-*Maidstone* of 1654) has a typical Restoration stern: the three-part quarter galleries, tending to resemble oriel windows; the statue in the panel above the centre part of the gallery; the lower part of the flat of the stern vertically segmented by lines of carving, while the space between the taffrail and the stern windows, almost square in shape, is dominated by the Royal coat of arms.
National Maritime Museum

Decorations of the sides, c1670: the *Prince* model has typical circular port wreaths, with carved figures supporting the entry port and ladder; other carvings form parts of the rails of the sides. The Van de Velde drawings of an unidentified ship (opposite) show some variations on this theme, with figurine rather than floreate port wreaths.
Model – The Science Museum; Drawing – National Maritime Museum

it would seem that gold leaf was in fact too expensive to use in the great majority of cases and it seems that a cheaper but less striking form of gold paint was normally used. The coat of arms on the stern is shown as gilded on most models, but the evidence of most paintings suggests that it was given the appropriate heraldic hues, thus providing a touch of colour as an effective contrast.

This, then was the style of decoration which we associate particularly with the reign of Charles II. In fact it was only refined and developed during that reign, for every feature of it had originated during the Commonwealth, or earlier. Moreover, it was not to remain in fashion for more than half of Charles's reign; it reached its height in the early 1670s, but there soon appeared a new influence, which was to change it drastically. This was Colbert's new French navy, which so impressed Charles II and terrified most of his

Bulkhead decoration, shown here on the *St Michael* of 1669, was normally confined to three-deckers until the late 1670s; smaller ships tended to have much plainer bulkheads. *National Maritime Museum*

1 The beginning of the revolution in stern decoration: the *Hampton Court* of 1678 shows one of the first examples of French influence, being fitted with stern galleries. Some attempt has been made to retain the vertical emphasis, in that the rail of the lower gallery has vertical supporters, but the Royal coat of arms is not in evidence. The carving of the taffrail is very ornate, completely overshadowing the taffrail itself. The tripartite arrangement of the quarter gallery is now rather vestigial, and the central pinnacle completely dominates the other two.
National Maritime Museum

2 The early eighteenth century head, on a 90-gun ship of 1702: the great depth of the head has led to the introduction of a fourth rail; the overall effect is rather regular and angular; the vertical head timbers curve inwards, whereas in the previous century they had normally curved outwards. The influence of Chinoiserie can be seen in the figures on the forecastle bulkhead, and in the shape of the lion figurehead.
The Science Museum

subjects. The French had put great artistic effort into the design of their ships, and in appearance they were very different from the English ones: much more angular on the stern and quarters, more florid and rounded in the bows. The carvings were perhaps a little less numerous, but generally more elaborate, and they carried open galleries in the stern for the comfort of the officers.

The French style of decoration first began to have effect in England in 1673, when Charles was so impressed by the *Superbe*, and ordered her design to be copied by Deane. Deane's two ships, the *Harwich* and *Swiftsure*, took much of their decoration from the French style, both in the method of placing the carvings and in the use of stern galleries.[4] By 1677 there was a general move towards the use of stern galleries. As yet many ships were not fitted with them, but about half of the 1677 ships carried them in one form or another: most had projecting galleries, which jutted out directly from the flat of the stern; others had recessed galleries, in which the row of stern windows was omitted, and a screen bulkhead placed a few feet forward, to allow a kind of covered balcony; yet others had a combination of the two, giving a rather wider gallery. Some of the two-deckers had two galleries, one on the quarterdeck and one on the upper deck. At first there was no general pattern, and much appears to have been left to the individual shipwright.

These galleries did much to alter the old system of decoration, for in time they naturally destroyed the vertical emphasis of the stern. It was now becoming common to fit a row of stern windows on the quarterdeck cabin, and this, even if it was not combined with a gallery, meant that the royal coat of arms, which had once dominated the stern, became much smaller. It was usually fitted between the quarterdeck and the upperdeck windows. Initially there was some attempt to retain the old vertical emphasis, with lines of carved figures running upwards despite the

1

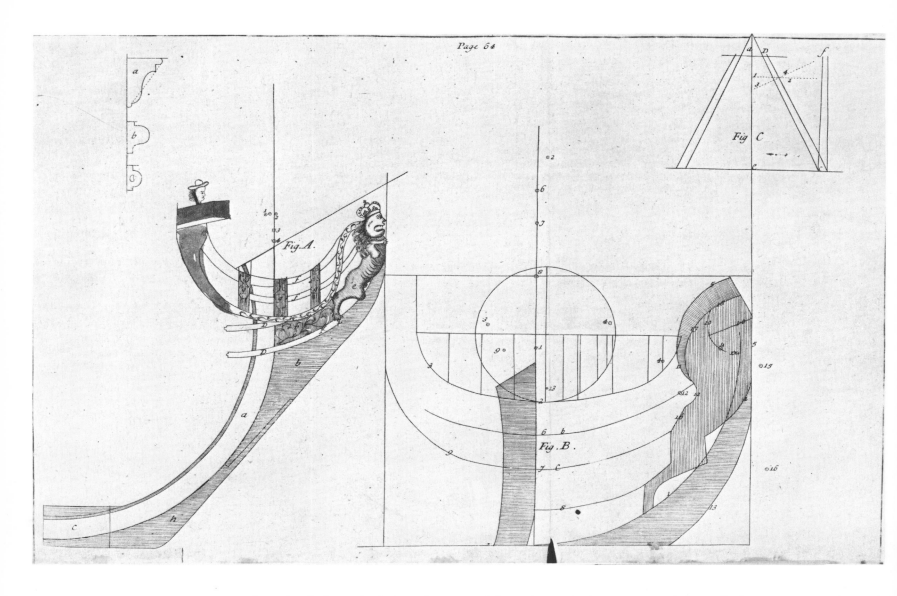

Ways of drawing the head, from Sutherland's *Shipbuilding Unveiled* of 1711. Around this time, the figurehead began to take on an increasingly standardised form.

interruptions of galleries and windows, but around the end of the century these had been replaced by heavily carved friezes, which usually had a horizontal emphasis.

The quarter galleries were now losing their tripartite form, and assumed a shape similar to a half-bottle, but angled slightly backwards. The upper part of the quarter gallery had once been purely decorative, but now there was a general trend to make the quarterdeck cabin more comfortable, and in some of the ships of the 1677 programme we can see that there is a real quarter gallery at that level. By the 1690s it was becoming common to have a window in the upper part of the gallery, and in some ships, such as the *Boyne*, the gallery was beginning to lean against the flat of the stern, thus making it rather larger.

The head did not change fundamentally after 1670, but many superficial details were altered. The heads of the ships of 1677, influenced as they were by French Baroque, were particularly florid, but this trend did not last long. In succeeding years there was a tendency for the upper rail to become higher, thus making the head deeper. On three-deckers this led to the introduction of a fourth rail, which gave a rather clumsy appearance. The lion figurehead, still common to the majority of ships, gradually became more standardised in form, and there was apparently a standard set of rules for drawing it on the draught. Around 1700, the

vertical supporters of the rails began to curve inwards instead of outwards, and this was to remain the fashion until the end of the age of sail.

King William III, despite his sombre Protestant background, did nothing to restrict the carvings of his ships, and there are signs that they became even more expensive during his reign. The figures on the stern, for example, had once been carved only in bas-relief, but they were now becoming more solid and elaborate. The peak of this style of decoration came with the rebuild of the *Sovereign* in 1701. Of course she was a prestige ship, the largest of her day and the replacement for the pride of the Stuart navy; but, even so, the cost of her decorations was considered excessive, and caused something of a scandal within the naval administration.

It was not the first time that the excessive cost of decorations had come to the notice of the administrators. In 1677 even Charles II had repented of his custom of ordering shipwrights to add extra decorations without consulting the Navy Board.[5] Two years later it was discovered that some master shipwrights were ordering joiner's work which was 'not only extravagant and profuse as to their charge, but also very inconvenient with respect to the service', and the Navy Board ordered, to little effect, that it be stopped.[6] Again, in 1700 the Board cited 'the many cautions which

The *Boyne* of 1692 represents the transition between the Caroline and Georgian styles of decoration. Painted friezes can be seen on the sides, as well as port wreaths. She was one of the first ships to have windows on the upper quarter galleries, and the upper part of the gallery is already tending to lean against the quarter piece. Almost every part of the surface of the stern and quarter gallery is covered with carvings.
National Maritime Museum

The stern of a 70-gun ship showing typical decoration of the 1690s.
The Earl of Pembroke

have been given by this Board to the officers of His Majesty's yards against the increasing of His Majesty's charge in the ornamental works of His Majesty's ships,' and imposed a 'limitation to be put on the charge of works for each rate', ranging from £500 for a First Rate, £130 for a 70-gun ship, and £25 for a Sixth Rate.[7]

But it was not until the orders of June 1703[8] that any real impact was made, for these gave detailed instructions about which carvings were to be employed, and which were to be omitted. It was ordered that

> the carved works be reduced only to a lion and a trailboard for the head, with mouldings instead of brackets placed against the timbers; that the stern have only a taffrail and two quarter pieces, and in lieu of brackets between the lights of the stern, galleries and bulkheads, to have mouldings fixed against the timbers.

Thus most of the elaborate carvings were abolished, and replaced with much simpler mouldings. The port wreaths of the sides were left out of the list of permitted carvings, and were in effect abolished.

For a number of years, the orders seem to have been effective, and models dating from this period show a very plain style of decoration (though this does not prove that the shipwrights did not alter the design after the model had been approved by the Navy Board); but within ten years of the order, a new style of decoration had begun to emerge, slightly less lavish than the old one, but nevertheless much more elaborate than the orders of 1703 would have allowed. This is commonly thought of as the Georgian style, though, like its predecessor, it had actually been evolved slightly earlier.

By 1710, the quarter galleries invariably leaned against the stern, thus causing a single flat surface, broken up by galleries and windows. All ships of over 40 guns had some kind of open gallery on the stern. The quarterdeck gallery usually protruded over the stern, and was also inset and separated off by a screen bulkhead. Three-deckers had an additional similar gallery at upper deck level; many two-deckers also had a gallery at upper deck level, but it did not normally jut out beyond the line of the stern but instead was recessed, with a screen bulkhead to separate it from the cabin. Such a gallery, although stronger than the protruding one above it, was nevertheless very weak for its position so close to the water, and must have caused some problems in a heavy sea. The Admiralty appeared to recognise this as early as 1710, and ordered that 'there be no screen bulkheads placed in the great cabins of any of Her Majesty's ships for the future'[9], but the order was ineffectual, and they continued to be fitted until well into the 1730s. After that, the galleries of ships of the line became standardised – one on a two-decker, at quarterdeck level: and two on a three-decker, at quarterdeck and upper deck level.

The rails of these galleries dominated the appearance of the stern. Usually they were supported by decorated wooden pillars, but around the middle of the century there was a fashion for other forms of rail. In the early part of the century the open gallery was continued around the quarter gallery at quarterdeck level, but this must have caused some inconvenience for the users of the quarter gallery, and

The stern of the *Royal Sovereign* or 1701 represented a new peak of elaborate decoration, with heavily carved figures dominating the whole of the surface of the stern.

The effects of the order of 1703, shown on the *Captain* of 1708: she is without port wreaths or friezes on her sides, and the quarter galleries have virtually no embellishment.
The Science Museum

A typical stern gallery of the early Georgian period, on the *Edinburgh* of 1721: the lower row of stern windows has a recessed gallery, while the upper row had a protruding one; the open gallery is continued round the sides of the upper quarter gallery; the taffrail and quarter pieces are dominated by carvings, and there is much painted frieze work on the stern and the upper parts of the sides, replacing the bas relief carvings and port wreaths of earlier periods.
The Science Museum

the custom died out. Nevertheless, the rails of the open stern gallery were continued round the quarter galleries in the form of false rails, thus providing much of the visual emphasis of the stern. Above the galleries and windows, the taffrail was curved over the stern itself, with two smaller curved pieces above the rear faces of the quarter galleries. These allowed suitable flat surfaces, which were generally covered with elaborate carvings. The largest single carvings on the stern were the figures which formed the corners of the quarter galleries.

Gun port wreaths disappeared soon after the orders of 1703, and never reappeared. The sides of the ships were generally devoid of carvings, except for the strips of moulding which followed the lines of the planking and gunwales. The ends of the mouldings, at the breaks of the forecastle and quarterdeck for example, were formed of scroll work which broke the regular lines of the rest of the hull sides. Most ships of any size were heavily painted with decorative friezes, usually filling the space between the channel wales and the top of the sides. The bulkheads of the poop, forecastle and quarterdeck were less elaborate than in the past, but usually had some form of panelling and moulding, perhaps picked out in gold paint. After about 1720 lanterns were no longer spherical: they were hexagonal in cross section, with flat sides, and tapered slightly towards the base.

The figurehead retained its standard form throughout the first forty years of the eighteenth century, with the equestrian figure for First Rates and the lion for smaller ships. The lion, and some of the other carvings, often showed some Chinese influence, for trading visits to China had established the fashion for 'Chinoiserie' in the country, particularly around 1710. In the 1740s, ships were allowed to carry individual figureheads, often, but not always, representing the name of the ship. First Rates often had the 'double equestrian' form, rather peculiar in shape but usually very well carved. Smaller ships had a single figure of a man or woman, often in classical dress. In general the

The figurehead of the *Centurion* of 1732 is completely typical of the times. The lion stands almost vertically, and retains the form it had achieved in the early 1700s.
National Maritime Museum

The 'double equestrian' head, standard for First Rates around the middle of the eighteenth century, here shown on the *Royal George* of 1756.
National Maritime Museum

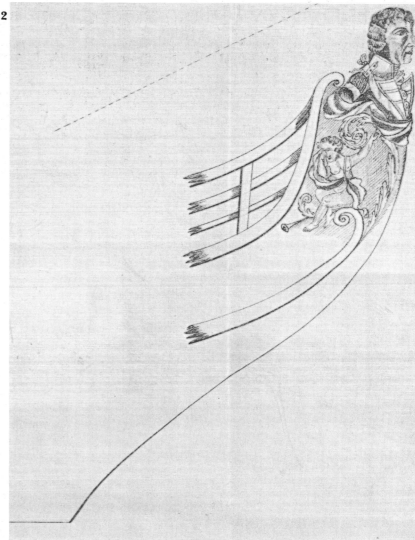

standard of carvings seems to have improved over the years, and none of the crudities of the seventeenth century were apparent.

The head itself became shallower in the 1750s. The rails of the head were brought closer together, giving a slimmer and more streamlined appearance. The rails were almost parallel to the waterline as they passed the stempost, but they curved sharply upwards just before they reached the figurehead. The head itself was close to vertical, and, in some cases around the middle of the century, it was angled slightly backwards. Below the head, the cutwater, which had been straight for almost a century, began to take on a slight inward curve around the middle of the century. Thus the head regained some of the features which it had lost in the 1650s, for it abandoned the straight cutwater and rounded rails of the last hundred years; but in fact it was very different in effect from the old head, being much smaller and less vulnerable, and more strongly supported.

It was not until 1771 that British warships began to carry their names painted on their sterns, though the French had carried them much earlier. In 1771 the British ships were to carry them painted on the second counter, in 12-inch high letters. In the following year this was amended, and the letters were to be 'as large as the second counter will admit'. This remained the standard practice, though in 1778 Admiral Keppel was allowed to obliterate the names from the ships of his fleet, for security reasons.

The Georgian style of decoration was restrained and almost sombre in contrast to the extravagances and frivolities of the later Stuarts. It still had little in common with land architecture, in that a ship could not be made to resemble the great Palladian country houses then being built. Nevertheless it does represent the spirit of the age, and the desire for order and stability is reflected in the regular lines of the ships' decorations, while the influence of a classical education is often to be seen in the figureheads. Though they resembled nothing on the exteriors of contemporary buildings, the friezes on the sides of ships may well have been influenced by the style of interior decoration then in use. The Georgian style was tasteful and elegant, which was fitting for an age of great architecture, but, although less extravagant than preceding styles, it was still too expensive for some.

The second version of the Georgian style, as settled

1 An example of the individual figurehead, introduced in the 1740s: it is from the *Egmont* of 1768, and is intended as a portrait of the First Lord of the Admiralty of the time.
The Science Museum

2 The short figurehead of the late eighteenth and early nineteenth century, as proposed for the *Victorious*, 74, in 1814.
Public Records Office

1 Stern galleries, second half of
the eighteenth century: the
recessed stern gallery on the
upper or middle deck has been
abolished, and replaced by a
simple row of stern windows.
The *Ajax*, 74, of 1767 has an
open gallery on the
quarterdeck only, as was
normal with two-deckers of the
period, although three-deckers
also had an open gallery on the
upper deck. The galleries
protrude over the stern, and are
also recessed and separated
from the cabins by a screen
bulkhead. The upper quarter
galleries are now completely
enclosed, but the rail of the
stern galleries is continued
round them in purely
decorative form.
The Science Museum

2 The *Victory* as rebuilt has the
typical plain stern of the early
years of the nineteenth century.
Stern galleries have been
abolished, and the flat of the
stern is closer to the vertical
than in earlier periods. Even on
a prestige First Rate, decoration is severely limited. The
quarter pieces are no longer
dominated by large carved
figures. Only imitation rails
and bas relief carvings are fitted
as relics of past glories.
CPL

1

around 1750, lasted through the Seven Years War and the American War with only slight alterations. The next war, against the French Revolutionaries, was altogether more intense, and closer to a twentieth century total war, as the British regime fought for its survival against a strong combination of European powers, and was obliged to set out enormous fleets to keep its enemies in check. In 1795, therefore, the Spencer administration began a new purge on decorations, more drastic even than that of 1703. It issued an order to 'explode carved works'.[10] Figureheads of larger ships had become increasingly elaborate over the years – the *Victory*, for example, had originally been fitted with an extremely complicated structure, whose official description occupied several hundred words.[11] By the new orders, figureheads were to become much shorter, with only a half length figure, instead of the full length one carried by the majority of ships. The painted friezes on the sides of ships were abolished. The carved figures which had

until now adorned the stern were no longer to be used, and only small bas-relief carvings, imitation rails, and mouldings round the edges were now to be fitted.

By a separate process, the stern galleries were removed and the stern became flatter. Captains had been showing dissatisfaction with their cabin arrangements for some time: the recessed screen bulkhead took up a great deal of space in the cabin, and was a considerable source of weakness, in that it gave very little support for the deck above.[12] With the fitting of carronades to the poop, such a situation could no longer be tolerated. There were some attempts to move the screen bulkhead aft, giving more room in the cabin, but this did nothing to increase the structural strength. With the building of the *Kent* and *Ajax* in 1795, a completely new type of stern was designed. It was closer to the vertical than the previous one, and formed a continous surface without interruption by galleries. In contrast to the old one, it was rather angular, and was almost flat, broken only by the

The round stern allowed some return of architectural influences. The rails and bow windows of the *Hibernia* are reminiscent of those to be found on seaside buildings of the late Georgian period.
The Science Museum

The elliptical stern of the *Albion* of 1842: in shape it resembles the stern of the second half of the eighteenth century, but decoration is minimal – only a rather crude moulding and a wrought iron rail, continued round the quarter galleries by an imitation rail.
The Science Museum

rows of stern windows. Furthermore, its carvings were small and light, and did not disturb its basic composition; as a radical break from tradition, large areas of the surface were left completely unadorned. This method was soon standardised by Admiralty Order.[13]

This style of decoration was to continue throughout the French wars, except that in the 1800s stern galleries began a partial revival, when the new First Rates of the *Nelson* class were allowed small protruding galleries, and other ships were similarly equipped later. These had no screen bulkheads, and so did not interfere with the structure.

Perhaps it was the basic simplicity of the new style which inspired greater interest in the painting of ships. In the past the sides of ships had been left in their natural wood colour, and payed with varnish for protection. Only the topsides, above the channel wales, had been painted – black in the seventeenth century, dark blue or red in the eighteenth century. By an order of 1780[14], captains were allowed black and yellow paint to cover the sides of their ships, but still retained much discretion in the manner in which it was to be applied. Over the next few years a wide variety of styles was used, especially since some captains could afford to add their own colours to those officially allowed. Usually they seem to have preferred yellow sides, with some of the wales and rails picked out in other colours, or in black. The famous 'Nelson chequer' came into use in the early 1800s, solely due to the influence of that famous admiral. The spaces above and below the lines of gunports were painted black, as were the gunport lids, and the spaces between

them were coloured yellow. The style was soon copied by the captains under Nelson's immediate command, then by the rest of the British fleet, and, before the Napoleonic wars were at an end, by many ships in foreign navies. By 1815 white had replaced yellow for the spaces between the ports on many ships, and this soon became established as the traditional style of the British warship, and was copied even by merchant ships.

Seppings' changes in the bows and sterns of ships further removed the opportunity for lavish decoration. The round bow made it impossible to fit the elaborate beakhead bulkheads which had been common in the past; the round stern further reduced the amount of space available for carvings. A small bas-relief carving was often fitted below the taffrail, but otherwise the stern was severely functional, with only cast iron rails and round quarter galleries to disturb its plainness. Sometimes these tended to resemble the balconies and bow windows fashionable in some houses of the 1820s and 1830s, and for once we can see a close link between land architecture and ships' decoration (though this may well have been accidental, and caused simply by the needs of the fleet as interpreted by Seppings).

The broad black and white stripes now began to extend to the extremes of both the bow and the stern. The rails of the head were now very close together, and the flat surface of the cutwater therefore became more prominent, and the black and white painting was continued along it. The coming of the elliptical stern after 1832 might have allowed some return of carvings, but the Navy had apparently become used to plain ships, and governments of the time were concerned to keep taxation down, and were unlikely to spend much money on such unnecessary articles.

The early Victorian warship was a complete contrast to her ancestor of Stuart or Georgian times, both because of the reluctance to spend money on frivolous decorations, and because of the design practices of the times. With very little sheer, a round bow and stern, and plain black and white painting broken only by a figurehead on the bow and a small frieze on the stern, she was severe, regular and functional. The ostentations of the master shipwrights had at last been brought under control, and governments had discovered that their security lay in the hard realities of ships and guns rather than in the prestige of decorations. The early Victorian warship looks rather ugly in draughts and in many drawings, but at sea her proportions gave her a functional beauty, and there is now an understanding that she had many advantages over her seventeenth and eighteenth century predecessors.

A plain head of the early Victorian period: the rails of the head have been greatly reduced in importance and elaboration, and the black and white stripes of the main hull dominate the area of the head. *National Maritime Museum*

4. Masts and Yards

Just as a modern ship would probably have its engines made by a different contractor from the firm that built the hull, so the main motive power of a sailing warship – the masts, sails and rigging – would not always be provided by the builder of the hull. It was not normal to include them in a contract with a merchant builder – a ship completed in a private yard would usually be towed to the nearest dockyard for fitting of masts and other accessories, and this was one of the main motives for restricting shipbuilding contracts to those who had yards near the dockyards. It was intended that masts and yards should be standard fittings, which could be kept ready in store in the dockyards, rather than built for an individual ship. Much effort was devoted to making this possible, and the Admiralty tried, by means of the establishments and by the use of standard designs, to ensure that 'all the principal sizes and measures requisite to be observed in the building of a ship and fitting her with masts, yards, blocks, etc be one and the same in every of the new ships of the same rank.'[1] Much of this effort was to no avail, as we have seen, and the establishments did not succeed in freezing ship design over a long enough period to be effective. Therefore the dockyards were obliged to keep large stocks of masts and yards of different sorts for the use of ships fitting for sea.

Ideally, the dockyards would have preferred to make the Navy's masts themselves, but this was not entirely practicable. A large proportion of the timber for mastmaking came from either New England or the Baltic,

Mastmaking tools c1790.
From Steel's Masting and Rigging

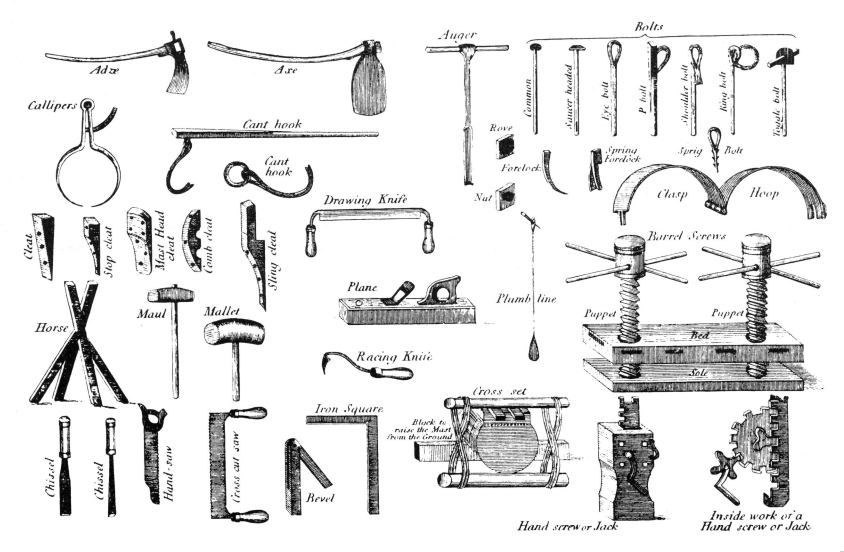

THE DEVELOPMENT OF THE SAIL PLAN 1670-1834

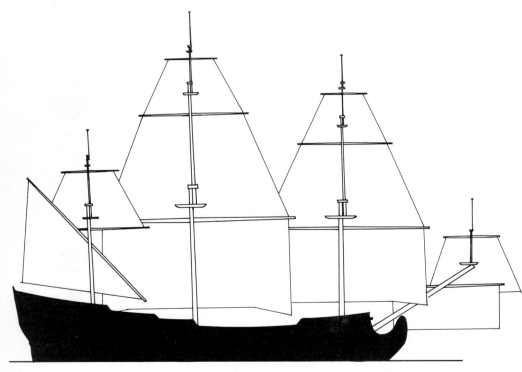

Third Rate 70-gun ship, based on Deane's *Doctrine* of 1670.

70-gun ship of 1692, based on plans taken off a model in Wilton House (see Volume I, p60): the fore mast has been moved slightly aft, and flagstaffs have been fitted above the topgallant masts.

and it was easier to have the trees trimmed to shape before transportation, though much of the finishing seems to have been done in the dockyards. Each dockyard had a master mastmaker who would supervise the work. Mastmaking was regarded as an integral part of the shipwright's trade, and labour could be assigned to the work out of the general pool of shipwrights.

Ships of the line invariably carried three masts. A fourth mast, the bonadventure mizzen, had been common on large ships in the sixteenth century, but it had died out in the 1630s, before the concept of the ship of the line had been evolved (though the *Prince Royal* had carried one in the earlier part of her career). Four and more masts were again carried by late nineteenth century ships, but only after the ship of the line had become obsolete, and only for fast, narrow clipper ships and ironclad battleships. The ship of the line, in contrast, was relatively broad in proportion to its length, and would not have been well suited to more than three masts:

> The masts being used to extend the sails by means of their yards, it is evident that, if their numbers were multiplied beyond what is necessary, the yards must be extremely short, that they may not entangle each other in working the ship, and in consequence, their sails will be very narrow, and receive a small proportion of wind.[2]

The three masts all fulfilled different functions. The main mast was easily the largest, and provided most of the driving force in most circumstances, and was therefore situated close to midships. The fore mast was a little smaller, and also provided much of the power of a ship, especially when the wind was aft. In these circumstances the main mast would not carry its full complement of sails, to avoid masking those of the fore mast. The fore mast was therefore situated well forward, to help keep the ship on a steady course. The mizzen mast was placed aft, but not so far aft as the fore mast was forward. Originally it had carried only fore-and-aft sails, and had been intended as an aid to steering rather than a means of propulsion; in later years it was to carry a full complement of topsails, topgallants and royals above, but the most important sail on the mizzen was still fore and aft, whether lateen- or gaff-rigged. If the mizzen was placed too far aft, the sail would overhang the stern, and be very difficult to handle.

The detailed positions of the masts varied somewhat over the years. In the seventeenth century it was believed that the main mast should be situated in the middle of the keel, and therefore somewhat aft of midships.[3] Models and documents of the later part of the century suggest that it tended to be moved forward over the years, ending just aft of the middle of the gun deck. In the mid-eighteenth century it was suggested that it should be placed 'at the axis of the equilibrium of the ships resistance', and experiments to find this point by hauling the ship sideways were recommended.[4] In the early nineteenth century there was apparently a rule, 'the result of long practice and experience', that the main mast should be five-ninths of the way along the length of the gun deck, from the stern, thus placing it forward of midships; but the writer urged caution: 'Perhaps, after all that can be said, there may exist more whim and fancy in the regulation than real truth.'[5]

In the mid-seventeenth century the fore mast was placed well forward, sometimes above the rake of the stem rather than the keel. Though this could have helped steering in a following wind, it must have affected the balance of the rig in other conditions, and it was gradually moved aft. By the early nineteenth century it was recommended that it should be one-ninth of the length of the gun deck aft of the stempost.[6] The mizzen mast varied considerably in position, even among ships of the same period, but the distance between the mizzen mast and the stern was generally about half to a third of that from main mast to the stern. The changes in the positions of the three masts over the years had the effect of spacing them more evenly, and placing them further away from the extremities of the ship. Nevertheless there remained a large gap between the fore and the main, caused partly by the fact that it was difficult to fit a mast in the waist, and by the need to keep the fore mast well forward to aid steering. A redistribution of the masts might have allowed a more balanced rig, but to achieve this it would have been necessary to alter much of the ship's layout, and it was never felt that this was necessary in the larger ships, though some experiments with smaller ships in the early nineteenth century tended in this direction.

Throughout the centuries, the two after masts were raked backwards, for it was believed that this helped the shrouds hold them more firmly in position. The fore mast, on the other hand, was almost vertical, perhaps because this would help carry its effect as far forward as possible. The rake tended to be reduced slowly over the years, but it remained even to the end of the age of sail. Its effect was slightly exaggerated in practice, for ships were usually trimmed to sink lower at the stern, and this meant that the masts were angled backwards even further.

The bowsprit, jutting forward from the bows and angled upwards, served a variety of purposes: it provided a lead for the bowlines, which held the edges of the fore sails forward when sailing close to the wind; it was important in the bracing of the fore mast; it also carried sails of its own, either square sails known as spritsails because of their position on the bowsprit, or fore-and-aft staysails hung on the fore stays. Its angle, or steeving as it was known, varied from time to time, and according to the sails which it was expected to carry. In the seventeenth century the spritsail topmast was fitted vertically to the end of the bowsprit, and this meant that the bowsprit itself did not have to rise very sharply: furthermore the lowness of the beakhead to which it was secured meant that it could not rise too steeply. As beakheads became higher, and the spritsail topsail less important, it began to rise more sharply, reaching an angle of about 30 degrees by 1670.[7] In the early eighteenth century the spritsail topmast was replaced by the jibboom, which was an extension of the bowsprit itself, and this meant that it had to rise even more steeply to allow the new topsail, fixed under the jibboom, to have any effect – an angle of 36 degrees was common around 1720. In the late eighteenth century spritsails were gradually superseded by staysails, and the bowsprit could again become flatter; 25 degrees was common at the end of the century.

The term 'mast' is to a certain extent ambiguous. It can mean the whole height of, for example, the fore mast,

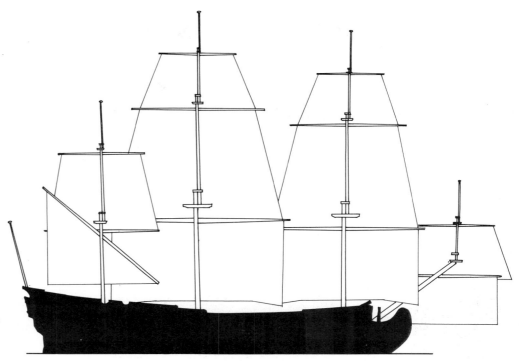

An 80-gun ship of the 1719 establishment: the topsail and topgallant yards have been considerably lengthened since the 1690s, making the topsails squarer and the topgallants larger.

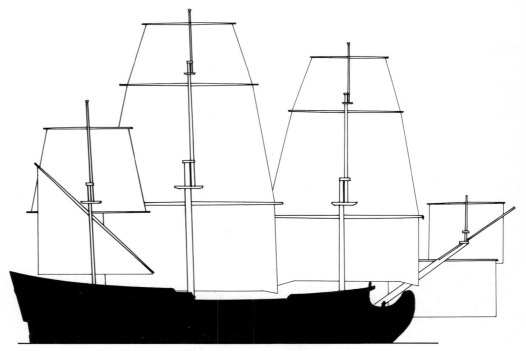

An 80 of 1745: the topsail and topgallant yards have been further extended. A jibboom is fitted, but the sprit topsail could still be carried on three-deckers.

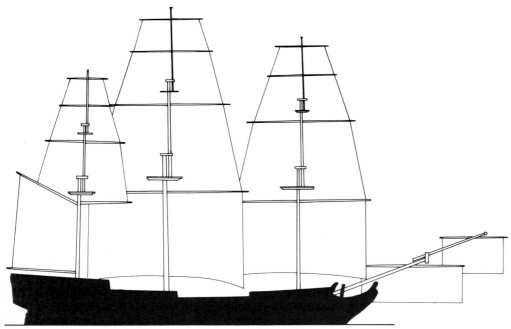

A 74-gun ship, c1795: royals have been introduced on the fore and main, and a topgallant on the mizzen; the sprit topsail is now carried under the jibboom; a gaff is fitted instead of a lateen sail on the mizzen.

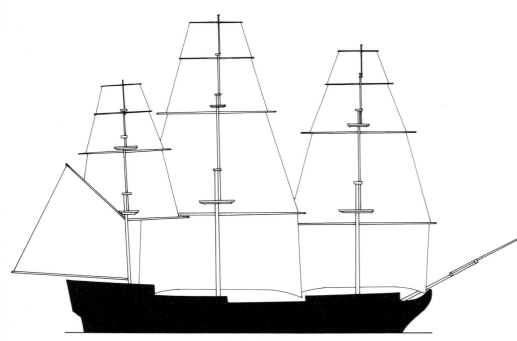

The *Revenge* of 1805, as rigged before the re-organisation of 1834: square sails are no longer carried under the bowsprit; the gaff mizzen has been considerably extended.

1 The *Edinburgh* of 1811, showing the rig she carried after the changes of 1834: the changes are only in the details, with minor adjustments in the sizes of certain sails.

2 Fore-and-aft sails as carried about 1800.

3 A Third Rate of about 1725 showing the combination of jibboom and sprit topmast fitted in the early part of the eighteenth century. *CPL*

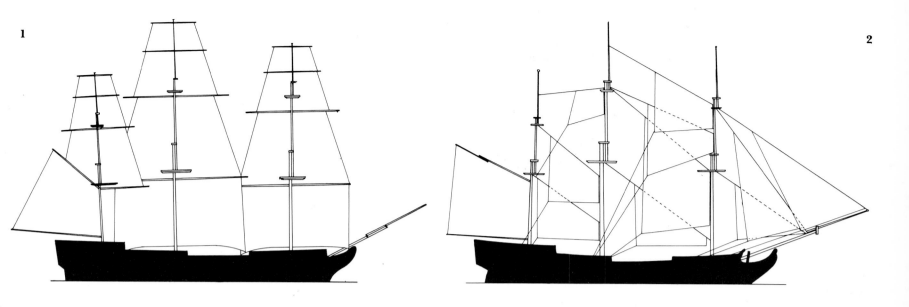

including the parts which support the topsail, topgallant, and royal (if any) up to the flagstaff at the top. On the other hand, it can refer only to each individual section of the mast; thus the fore mast in the former sense would consist of the lower mast (or fore mast proper), the fore topmast, the fore topgallant mast, and the fore royal mast. In the latter sense, it is reasonable to say that there was one mast and one yard for each sail, with the exception of staysails and studding sails which had no masts or yards of their own. In large ships it was not possible to construct a single mast which would support the lower sail, the topsail, the topgallant and the royal, and so several parts were made, and secured together by means of overlapping sections. Thus a ship of the line invariably had three lower masts; above each of these was to be found a topmast. Seventeenth century ships did not always carry sails above that, for the topgallant mast, though provided for all ships of the line, was not always carried, especially in winter. The *Sovereign of the Seas* took matters a little further, and from her first building in 1637 she was provided with royal masts and sails above the topgallants. She was probably the first ship to carry these, and remained unique in the British fleet of the seventeenth century. Royals were not to become standard on British ships of the line for nearly a century and a half after the building of the *Sovereign.*[8]

The lower portion of each mast was held securely to the hull of the ship. Its bottom end was fitted into a block of wood on the kelson, known as the step, except in the case of the mizzen mast, which after about 1690 was usually stepped on the lower deck. As the mast passed through each deck in turn, it was held firmly in place by partners – pieces of timber which linked it to the deck beams. The mast was at its widest where it emerged into the daylight, at forecastle and quarterdeck level, or at the level of the poop deck in the case of the mizzen. Below decks it tapered somewhat down to the step, and it also tapered rather more above decks. It was generally circular in cross section, but the section above the hounds, which was intended solely to form an overlap with the mast above, was rectangular in section. Just below the hounds were the cheeks. These were pieces fixed to the sides of the mast to help support the trestletrees above. In the mid-seventeenth century the cheeks were very short, but they were gradually extended downwards over time, and by the 1770s they were two-thirds of the way down the mast. They were fixed to the mast by rope woldings, and later by iron bands. Outside the cheeks, immediately below the trestletree, were the hounds. These were flat pieces of timber, with an extension forward known as bibs, which gave extra support to the trestletrees.

The topmast was slightly simpler than the lower mast in construction. It was naturally rather thinner, and basically tapered continuously from heel to head. Again it was mostly circular in section, except at the head. Its lower part, for about a fifth of its length, overlapped with the head of the lower mast. Its hounds were different in construction from those of the lower mast, consisting of a section of reverse-taper just below the siting of the trestletrees which usually became hexagonal in section instead of circular. Above that, the mast again became square where it was intended to overlap with the lower end of the topgallant mast. Topgallants and royals, if fitted, were yet smaller, and

The masts and yards of a 60-gun ship, *c*1760: all the lower masts appear to be constructed in one piece, except for the hounds and bibs which support the trestletrees. This was the most common method before the 1770s, especially for a relatively small ship such as a 60. *National Maritime Museum*

of similar construction to the topmast. The whole structure, whether it ended with the topmast, the topgallant or the royal, ended with a flagstaff, with a rounded head (or truck).

The trestletrees consisted of five pieces of timber. Two of these, the trestletrees proper, ran fore and aft, one on each side of the mast, and the other three, the crosstrees, ran athwartships, two before and one after the mast. They crossed over one another, and were rebated together. They served several purposes: they formed the join between the hounds of a lower mast and the heel of an upper one; they helped spread the shrouds which were intended to support the upper mast; and they provided a platform for the men working on the upper yards, and for lookouts.

Trestletrees were sufficient for the upper masts, but the head of the lower mast needed something more. This position served as a base for the men working the upper sails, and in action it was used by parties firing small arms and light artillery onto the enemy's decks. A stout platform, known as the top, was therefore built above the trestletrees and planked over. In the seventeenth century tops were circular, and had slightly raised edges, but by the beginning of the eighteenth century they had begun to assume a rather different shape. First, the rearmost edge was flattened, and then squared off, so that the top became D-shaped. The curved surface forward prevented interference with the sails, while the square corners aft allowed more working space for a given weight, and the flat parallel sides spread the shrouds more efficiently than rounded sides would have done. This shape changed only slightly during the next century, but the flat sides tended to take up a greater proportion of the length, the corners aft became squarer, and the curve forward was slowly made flatter; after 1815 the sides of the top began to taper forward.

The trestletrees and the tops served as one part of the join between an upper and a lower mast. This was reinforced by another join, between the partners of the upper mast and the head of the lower, which were linked by a piece of wood known as the cap. This was simply a rectangular piece of timber (with rounded corners in later periods), pierced with two holes – a round one for the partners of the upper mast and a square one for the head of the lower.

The bowsprit was generally similar in shape and construction to the lower masts, but its siting and function caused some important differences. For most of the seventeenth century it was placed to one side of the centreline, usually to the starboard. By around 1675, it was moved to the centreline, which was made possible by its changing angle. In the early period, it had risen at only a slight steeve, and had it been carried directly back along the centreline it would have interfered with the fore mast. In the later seventeenth century the bowsprit followed the beakhead in rising at an increasing angle to the horizontal,

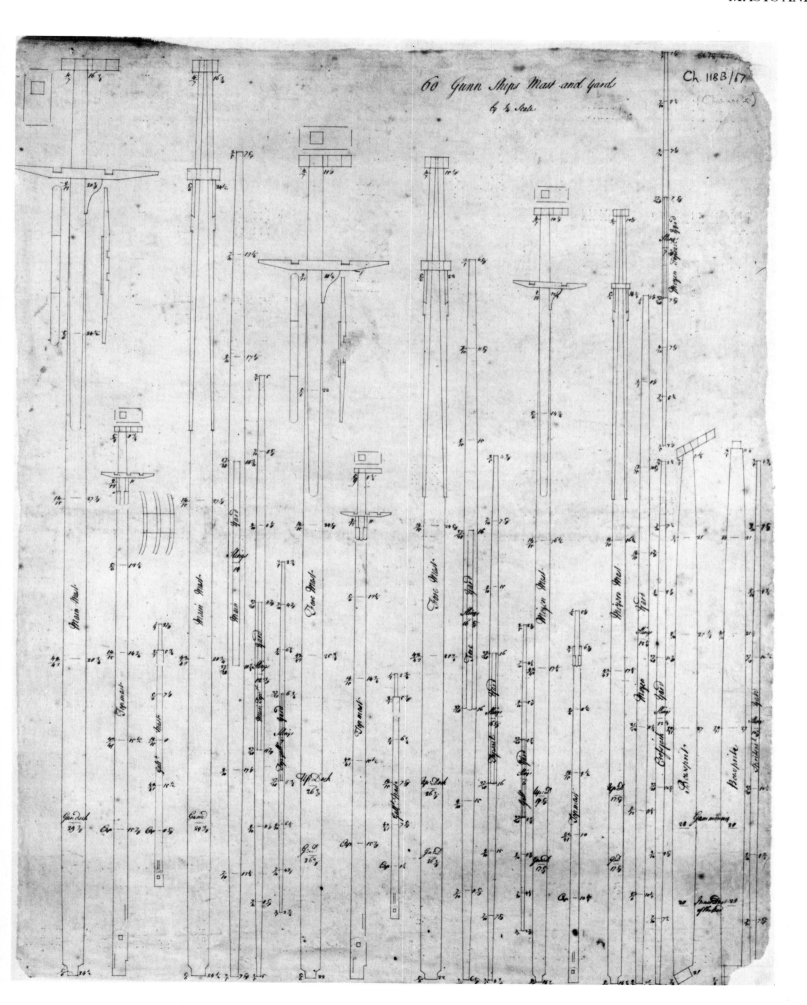

60 Gunn Ships Mast and Yards
by ¼ Scale

Ch. 118 B/57

The bowsprit, jibboom, flying jibboom and dolphin striker as fitted about 1815.
From Lever's Sheet Anchor

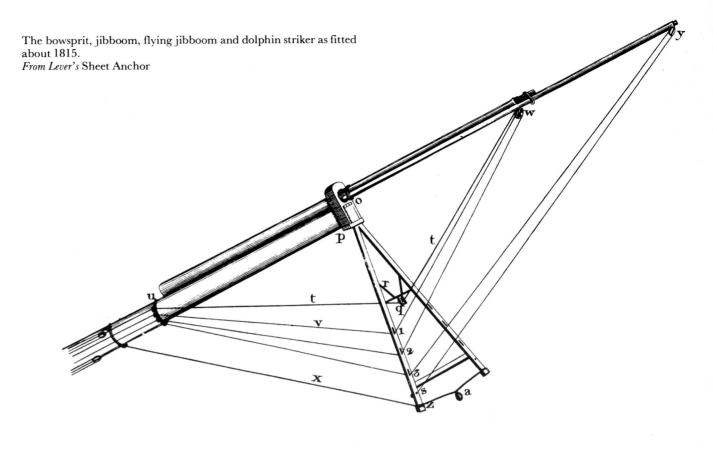

The made mast of a 74-gun ship, late eighteenth century.
Rigsarkivet, Copenhagen

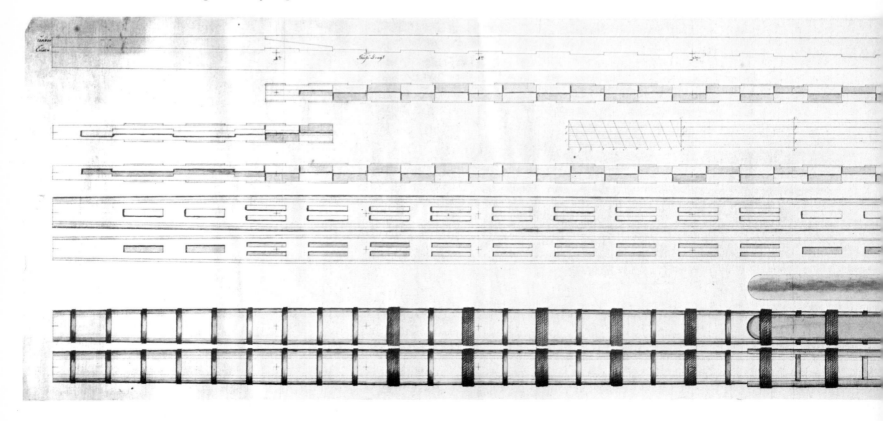

and thus it became possible to end it before meeting the fore mast; this was further helped by the fact that the fore mast now tended to be placed further aft. Its after end was held in position by the step, a large piece of timber with a square hole to receive the end of the bowsprit. The step was fixed to the upper deck, and met the bowsprit at right angles, so that the step itself was at an angle of several degrees to the vertical. The bowsprit was also secured to the hull by means of the knightheads. These pieces of timber arose vertically out of the main structure of the bows, and were intended to prevent the bowsprit from moving from side to side. They were so called because in the seventeenth century their tops were usually carved in the form of human heads.

The form of the outer end of the bowsprit varied according to the function it was intended to perform. Up to 1720 (and later in three-deckers) it usually had to support a spritsail topmast arising vertically out of its end. This meant that it had to be fitted with a top, similar to those of the fore, main and mizzen masts, to spread the shrouds of the topmast. Even so, the join was rather tenuous, for, in contrast to the masts themselves, there was little room for overlap between the bowsprit and the spritsail topmast, and it appears that the topmast was simply butted into a recess in the end of the bowsprit. Otherwise the spritsail topmast was similar in construction to one of the upper masts. It usually ended with a flagstaff and a round truck.

The spritsail topmast had other disadvantages besides the weakness of its join to the rest of the structure. Because of its position, its sail must have been very difficult to handle; it must have been virtually useless in a following wind, for it would have been masked by the other sails; and in any other position it could have borne little strain, for it was impossible to spread its shrouds sufficiently. It may have

been of some use in tacking and wearing, but it would have been clumsy to handle, and less efficient for such purposes than a fore-and-aft sail. Its supersession began around the beginning of the eighteenth century. In 1705 it became normal to lash an extension to the end of the bowsprit, carrying it directly forward; this soon developed into a regular spar, known as the jibboom, and acquired a yard to carry a new type of spritsail topsail, less clumsy than the old. The jibboom also allowed the increasing use of fore-and-aft sails, the flying jibs, fixed to the stays of the fore mast. The use of these obviously conflicted with the spritsail topmast, and it was abolished for all ships lower than the Second Rate in 1720. Three-deckers retained it until around 1750, but in form it became increasingly vestigial, and was perhaps used as a flagstaff rather than a true mast.

Even the new arrangement of spritsail and topsail was not entirely satisfactory, and it began to fall into disuse as the numbers of fore-and-aft headsails multiplied. The spritsail was still difficult to handle and insecurely stayed, and tended to be masked by the effect of the hull and the other sails. In addition, its closeness to the water must have caused some problems. Nevertheless it survived almost until the end of the age of sail, for the spritsail yards helped to spread the shrouds of the bowsprit. By the beginning of the nineteenth century, the spritsails themselves were apparently little used.

Ideally, most shipwrights would have preferred to make each mast from a single tree, and this was usually possible with the upper masts. With the lower masts, however, it became increasingly difficult to find suitable pieces of timber, especially as ships became larger, and the forests were depleted. From the late seventeenth century builders were forced to look elsewhere for supplies, and for a time

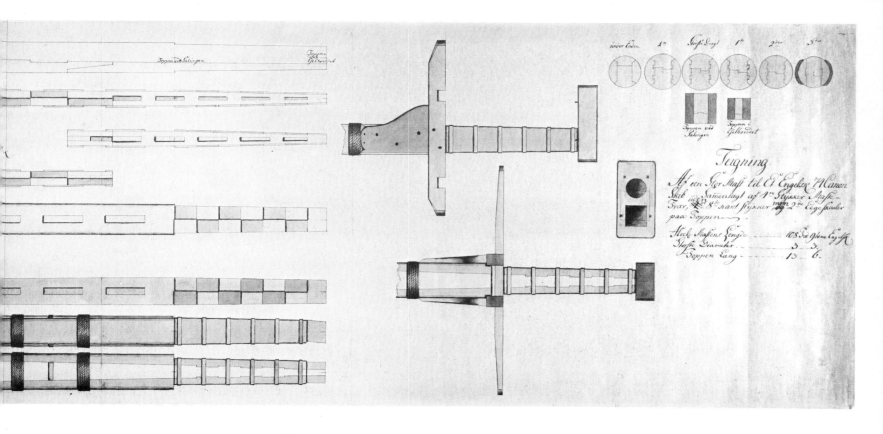

The different pieces which compose the made Mai

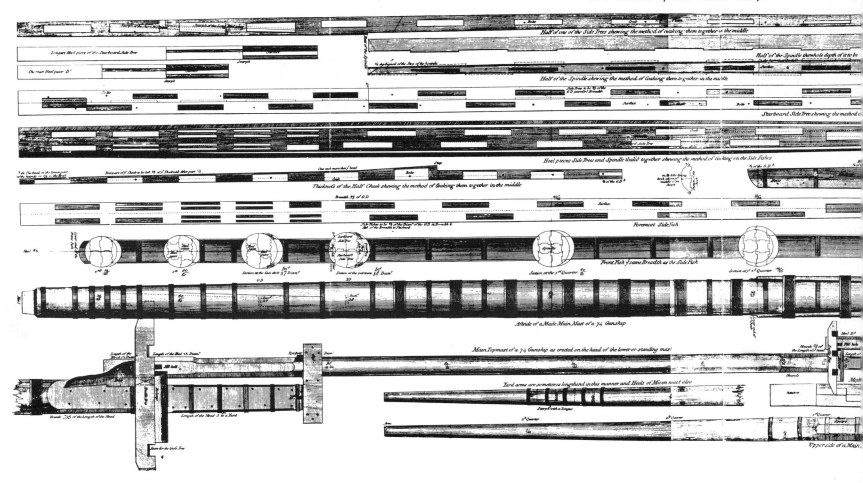

A 74 Gunship's Fore, Main, and Mize

f a 74 Gunship, etc.

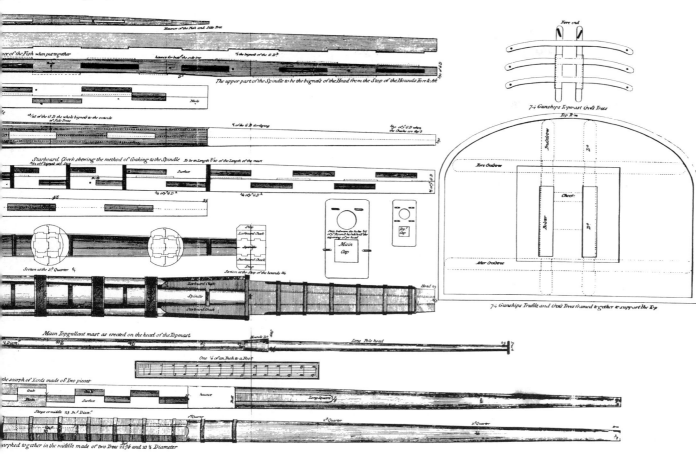

The constituent parts of a 74's main mast, including top, topmast and topgallant, as constructed *c*1800.
From Steel's Masting and Rigging.

and Bowsprit.

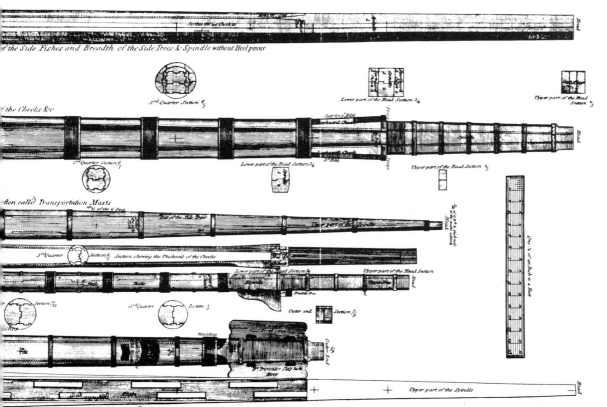

The lower masts and bowsprit of a 74, *c*1800.
From Steel's Masting and Rigging

1

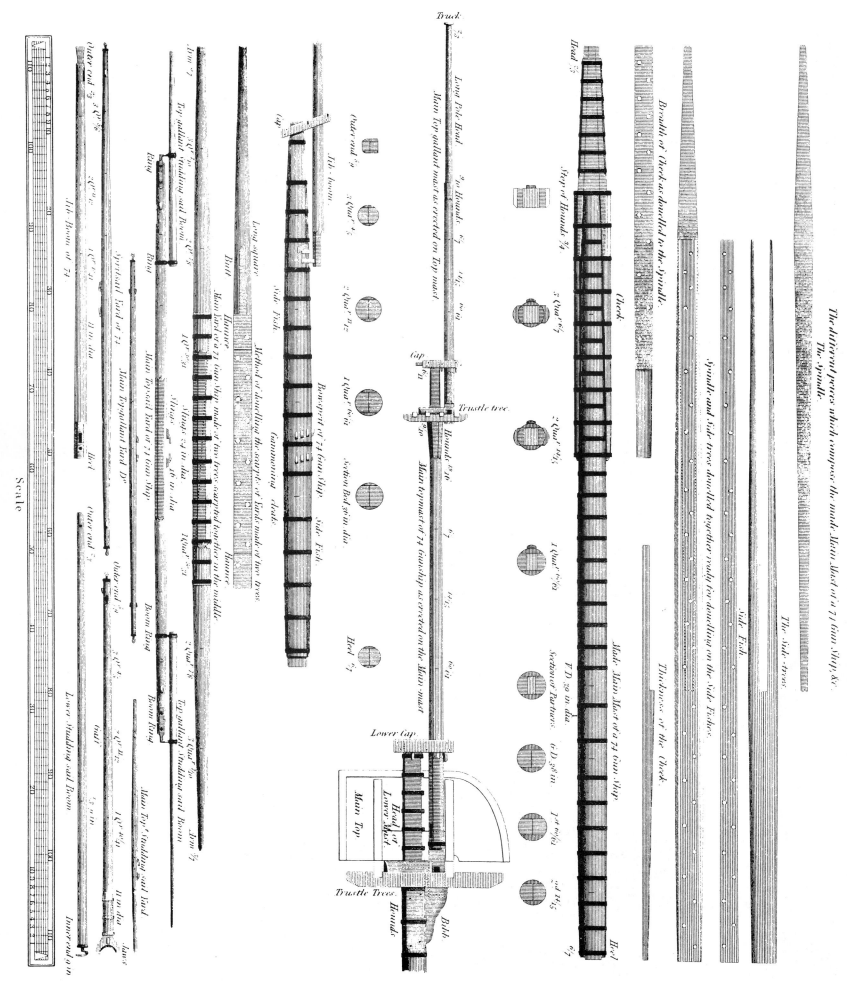

they found the answer in New England, with its almost inexhaustible forests. It was not the very best of timber: most shipwrights preferred that from the Baltic, and insisted on making a New England mast slightly thicker than one of English or Baltic origin[9]; but it was cheap, and, until the 1770s, its supply was not likely to be interrupted in time of war. As early as 1652 supplies of masts were being obtained from New England, and this source was increasingly used over the years. The Navy became increasingly dependent on this supply over the first three-quarters of the eighteenth century, though the 'made mast', constructed from several pieces of timber carefully joined together, did not entirely disappear. In 1779, however, the 'mast crisis' developed. The supplies from New England were no longer easily obtainable, and the battles of the American War, particularly that of Ushant, caused heavy damage to British rigging and spars. The dockyards were forced to turn increasingly to making masts from several pieces, but this process was time-consuming and expensive

of skilled labour, and the dockyards never fully caught up with the needs of the fleet at sea.[10]

There were several variations in the method of making a composite mast, as the Navy Board found in 1779-80, when it began to collect information from the different dockyards on their established practices, but essentially all relied on similar principles. The core of the mast was formed by the spindle, made of two pieces fitted together, one behind the other. The spindle was rectangular in cross section, except for the tables and coaks which disturbed its surface and aided its join with the other parts. Except at the head above the hounds, where the section of the completed mast was rectangular, no part of the spindle was exposed when the mast was finished. The spindle began at the partners, where the completed mast was at its thickest, and continued to the head. It had its greatest thickness just below the hounds, and tapered to nothing at the partners. Other pieces were joined to the spindle to complete the mast. The side trees formed the basic structure of the lower part, where the

1 The early nineteenth century method of making masts, using dowels instead of tables and coaks; and (centre) the topmast and topgallant mast, showing the method of fixing them with trestletrees and caps.
From Rees' Cyclopaedia

2 A sheer hulk, early nineteenth century: this was an old warship, fitted with sheers, or legs, and used to hoist the lower masts of ships into position.
From Cooke's Shipping and Craft

2

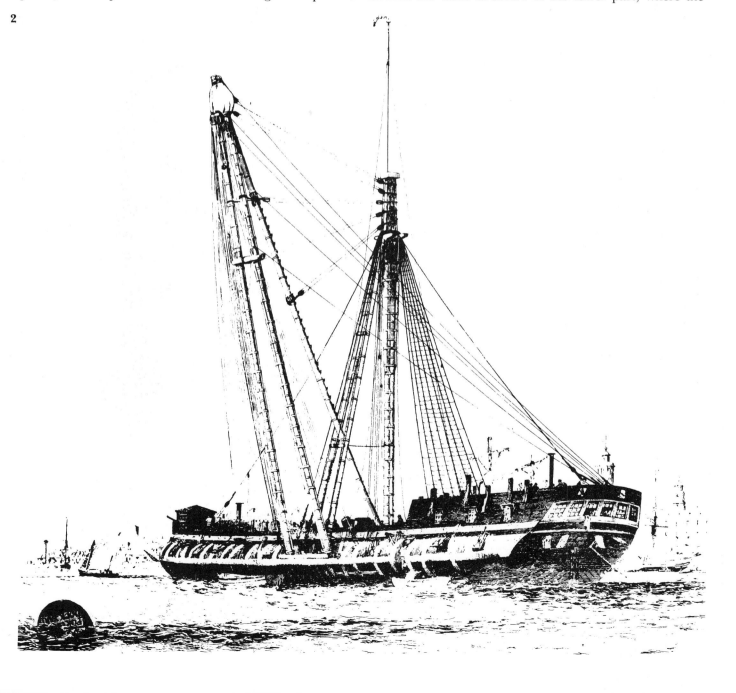

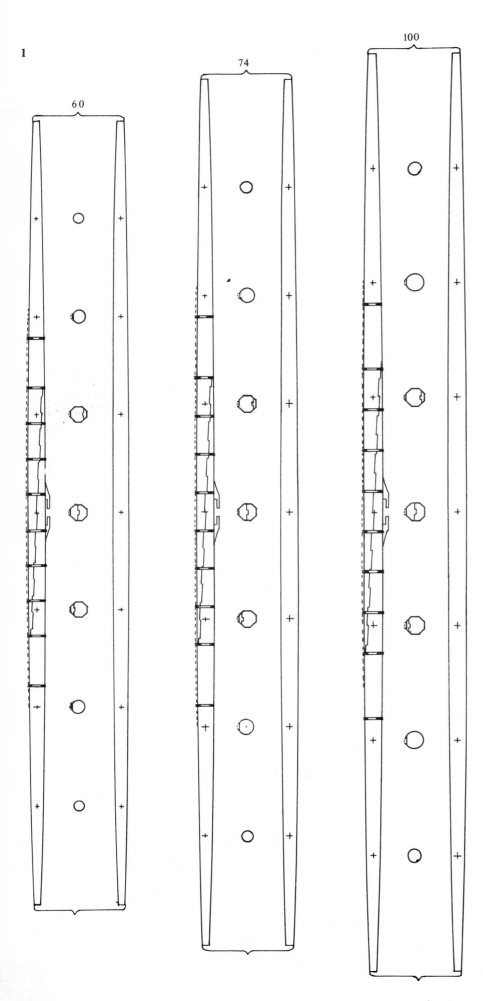

spindle did not exist. Beside them were the fore side fish and the aft side fish and the front fish, all of which contributed to the rounded shape of the completed mast. All of these pieces began at the heel of the mast, and ended at the hounds. The sides below the hounds were thickened by the cheeks, which began about the middle of the mast's total length, and continued right up to the head. Other minor components, such as fillers, stops, and cant pieces, were inserted into any spaces left between the major parts. The different parts were secured together by means of tables and coaks – a rectangular hole was cut into each of the surfaces to be joined, while a square peg (the coak) fitted tightly into both holes, holding the two parts together. The number and size of these tables and coaks suggests that they must have taken up most of the man-hours used in making such a mast; in the early nineteenth century this part of the process was simplified slightly, and dowels were used instead of tables and coaks. In the early period the parts of the mast were held together by rope woldings, turned several times round the mast at intervals of a few feet. These were replaced by iron bands in the early nineteenth century. These processes were only used for the lower masts; the upper masts were rather smaller, and were made from a single tree.

Lower masts were generally fitted by means of a sheer hulk. This was an old warship which had become unfit for sea service, but was cut down and fitted with sheers – a triangular system of legs which could be used to lower the heel of the mast through the spaces left in the deck for its accommodation. The partners were then fitted to secure the mast, and the standing rigging put on to hold it in place. If the ship was to be laid up in ordinary, it is unlikely that it would be fitted with any more than the three lower masts and the bowsprit. If she were to be fitted for sea, the upper masts would have to be fitted and rigged, and these were hoisted into place using a complicated system of tackles.

Each mast or part of a mast carried a sail of its own, and a yard to stretch it out. With the exception of the lower mizzen mast, which carried a fore-and-aft sail, all masts carried a square sail, and a yard. The length of the lower yards was determined by several factors. They could not be much longer than the beam of the ship, for if the lower corners (clews) of the sails were too far from the sides of the hull they could not be sheeted properly. Moreover, yards that were too long would interfere with those of the other masts before or aft of them. Nevertheless the main yard of a large ship was a substantial piece of timber: that of a 110-gun ship in the early nineteenth century was 102 feet long and 2 feet in diameter.

The upper yards were shorter and narrower than the lower ones, for it had long been appreciated that an unduly heavy force acting a long way above the hull of the ship would cause a great strain. Indeed, the early sailors were particularly cautious in this respect. When, in the fifteenth

1 The method of producing main yards by scarphing them in the middle.

2 The sail plan as it was around 1700: long mizzen yard, with square mizzen topsail above; no royals; sprit topmast and spritsail on bowsprit.
From Sutherland's Shipbuilding Unveiled

century, they first added topsails above the main sails, they made them so small that they must have had an almost negligible effect. By the seventeenth century, however, the topsail had greatly increased in size and importance, for in many ways it was safer and more manageable than the main sail below it, and it often approached it in effective area. This was only achieved by giving the topmast great depth. The topsail yard was kept much smaller than the lower yard, and this caused the sail to taper sharply upwards. After 1700, this taper began to be reduced, when it was discovered that French ships were able to carry larger, squarer topsails, and longer yards.[11] The process continued for the next few years: in 1678 the topsail yard was half the length of the lower yard; by 1711, five-ninths: and by 1719 it had reached 0.72 of the length of the lower yard, where it was to remain for the rest of the century.[12] The other yards, the topgallants and royals, were similarly smaller than the topsail yards, but less so as the eighteenth century progressed.

A yard was circular in cross section for most of its length, having its maximum diameter in its centre, and tapering outwards towards its ends in a circular fashion. Until 1690 yards were circular in cross section for the whole of their length. After that they had an eight-sided cross section in the centre, and for about a quarter of their length.

The great size of the lower yards of ships of the line caused problems of timber supply, especially during the mast crisis around 1780, and, as in the case of masts, it became necessary to make them out of more than one piece of timber. There were two main methods of doing this: one was by scarphing two pieces together, with a long overlap in the centre; the other was by 'tonguing' – by fitting an extension to each end, having a long pointed end of the centre piece fit into a hollow on the outer part. In 1780 shipwrights were evenly divided about the advantages of the two systems. The officers of Deptford believed that 'a yard scarphed in the middle is much stronger than tongued pieces at each arm, and requires less trees', while the Master

Shipwright at Sheerness had 'always considered scarphing lower yards in the middle to be the most expensive method', and believed that 'all lower yards as well as topsail yards will be best made out of Riga masts tongued at each end'.[13] Nevertheless the scarphing system seems to have prevailed, and to have become the most common in the nineteenth century.

In the earliest part of our period, the mizzen was the only fore-and-aft sail carried, and it was to remain the only one which had a mast and yard of its own, for the others were staysails, supported by the rigging rather than the yards. The mizzen sail was originally a lateen sail, derived from those used by ships and galleys of the Mediterranean. It was shaped like a right-angled triangle, so that the yard lay at an angle of 45 degrees to the horizontal. Only about a quarter of the sail area was placed in front of the mizzen mast, and this part was less than effective, and merely helped to make the sail more difficult to handle. Between 1730 and 1750, therefore, it became common to abandon the fore part of the sail and lace its fore edge to the mizzen mast. The yard continued to stretch forward of the mast, partly due to conservatism, and to the fact that it could perhaps be useful as a spare main or fore yard. Towards the end of the eighteenth century the forward part of the yard was abandoned, and it was replaced by a gaff. Around the same time a boom was fitted to extend the lower part of the sail, thus allowing it to be made rather larger.

The early mizzen mast had carried only a single lateen sail, but by 1620 square mizzen topsails were common. The upper sails and yards of the mizzen tended to resemble those of the fore and main masts, but often to lag behind them in development. When royals were introduced in 1779, for example, they were intended only for the fore and main masts, though in the 1790s they were eventually fitted to mizzens. The upper mizzen sails were much smaller than their counterparts on the other masts, and less useful in most circumstances, so they attracted less attention and developed more slowly. The lower mizzen was unique in carrying two yards: as well as the lateen or gaff which formed the mizzen yard proper, a square yard, known as the crossjack, was necessary to spread the foot of the mizzen topsail. It carried no sail of its own.

Other pieces of timber helped to support the sails and rigging of the ship. From about 1710 boomkins projected forwards and downwards from the beakhead, to spread the tack of the fore course. After 1794 the dolphin striker projected down from under the bowsprit. This was shaped like an inverted V, and intended to spread the ropes which braced the bowsprit against the lifting effect of the forestays. The channels projected from the sides of the hull, at different heights at different periods, to help spread the shrouds of the lower masts. The bees, so called from their shape, projected from the fore end of the bowsprit after about 1700. They formed a lead for some of the stays. Studding sails (or stunsails), used to extend the width of the normal sails in very light winds, are known to have existed from the 1650s onwards, though they came into increasing prominence in later years. They required small yards of their own, which were not permanent fixtures but were stored on deck in usual weather conditions. The stunsail boom was used to extend the principal yard and hold the stunsail yard; it was fitted above the main yard, and could be pulled out to give greater spread when necessary. It appears that in early times stunsails were carried only on the lower main yards, but by about 1680 they were also carried on the topsail yards of both the main and the fore mast, and after 1773 they were fitted to topgallants as well. They were never fitted to royals or to the square sails of the mizzen, though in the later period the gaff sail of the mizzen could be extended by means of its own stunsail. The lower edge of the lower stunsail was stretched by means of a boom extending from the side of the hull, which could be folded back against the side when not in use.

5. Sails and Rigging

THE RIGGING OF A SHIP OF THE LINE CONSUMED AN enormous amount of rope. As early as 1655, the *Swiftsure*, a Second Rate, needed 9060 fathoms (more than 10 miles) of rope, ranging in circumference from ¼ inch to 16 inches. By the early nineteenth century ships were much bigger, and the amount of rope used for rigging was even greater. Yet it is not clear exactly how much control the central naval administration had over the rigging of ships. From around 1700 rigging warrants were in use; these ordered the storekeepers of a dockyard to issue a certain amount of rope of varying sizes to a particular ship being fitted out, but few of these have survived. The Surveyors of the Navy had some responsibility for the supervision of these stores, but as naval architects they showed little interest. The rigging of a ship, according to Sir Anthony Deane, was 'a labour more fit for a master of attendant than a shipwright'[1], and we can assume that later designers shared his views for very little information on rigging is to be found either among the Admiralty collection of draughts or among the Navy Board correspondence.

Much of the decision-making, then, descended to the officials of the dockyard, especially the master attendant, the boatswain of the yard, and the storekeeper. Most shipwrights had some system of proportions by which they

The standing rigging of a 74-gun ship, *c*1800.
From Rees' Cyclopaedia

Ropemaking tools and practices, late eighteenth century.
National Maritime Museum

could decide the appropriate thickness for a particular rope, based on the thickness of the masts and yards to which they were to be attached. The ship was rigged only when she was ready to put to sea, and the job was largely done by the crew of the ship. Even if the dockyard officials supervised the process while the ship was fitting out, there was nothing to stop the captains, masters and boatswains from making amendments when at sea. This of course was not a purely negative phenomenon; the sea officers could often improve the performance of a ship by experimentation. In any case, the process was not completely anarchic. As with many things in the Navy, custom and tradition dominated, and it is not difficult to follow the customs and trends which prevailed at particular times. Small amendments to particular ropes did not greatly affect the general picture, and few captains and boatswains had the initiative to do more than that.

Most of the Navy's rope was made in the dockyards, which had their own rope-walks – long buildings in which the yarn was spun, after being combed out, or hatchelled. After that it was stretched, tarred and laid.

The rigging of a ship divides naturally into two types: the standing rigging, which supports the masts; and the running rigging, which supports and operates the yards and sails. The standing rigging was so called because it was more or less fixed in its position. Apart from a few minor adjustments to improve the trim, or take up slack caused by stretching, it was expected to remain in place throughout the ship's commission, and was therefore tarred, to protect it from the elements. Each mast was supported by a triangular system of standing rigging – by the forestays which led directly forward from the mast, and by the shrouds which led aft and to the sides. In the case of a lower mast, the forestay led directly to the deck near the mast ahead, or to the bowsprit in the case of the fore mast stay. The stays of the main and mizzen topgallants, topmasts and royals led diagonally downwards to a block on the mast ahead, and then onto the deck below. Those of the fore mast led to the jibboom or the spritsail topmast. The stays of the upper masts were generally single lines, but those of the lower masts were usually doubled, with a slightly lighter line known as the preventer stay, to give extra support. This was laced to the stay itself, by means of a rope which criss-crossed between the two.

The stays of the lower masts had to bear a great deal of strain, and were often the thickest ropes on the ship, apart from anchor cables and the like. The main stay of the *Sovereign* in 1640 was 17 inches in circumference.[2] The method of securing the stay to the masthead varied according to its position. On a lower mast, a small loop was formed at one end of the rope by seizing. This was passed round the masthead, and the other end of the line was passed through the loop, where a bulge – known as a mouse – was made in the rope to stop the loop slipping. The stays of the upper masts were usually fixed by rather simpler methods.

Naturally the stays tended to stretch in use, and a means had to be provided of tightening them when necessary. This was usually done by a system of lanyards. One block was fitted to the end of the stay proper, another to the deck where the stay was to be led. The lanyards passed between

LEFT: A typical shroud and its attachments – starting from the bottom left, the chain plates and chains, leading to the lower deadeye (8), the lanyard (7), the upper deadeye (3). The shroud itself is seized round the upper deadeye, looped round the mast, seized, and led back to form another shroud.

RIGHT: A main stay – the collar (3) is looped round the mast, held by the mouse (2) and the eye (1); a combination of heart blocks and lanyards (9) allows the stay to be tightened to take up slack caused by stretching of the stay; the lower end of the stay is fixed round the lower part of the fore mast.

From Rees' Cyclopaedia

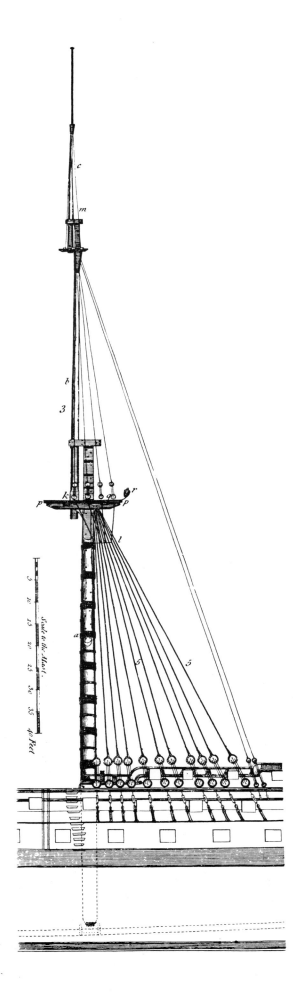

the two blocks, and could be tightened as necessary.

The shrouds supported the mast against forces acting from behind, and from the sides. In 1640 a large ship like the *Sovereign* carried 20 on the main mast alone, 10 on each side. Most ships of the future were to carry a similar number, the *Victory*, for example, having 13 on each side of the main mast, while a contemporary 74-gun ship had 9 per side on the main mast, the same number on the fore mast, and 7 on the mizzen.[3] The shrouds of the lower masts led from the top down to the channels (pieces of wood jutting out from the sides of the ship specially provided in order to help spread the shrouds). They were spaced unevenly along the channels, to allow room for the gunports. The foremost shroud on each mast led outwards and reached the channel almost at a level with the mast itself. The aftermost one led outwards and backwards at an angle of about 15 to 20 degrees, while the intermediate ones led backwards at lesser angles. The shrouds were formed in pairs. One shroud led up from the channel, round the masthead, and back to the channel thus forming the next shroud in line. Again, there had to be some method of correcting the stretching of the shrouds in service, and again lanyards were used. This time they were led through round blocks of wood known as deadeyes. The end of the shroud was looped round the circumference of one deadeye, and seized. The other deadeye was fixed to the channel by means of the chains, which were bolted to the side of the hull a little below the channels, led up through the channels, and fixed round the lower deadeye, situated just above the channel. Each deadeye had three holes in it; through these was passed the lanyard, alternating from one deadeye to the other, thus giving a means of securing and tightening the shroud.

The topmasts and topgallants also had shrouds, usually three to five on each mast. In the case of the topmast they ended at the edges of the top, while those of the topgallant were led to the trestletrees, with deadeyes and lanyards as on the lower shrouds. The shrouds of the upper masts were braced from below by the futtock shrouds. These led from the underside of the deadeyes on the top or trestletrees, and onto the lower set of shrouds. Shrouds were not sufficient to support the upper masts, and so backstays were used as well. These led from the head of the topmast or topgallant directly down to the channel, to give additional bracing.

Crowsfeet were used to spread the strain of the upper part of the lower stays, and to protect the sail from rubbing against the top or the stay. A number of ropes, perhaps twenty, led from a single point on the stay to various points evenly spread along the forward edge of the top. This custom, introduced in the middle of the seventeenth century, died out during the latter part of the eighteenth. Crowsfeet were also used for other purposes in the latter part of the seventeenth century: to spread the end of the sprit topmast backstay, which led to the fore stay, for example.

Shrouds, futtocks and backstays of a 74-gun ship, *c*1760: there are 11 shrouds to the main mast; aft of them are two backstays leading to the head of the topmast. There are four shrouds to the topmast, braced by futtock shrouds, which lead from the lower side of the top to the main shrouds.
From Falconer's Marine Dictionary

The bowsprit was an important anchorage point for the rigging of the fore mast, and it too had to be braced against the strain. Firstly, it was gammoned: that is, several turns of rope were taken round the bowsprit itself and passed through specially provided holes in the knee of the head. Secondly, from about 1685 the bobstay was led down from a point near the foremost end of the bowsprit to a position on the fore edge of the knee of the head. The spritsail topmast, while it existed, was braced to the fore stay by a complicated system of crowsfeet. After its replacement by the jibboom, methods had to be found to support the latter from below. A piece of timber was fitted under the cap of the bowsprit, known as the dolphin striker. A new line, known as the martingale stay, was led from the end of the jibboom, through the lower end of the dolphin striker, to the head of the ship.

THE FORE AND MAIN TOPS OF THE *ST GEORGE* OF 1701

1. The stay and preventer stay, laced together.
2. The crowsfeet, used to spread the effect of the stays, and protect the topsail from wear.
3. Shrouds and ratlines.
4. Futtock shrouds.
5. Topmast shrouds and lanyards.
The Science Museum

RIGGING TO THE BOW-SPRIT OF A 74-GUN SHIP, 1757
1. Forestay and preventer stay.
2. Fore topmast stay and preventer stay.
3. Bobstay.
4. Jib guys.
5. Spritsail topsail halyards.
National Maritime Museum

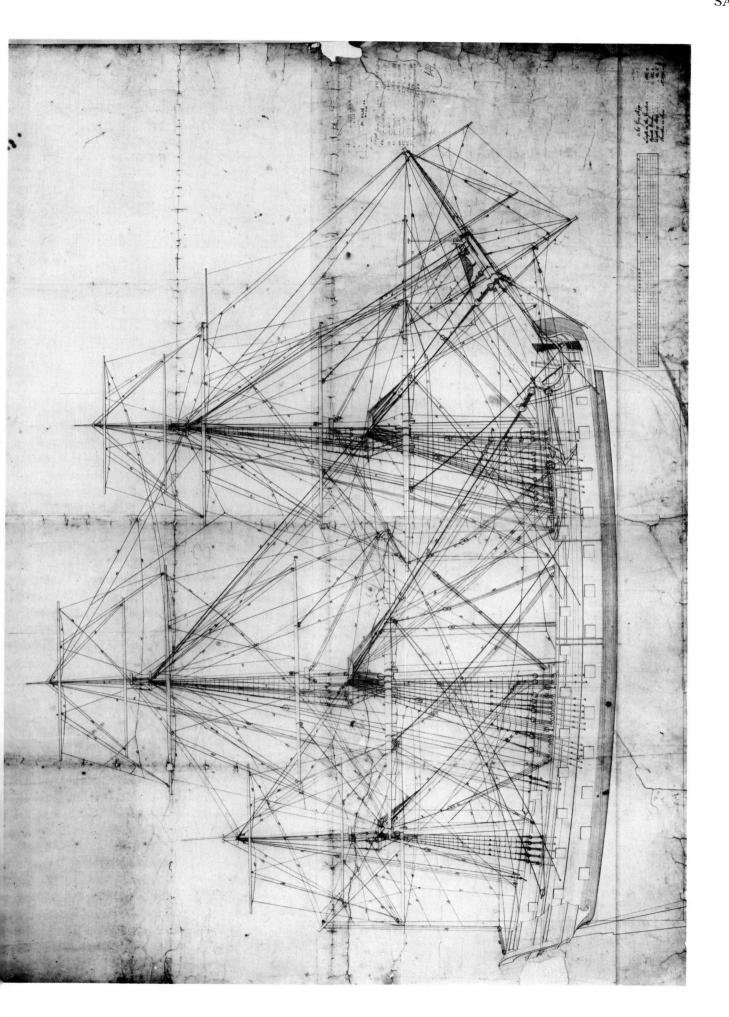

The rigging plan of a 60-gun ship of the 1745 establishment.
Sjöhistoriska Museum, Stockholm

1

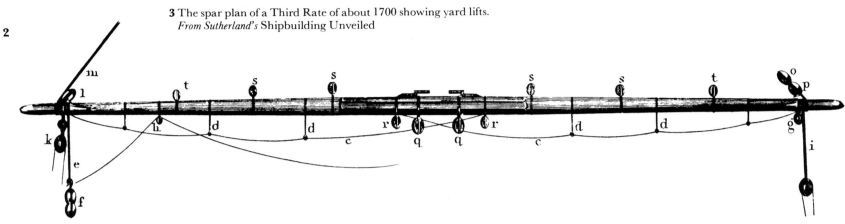

1 A parrel of around 1750, used to hold a yard against a mast.
From Blanckley's Naval Expositor

2 The rigging of a lower yard, *c*1810.
From Lever's Sheet Anchor

3 The spar plan of a Third Rate of about 1700 showing yard lifts.
From Sutherland's Shipbuilding Unveiled

2

3

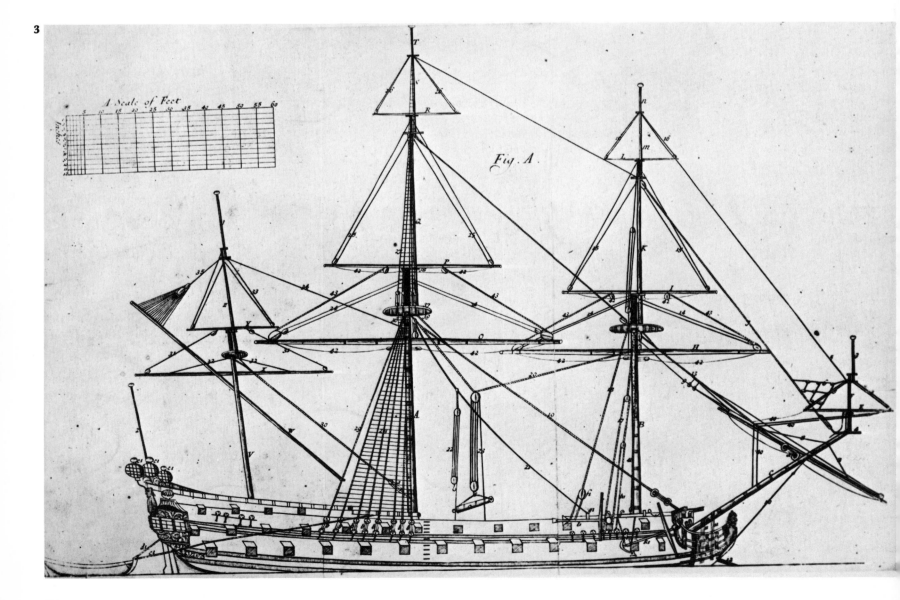

The running rigging was generally lighter than the standing rigging, and it was not tarred, for it was constantly being moved to control the performance of the ship. The running rigging can also be divided into two types: that which supported and controlled the yards and spars; and that which operated directly on the sails. Each yard had to be able to move in several directions – they had to be able to swivel around the mast, so that the sails could be turned according to the wind direction; the upper yards also had to be able to move up and down easily, so that they could be brought close to the top for furling sails, and raised again when the sail was in use. Even the lower yards needed some up and down movement, for it was common to lower and remove them if the ship was to spend any length of time in port. In addition the yards had to be braced against the wind pushing from behind or from the quarter, and they had to be able to support the downward pull exerted by their own weight and that of the sails.

In the earliest days of the ship of the line yards were still hoisted into place by means of halyards. A line was simply led from the centre of the yard to the head of the mast, and then down to the deck. Around 1660 these were replaced by jeers, in which case the blocks were placed between the yard and the masthead; usually there was one system of jeers on each side of the centre of the yard. The jeer blocks were supported from the masthead by specially placed cleats. The details of the fitting of jeers varied somewhat throughout the centuries, but the principle remained the same.

Trusses were also used in the early period, to hold the yard against the mast at its centre. They were also abandoned around 1660, and replaced by slings. These were fixed round the centre of the yard (which itself became known as the slings because of this) and then passed over the masthead, and back again to the centre of the yard. They served to assist the jeers in supporting the weight of the yard, and also helped to hold the yard against the mast. In wartime, chain slings were used, to reduce the risk of the supports for the yard being shot away in action. The main work of holding the yard against the mast, however, was done by the parrels, which were carried round the mast on a level with the yard. They were fitted with ribs and trucks (small beads of wood), to allow the yard to pivot freely around the mast. After about 1760 they were superseded by truss pendants and falls, whereby a line was fixed round the centre of the yard to one side of the mast, round the mast, and then round the other side of the centre of the yard. Until 1810 the ends of this line were led down to the deck, to allow for tightening and slackening as needed; after that, they were led to the top or trestletrees above.

All these lines were designed to support the centre of the yard, but it also needed to be supported at its ends, which was provided by the lifts, which kept it horizontal. In the seventeenth century, a lift line led from under the top to a block at the end of the yard, back to a block under the top, and down to the deck below. After 1680 the lifts led to the head of the mast instead of under the top, thus giving slightly more effective support to the yard.

The braces supported the ends of the yards against the effects of the wind, and allowed it to be moved round according to the wind direction. The braces of the fore mast and main mast began at the ends of the yards, led backwards to a block fixed to a stay, and then down to a belaying point on the deck. The mizzen yards had no mast behind them, and so it was necessary to lead the braces forward, but the principle was similar. The spritsail yard also had to be braced, but in this case the braces were led up to the head of the fore mast, and served part of the function of lifts as well. The spritsail topmast, while it existed, was generally fitted with lifts and braces similar to other yards.

Under each yard (apart from the crossjack which carried no sail) was fitted a footrope, which ran the length of the yard, and was allowed to hang a few feet below it, to permit the men working at furling or bending sails to stand on it. It was supported at intervals by stirrups, which hung vertically from the yard and prevented it from sagging too much in the centre.

The old-fashioned mizzen yard, which carried a triangular sail that stretched forward and aft of the mast, was secured at its aftermost (uppermost) end by a lift supported by a complicated system of crowsfeet. After 1710, around the time when the forward part of the lateen sail began to fall into disuse and the fore edge of the sail was laced directly to the mast, the lifts became rather simpler, but a system of blocks continued to spread the effect of the lift. The lower end of the old lateen yard was held in position by a bowline, which helped both to hold the yard in position and to control its lateral movement – larger ships had up to three, spread along the foremost part of the yard, and leading to the sides of the ship, or to the aftermost main shroud. The gaff which replaced the mizzen yard in the late eighteenth century was supported by halyards, similar in principle to the lifts which had supported the yard in the earlier part of the century. The lateral movement of the mizzen yard or gaff was, after about 1710, controlled by the vangs – lines which led from the uppermost part of the spar to the deck near the stern, on both sides.

In the early nineteenth century booms were also fitted to extend the foot of the gaff mizzen. These were supported by topping lifts, which led from the end of the boom to the head of the mast.

A ship of the line used an enormous number of blocks in its rigging – a 74-gun ship of around 1800 needed 922. The blocks served two purposes: either to alter the lead of a rigging line, so that it could, for example, be allowed greater purchase while still ending up at its belaying point, or merely to prevent it fouling other lines; or to be used, in combination with other blocks, in a system of tackles so that the extremely heavy weights of, for example, yards and boats, could be lifted by human muscle power alone. The simplest kind of block was the single block. It consisted of: a sheave – a circular piece of lignum vitae with a groove round its rim through which a rope could pass; a metal pin round which the latter could revolve; and a wooden shell, which would enclose the whole, with space for the line to lead out of it, and grooves for the rope which would secure it to the appropriate position. Other blocks, generally used in more complex block and tackle systems, were double, triple and quadruple, and had several sheaves laid side by side. A fiddle block, so called because of its likeness to that musical instrument, had two sheaves, probably of varying sizes, laid end to end. These, in many variations, formed an essential

1 THE RIGGING OF A MIZZEN YARD, c1730

1. Gaff topping lift.
2. Brails.
3. Mizzen bowlines.
The Science Museum

2 Types of block, c1750.
From Blanckley's Naval Expositor

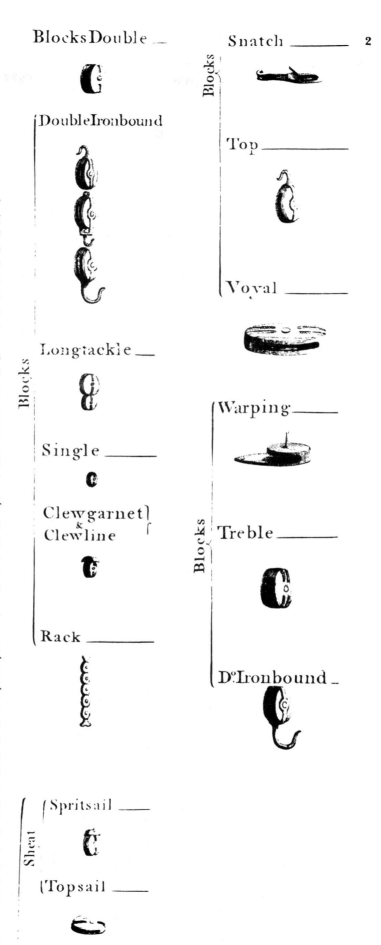

part of the rigging of any sailing ship.

Until the early nineteenth century blocks were made by hand, by skilled craftsmen, though mechanical sawing devices were coming into use even then. From 1759 the Taylors of Southampton were the main suppliers of blocks to the Navy. However, blocks were required in such large numbers that they were among the first items in the world to be manufactured by mass-production methods; from 1805, Brunel's blockmaking machines were in use in Portsmouth dockyard, to the admiration of all interested in the development of industrial technology.[4]

The method of making sails, on the other hand, appears to have changed very little over the centuries in which the ship of the line dominated the seas. A sail was defined as 'an assemblage of several breadths of canvas sewed together.' The strips of canvas, known as cloths, were usually 18 inches wide, and they had 'a double flat seam, and should be sewed with the best English-made twine of three threads, spun 360 fathoms to the pound, and have from 108 to 116 stitches in every yard in length.'[5] They were sewn together by sailmakers working in a sail loft, using large needles and similar implements. The Navy employed large numbers of sailmakers in the dockyards: in 1722, in time of peace, there were 26 sailmakers in Portsmouth yard; in 1748, during wartime, there were 34 in Deptford yard.[6] The width of a sail was often defined by the number of cloths used in it; in 1640 the *Sovereign* had a main sail of 49 cloths, while the smallest sail, the foretop royal, had only 6.[7] Around 1790, the main course of a 74-gun ship had 48 cloths, while her mizzen royal had 11.[8]

A bolt rope was sewn round the edges of the sail, to give it extra strength; in a 74 of the late eighteenth century, that of the main course was 5½ inches in circumference.[9] Along the edges of the sail, fitted to the bolt rope, were various loops of rope for fixing different lines. At the upper corners were the earrings, which helped secure the sail to the yard. At the lower corners were the clews (or clues), used for fixing the sheets, tacks, and the clew garnets which helped in furling the sail. Along the sides of a square sail, known as the leeches, were several reef cringles and bowline cringles. The head rope, along the top of the sail, had numerous holes in it to take the bands which would fix the sail to the mast or stay. After 1680 the larger square sails – courses and topsails – had several lines of reef points. Extra bands of cloth were fitted horizontally along the line of reef points, and through these were threaded numerous reefing lines, so that the upper part of the sail could be furled when it was not needed. Before that time, the size of the sail could be varied in rather a different way. An extra piece, known as a bonnet, was fitted to the lower edge of the sail, usually the course, and could be removed when not needed. The

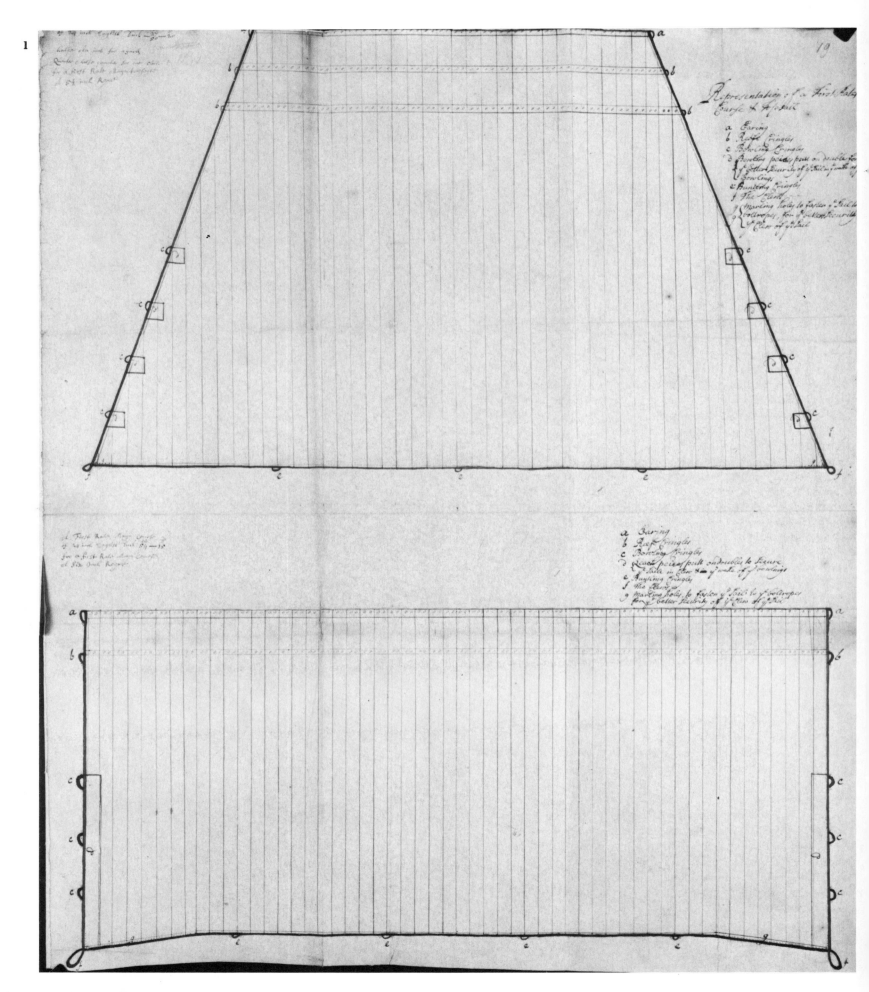

number of lines of reef points tended to increase over the years, particularly on the topsails. A topsail of around 1800 had four reef bands. This was mainly because the topsail was the most useful in dangerous situations – in action or in storm. In the latter case ships would sail under topsails alone, taking in reefs as the strength of the gale dictated.

Sails usually had some 'bag' in the middle. This meant that the cloths were drawn closer together around the edges, but allowed to be widely spaced in the centre, so that the sail, when filled, took on a rounded appearance. It was believed that this made the sail more effective when running before the wind, but of course it had the serious disadvantage that it made it more difficult to turn the edge of the sail into the wind when tacking. Bagging tended to be reduced over the years: by the end of the eighteenth century one-twelfth of the head and foot of a sail was taken in this way, and a twenty-fourth on the leeches.[10]

The square sails, which provided the main driving power of the ship, were so called because in their neutral position they were placed at right angles to the line of the ship's motion, for none of them was square-shaped in any strict sense. The courses were nearest to square, in that their sides were approximately parallel, and at right angles to the head. But they were much broader than they were deep, and the foot of a course had a deep gore: that is, its edge curved sharply upwards, to lift its centre clear of the deck over which it would operate. Topsails, topgallants, and royals had no gore until the early nineteenth century; their lower edges were flat, and parallel to the head, but their leeches tapered sharply upwards, since the upper yard was invariably rather smaller than the one below it.

Several types of fore-and-aft sails were carried. The oldest was the lateen sail, which was triangular in shape and supported from the diagonal mizzen yard by its longest edge. At certain periods it too had a row of reef points, running at an angle to the head of the sail. After the fore part of the lateen sail was abandoned, in the early eighteenth century, the sail was laced both to the yard above it and to the mast ahead of it. In the late eighteenth century the sail became more of a true gaff sail, as the fore part of the mizzen yard was left off, and eventually a boom was added. By this time the sail carried another set of reef points, near the bottom rather than the top of the sail, for the sail was reefed by lowering the gaff and lashing the unused parts of the sail to the boom.

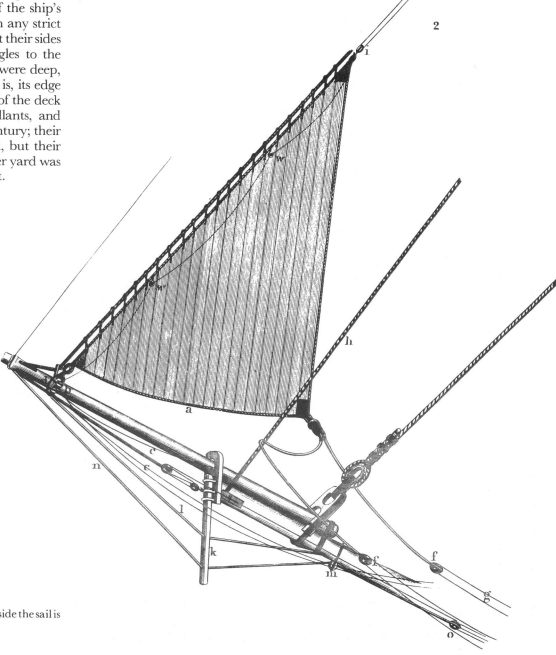

1 Sails of a First Rate, c1690.
The British Library

2 **A JIB SAIL AND ITS RIGGING, c1810**

w & b. Downhauler.
i. Halyard.
f. Sheets: one on each side, to be used according to which side the sail is set.
From Lever's Sheet Anchor

Staysails were, as their name suggests, fitted to the stays rather than the yards. They came into common use in the mid-seventeenth century, and a typical ship carried a sail on the main stay, the main topmast stay, and perhaps on the fore topmast stay. More were added in later years, so that by 1800 a 74-gun ship had seven staysails, rigged between the fore and main mast, and between the main and the mizzen.[11] Additional to these were the jib sails, which only came into their own after the demise of the spritsail topsail. These were rigged on the stays of the fore mast, and overhung the bowsprit. They were therefore very useful in the steering of the ship, and in tacking and wearing.

The original staysails were triangular, but in the eighteenth century they were usually made quadrilateral, in order to give them greater area. The jibs were invariably triangular, to fit into the space between the bowsprit and the stay. Staysails were laced to the appropriate stay, in the same way as the square and mizzen sails were fixed to the yards and the gaff.

Stunsails were made of the thinnest canvas, since they were only used in very light winds. They were deep and narrow, with the head parallel to the foot, as in other square sails. Those of the lower yards were rectangular, while those of the topsails and topgallants tapered in accordance with the shape of the square sails to which they were added.

Sails were made of different types of canvas according to the uses to which they were put. In the 1650s we hear of 'noyals', 'Ipswich warped', 'Ipswich double', and 'vittery'.[12] In later years canvas was classified according to its strength and thickness, from Number 1 to Number 8. Stunsails and the like were made of the thinnest material, Number 8, while the strongest topsails, used only in storms, were made of Number 1. In the seventeenth century, when the English canvas industry was relatively new, there was some lack of confidence in the native material, and ships carried sails of thick canvas. In 1670 a typical ship carried 40 sails, of which 20 were spare – 3 courses and topsails for each mast, and 2 of most of the other sails. The ships of 1677 apparently carried less, a total of 28 sails, of which 7 were spare.[13] By 1728 there was more faith in English canvas, and a new establishment of sails was ordered. By this time a total of 33 sails was carried, of which 11 were spare, with the fore and main courses, topsails and topgallants being supplied in duplicate, and the fore courses and topsails in triplicate.[14] By 1746 a Third Rate on foreign service carried a total of 41 sails, of which 12 were spare.[15]

The spare sails were stored in the sailroom, amidships on the orlop deck, between the cable tiers. Like the magazines, they were to be sited well away from the sides of the ship, for sails, like gunpowder, could be damaged by storage in damp conditions. Their care and maintenance was the responsibility of the sailmaker – a petty officer under the boatswain – and his assistants. The boatswain also had his

Bending a sail, c1810.
From Lever's Sheet Anchor

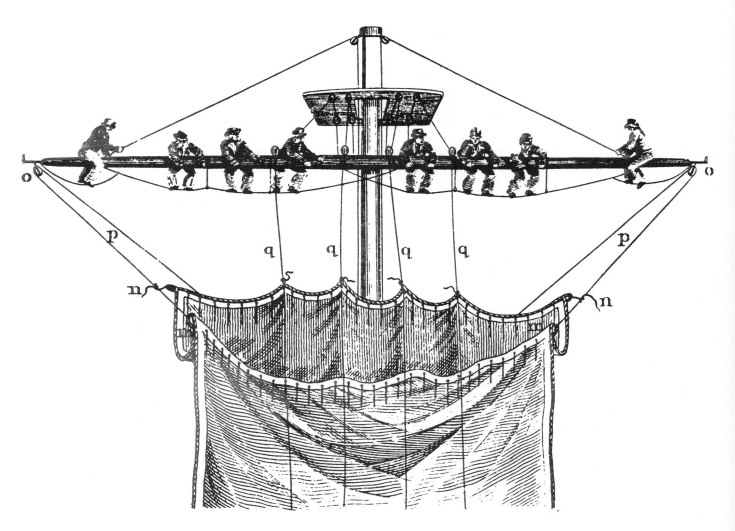

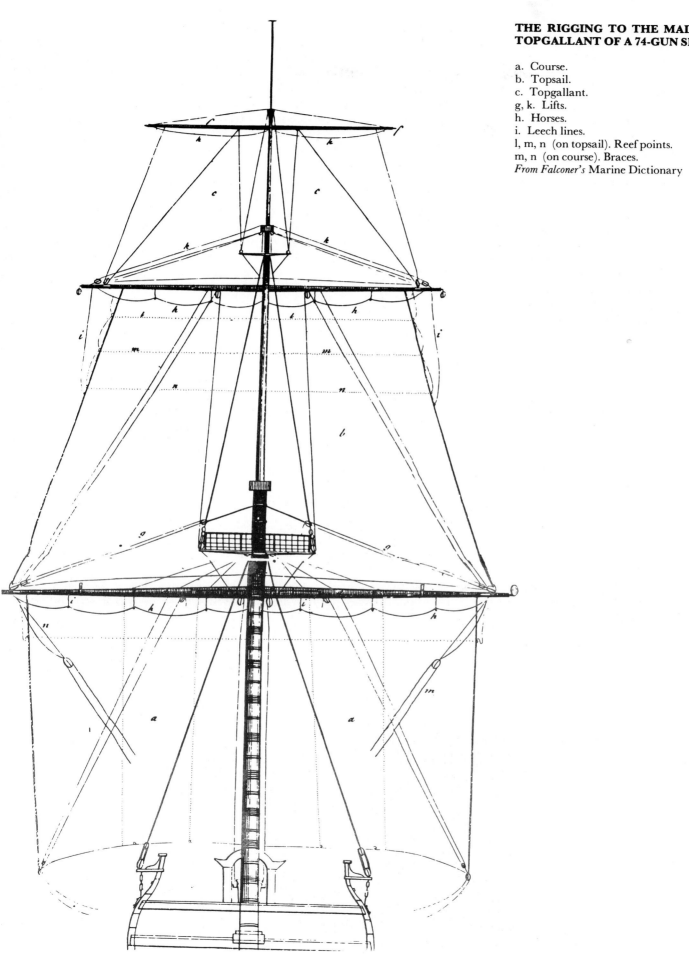

THE RIGGING TO THE MAIN COURSE, TOPSAIL AND TOPGALLANT OF A 74-GUN SHIP, *c*1760

a. Course.
b. Topsail.
c. Topgallant.
g, k. Lifts.
h. Horses.
i. Leech lines.
l, m, n (on topsail). Reef points.
m, n (on course). Braces.
From Falconer's Marine Dictionary

store room, forward on the orlop deck next to that of the carpenter. It was used for spare cordage, blocks and other parts of the rigging.

Sails were hoisted up to their yards by means of lines attached to their earrings, reef cringles, and head ropes. Once they had been raised into position, they were fixed to the yard by means of lines, known as robbands (or rope-bands) which ran through the head rope, and were tied round the yard.

Once fixed to the yard, sails had several lines fitted to them to control them. The sheets were fitted to the clews of the square sails; they were used to loosen or slacken the sail according to the strength of the wind, and to alter the setting of the lower part of the sail, as the braces on the yards controlled the upper parts. The sheets of the courses led aft to fixed blocks – apertures cut in the bulwarks or sides of the ship, into which sheaves were fitted. On the upper sails, they led through a block on the end of the yard below. In the early eighteenth century it had been the custom to make the sails a little deeper than the distance between the yards really required, but this practice was forbidden by an order of 1762.

The tacks led forward from the clews of the lower sails, as the sheets led aft. Their purpose was to allow the edge of the sail to be held forward when the wind required it. The edges of all the square sails, upper and lower, could also be held forward in a similar way, by bowlines. Each sail had one bowline attached to each leech, divided into several parts as it neared the edge of the sail, so that a topsail of the early nineteenth century had three bowline cringles, with a line attached to each. These parts, known as the bridle of the bowline, were joined together to form a single line. The bowlines of the fore sails led forward to the bowsprit; those of the courses led directly to the deck just inside the bulwarks; while those of the upper sails of the main and mizzen led to the rearmost shroud of the mast ahead before about 1680, and to the top or trestletrees after that date.

Several different types of rope were used for hauling up the sail for furling. The clew lines led from the lower corners of the sail to the ends of the yard above, and were normally fitted on courses. On topsails, topgallants and royals, where the head of the sail was much narrower than the foot, it was necessary to haul the corners inward, since the yard above was smaller than the width of the foot. These were therefore fitted with clew garnets, which led to the centre of the yard rather than the ends, and allowed the clews to be hauled inwards rather than directly upwards. Other lines, the buntlines, were fitted at points along the foot of the sail to

aid in furling. They led behind the sail, directly up to a point on the yard above. Slab lines were sometimes fitted ahead of the sail in a similar way, to aid in the process of hauling up the sail. Leech lines led from cringles on the sides of the sail to a point on the yard, to take some of the weight of the middle of the sail. When furled, the sail was secured to the yard by means of gaskets, ropes which were tied round the sail and the yard by seamen standing precariously on the footropes under the yard.

Triangular staysails, such as the jib sails, had three types of lines attached to them. The halyard was used for hauling the sail up, along the stay to which it was attached. The downhauler, as its name implies, served the opposite purpose, to pull the sail down when it was not needed. Two sheets were fitted to the free corner of the sail, one leading to each side, to be used according to the direction of the wind. Quadrilateral staysails, including most of those fitted between the fore, main and mizzen masts, had one extra line, the tack, which controlled the extra corner.

The mizzen sail, whether lateen or gaff, was hauled up by brails. In the case of the lateen mizzen, these were divided into two types: the foot brails, which led from the foot of the sail diagonally upwards to the yard; and the peak and throat brails which led from the after edge of the sail.

After the abandonment of the fore part of the lateen sail, three brails were usually fitted, all leading from the after edge of the sail – the throat, peak and mizzen brails.

Reef lines were fitted to square sails which had reef points. They were attached to reef cringles, on the leech of the sail on a level with the line of reef points. They were used to haul the upper part of the sail up to a level where the topmen, again standing on the footropes, could tie the reefing points round the yard.

After 1745 lower studding sails (stunsails) were held in position by their four corners. The top outer corner was attached to a short yard, which was held to the stunsail boom by the outer halyard. The inner halyard, leading along the yard to which the stunsail was attached, held the inner corner. A tack held the lower outer corner, and a sheet the bottom inner, to the lower stunsails boom. Before 1745 the system had been rather simpler and more precarious, with a single halyard holding the stunsail yard near its centre, and a sheet, divided into two, holding the lower edge. The upper stunsails had much narrower heads, and they continued to be held only by a single halyard.[16]

Most of the lines of the running rigging led eventually down to the deck, where they could be hauled by parties of less skilled seamen, unable to work on the tops and yards.

The *Ramillies* takes in sail on the approach of a storm, 1782. *National Maritime Museum*

1 The *Prince George*, 100 guns, of 1723, at sea: the jibboom is beginning to take over the function of the spritsail topsail yard, though the latter still finds some use as a flagstaff. The lead of the bowlines and bridles can be clearly seen.
National Maritime Museum

2 The *Worcester*, 60 guns, of 1735, showing the use of studding sails in a light wind: the driver, intended as an extension to the fore-and-aft mizzen sail, is here used virtually as a square sail.
National Maritime Museum

2

Numerous points were needed to belay these lines, of varying strength according to the strain to be put on the line. Among the most important were: the jeers, which supported the weight of the yards; they were belayed to the jeer bitts, anchored to the deck around the masts, and extending down to the deck below; the braces and sheets, which were similarly fixed to bitts around the masts, or to the staghorns (U- and V-shaped structures on the inside of the bulwarks) and kevels; and the tacks, which led round a fixed block or a chesstree, to be belayed on the inside of the bulwark. Other lines were fixed to various points – to cleats on the inside of the bulwarks, to the lanyards of the shrouds, to spare points on the bitts, or to the timber heads on the forecastle. By the end of the eighteenth century belaying pin racks had begun to appear. These were shelves fitted to the insides of the bulwarks, and drilled with holes to receive belaying pins. A ship of the line required hundreds of lines of standing rigging, and the arrangement of their belaying points was very complex; but there seems to have been a standard system, so that a seaman could transfer from one ship to another and still find the end of the appropriate line.

The rigging so far described was used solely for the actual sailing of the ship. Many other lines were needed, for multifarious purposes. Tackle was required for hauling aboard boats, stores, guns, and other heavy weights. Permanent ropes, known as the burton pendants, were fitted to the fore and main mastheads to provide an anchorage for this equipment, while other lines, kept in the boatswain's store when not in use, stretched between the main and the fore yards for lifting heavy weights. In the case of especially weighty items, such as guns, extra lines were fitted to reinforce the lifts of the yards. Other lines were used for anchor work, for towing boats, and for a variety of other purposes. A boatswain, or any skilled seamen, had to be a considerable expert on work with ropes and with blocks and tackle, and needed great adaptability to deal with emergencies, such as the setting up of a jury mast, or the repairing of rigging damaged in storm or action. It is not surprising to hear that in 1761, during the capture of Martinique, the soldiers were amazed at the skill of the seamen in hauling guns over obstacles on land: 'A hundred or two of them, with ropes and pullies, will do more than all your drayhorses in London.'[17]

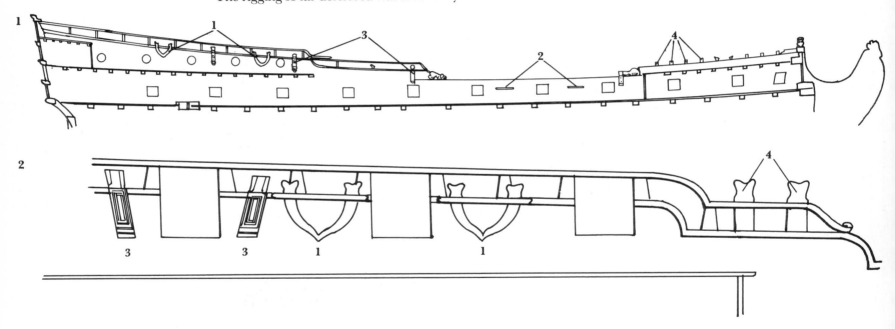

1 Belaying points on the *St Albans* of 1687.

2 Belaying points on the quarterdeck of the *Dorsetshire* of 1757.

1. Staghorns.
2. Cleats.
3. Kevels.
4. Timber heads.

6. Fittings

BESIDES THE SAILS WHICH PROVIDED HER MAIN MOTIVE power, a ship of the line required many other fittings to keep her afloat, seaworthy, and operational. She needed anchors to hold her at her moorings, and systems of raising and lowering them; methods of keeping the water out of the hull, and removing that which entered despite precautions; a system of steering, and boats to move anchors, take on stores and men, and tow the ship in or out of harbour in a calm.

The old sailing ship anchor – with its long metal shank, its arms and flukes angled upward from, and the wooden stock at right angles to, the arms – is perhaps the best known symbol of maritime affairs; justifiably so, since it can be dated, in almost unchanged form, from classical times. It was an expensive item, for most if it had to be made of iron, and it represented many hours of skilled work for the blacksmiths. Its basic principle of operation was simple. When it reached the bottom, the wooden stock would hold it level, allowing one of the flukes to sink into the mud. Any pull on the cable would only cause the fluke to sink deeper, giving the anchor a very strong hold. The basic type of anchor saw little change during two centuries of service with the ship of the line: for most of our period ships were fitted with the 'angle crown' type, in which the arms were angled upwards from the end of the stock, and then carried slightly more sharply upwards by another angle halfway along the arm. Early in the nineteenth century these were replaced by anchors in which the arms formed an arc of a circle, known as the 'round crown' type.

A ship of the line carried several anchors, serving different purposes. The main ones were the two bowers, so called because they were carried in the bows, and thus

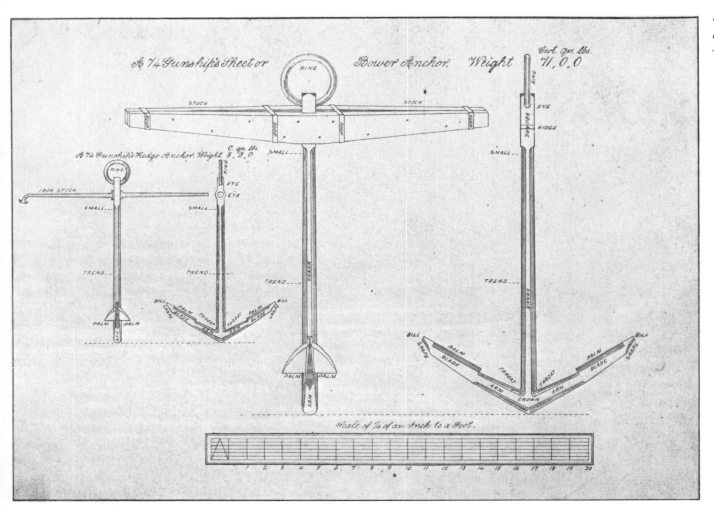

The anchors of a 74-gun ship, c1800.
National Maritime Museum

ready for immediate use. These were the general purpose anchors, useful for most tasks. More specialised was the kedge, the smallest of the anchors. Because of its size, it could be slung under the ship's longboat and let go some distance from the ship; and the ship could then be moved by hauling on the capstan, when wind and tide did not permit movement by the use of the sails. Slightly larger was the stream anchor, used in a similar way for pulling the ship against the tide or current. The largest was the sheet anchor, 'the largest and strongest, being that which seamen call their last hope, and never to be used but in great extremity.'[1] Despite their different names, the sheet and bower anchors were usually all the same size by the end of the eighteenth century. In the 1670s a Third Rate had eight anchors; by 1809 a Third Rate generally had six, comprising four bowers, a stream and a kedge.[2]

The anchors were held to the ship by the cable, a very thick rope. In the early nineteenth century the thickest cable, that of a First Rate, was $23\frac{1}{2}$ inches in circumference, while that of a Third Rate was $20\frac{1}{2}$ inches.[3] The length of the cable had to be much greater than the depth at which the ship was likely to anchor, for if the ship was directly above the anchor it would not be able to hold securely. Therefore, although ships did not normally anchor in more than 40 fathoms of water, the standard length of cable was 120 fathoms, and two could be joined together to give greater length when necessary. Ships normally carried more cables than they had anchors: for example, a Third Rate of the early nineteenth century had eight cables, and only six anchors. One of the cables was lighter than the others, and was known as the stream cable or hawser. It was used with the kedge and stream anchors for manoeuvring and light mooring. On a 100-gun ship of around 1810 it was only 14 inches in circumference.

The method of stowing the anchors of a ship of the line is shown here on a 70-gun ship of the early eighteenth century, but is applicable to most of our period. The bower anchors are suspended with the head under the cathead, but not directly attached to the cathead itself, while the arms are held against the fore channels. The sheet anchor is secured aft of the fore channels, without a cable attached to it. A kedge or stream anchor is held against the stock of the larger anchor. The moveable anchor davit, in common use during this period can be seen protruding from the port side. An anchor buoy is stowed against the shrouds, just above the fluke of the bower anchor.
National Maritime Museum

Obviously the cables, of great length, thickness and weight, took up a great deal of space on a ship, and it would be rare to have more than two of them in use at once. They were stowed in large coils on the orlop deck, taking up much of the space between the warrant officers' cabins near the stern and the store rooms in the bows. One end of the cable was fixed to the ring at the end of the anchor shank. The other passed through the hawse holes in the extreme bows of the ship and down through a hatch into the cable tier on the orlop.

When not in use, the anchor was hung from a heavy davit in the bows, known as the cathead. This supported the anchor by its upper end, where the stock was fixed, and was used for raising it out of the water by means of blocks and pulleys. If the anchor was ready for immediate use it would be hung from the cathead with its shank vertical. Otherwise, it would also be fished – a rope would be fitted

to one of the flukes, and that would be hoisted up until the shank was almost horizontal. A large piece of timber, called a billboard, was fitted under the channels to prevent the anchor from damaging the sides of the ship when being fished. A moveable fish davit, which could be swung from one side of the ship to the other, was used for this operation. Each cathead could only hold one of the bower anchors at once; the others were slung behind, sometimes with the smaller anchors fixed to the larger ones. Anchor buoys, used to mark the position of an anchor when it was in the water, were sometimes stowed in the shrouds above the anchors.

The main work of hauling up the anchors was done by the capstans. These were simple mechanical devices, consisting basically of vertical cylinders with bars attached, allowing a large number of men to apply a great deal of leverage to the task. Early capstans were simply cylinders, with supports known as whelps to give the ropes greater

The seventeenth century capstan, seen here on the *Prince* of 1670: only four arms, each passing right through the barrel of the capstan, can be used, and each bar is at a different height.
The Science Museum

1 A late eighteenth century capstan, basically similar to those in use from about 1680 until the end of the age of sail.
National Maritime Museum

2 The fore jeer capstan of the *Stirling Castle* of 1779.

3 Method of raising the anchor, *c*1800: a total of 84 men are operating the main capstan, though the lower part is not in use, except to receive the messenger. The messenger is passed forward, and held against the cable by means of nippers, then passes through a system of pulleys back to the capstan. In the main hold, a large party works to stow the cable after it has been passed through the hatchway. On the forecastle another party stands by to raise the anchor out of the water, by means of the cathead, and then to stow it against the side.
National Maritime Museum

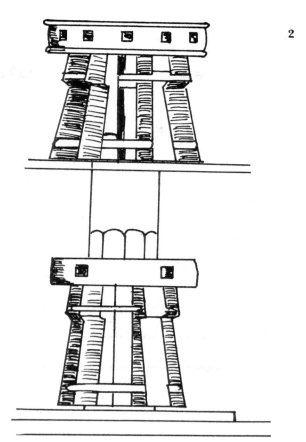

2

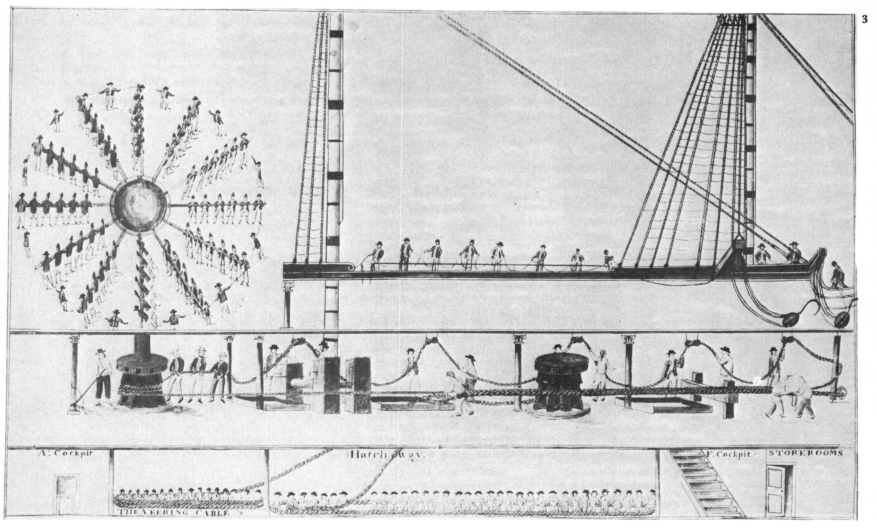

3

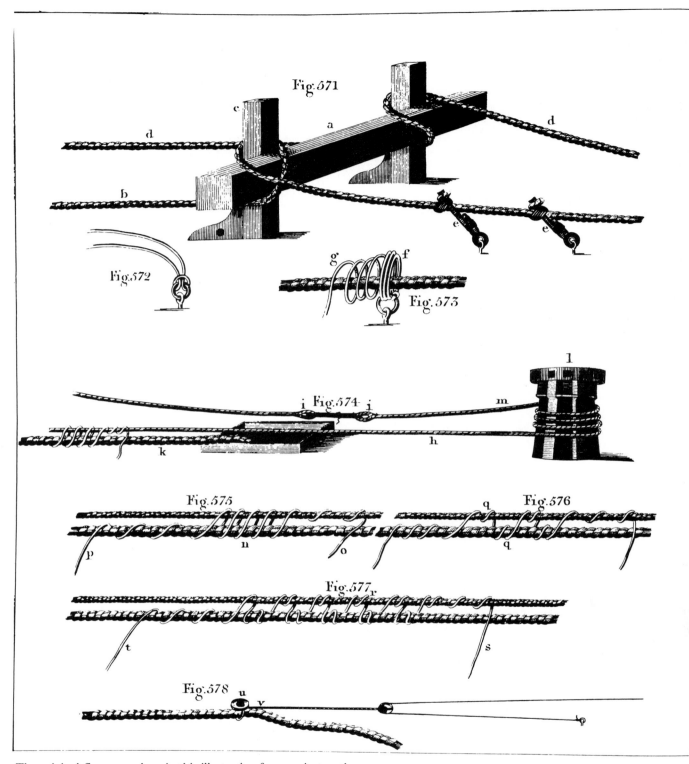

The original figure numbers in this illustration from a nineteenth century manual refer to the following – Fig 571: The anchor cable coiled round the bits, and secured to the deck by stoppers (e). Fig 572, 573: Different types of stoppers. Fig 574, 575, 576, 577: Different means of securing the cable to the messenger to the cable by means of nippers, used according to the amount of strain on the cable.
From Lever's Sheet Anchor

grip, and increase the diameter of their sweep. Through the top of the capstan four square holes were bored, and a long bar was passed through each, thus providing eight arms for the crew to push against. Of course it was impossible for all of the holes to be at the same height, and so only one of the bars could be situated in an ideal position for the men to push against. Efficiency was lost as the others worked with bars which were either too high or too low. This difficulty was solved around 1680,[4] when a new type of capstan was installed, known as the drumhead capstan. It took its name from the large circular piece at its head, which had holes for the bars. Since the head was now much larger, it was not necessary for the bars to pass right through in order to be secure, and so a separate bar could be fitted to each side. This gave two advantages: firstly, the bars could all be fitted at the same height, thus adding to efficiency; secondly, more bars could be fitted, and most capstans of this type had twelve. With 6 men at each bar, this would allow 72 men at a single capstan, with the addition of others who pulled on lines stretched between the outer ends of the bars, where leverage was greatest. The bars were of course removeable on both types of capstan, in order to save space when it was not in use. A capstan was held rigid against the deck by means of strong pieces of timber known as partners, and a lever known as a pawl was fitted to prevent it from surging backwards and causing injury among the crew. The main capstan had its head on the upper deck, but it extended down to the deck below, where the trundle-head was fitted. This could take another set of bars, and thus allow yet more men to work at it. Another capstan, the fore jeer capstan, was fitted forward; it was generally used for lighter purposes, such as hauling in cargo or spars.

The anchor cable, being very heavy and unmanageable, could not be directly hauled against the capstan, and did not come into direct contact with it. Instead, it was linked to it by means of the messenger, a lighter piece of cable. This was fixed temporarily against the piece of anchor cable which at that moment was passing along the deck, by means of light ropes known as nippers. These were constantly coiled and uncoiled against the messenger and cable as the latter passed along the deck. The messenger was endless: several turns were taken round the capstan, and it was passed along the cable, and then back to the capstan by means of a system of pulleys. The cable was passed down into the orlop, where a large party worked to stow it. Another party was based on the forecastle, ready to cat and fish the anchor when it appeared at the surface of the water. When the anchor was holding the ship, the cable was belayed against the bitts. These were stout horizontal pieces of timber, supported by strong verticals which extended down through the decks below. The cable was turned round the bitts, and then fixed to the deck by means of stoppers.

The stern rudder, hinged against the sternpost of the ship, had been used since at least the twelfth century, and the principle remained the same throughout the age of the ship of the line. The rudder was of approximately the same width as the sternpost, which made it rather thick, but sufficiently strong for its crucial role. It reached along the whole length of the sternpost, beginning at the level of the keel and continuing slightly above the post, to allow the

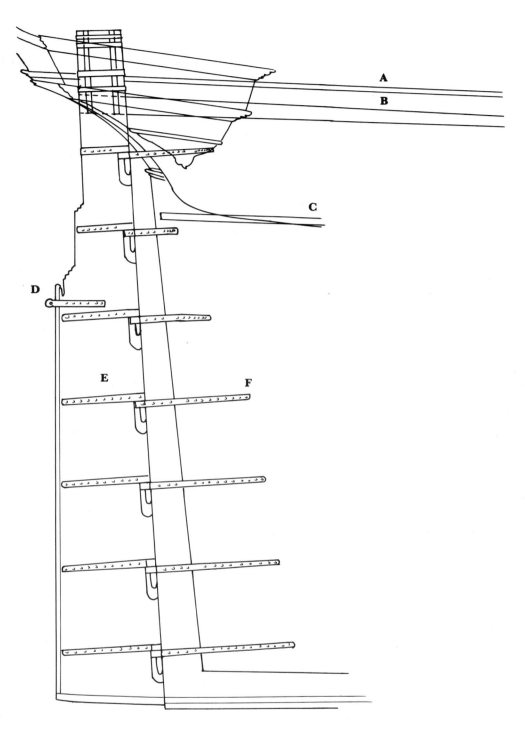

THE RUDDER OF THE *GOLIATH*, A 74 OF 1781

A. Upper deck.
B. Tiller.
C. Gun deck.
D. Point for fixing emergency chains.
E. Pintle.
F. Gudgeon.

Gudgeons and pintles of the
rudder of a 90-gun ship, c1780.
*Based on a drawing in the Public
Records Office*

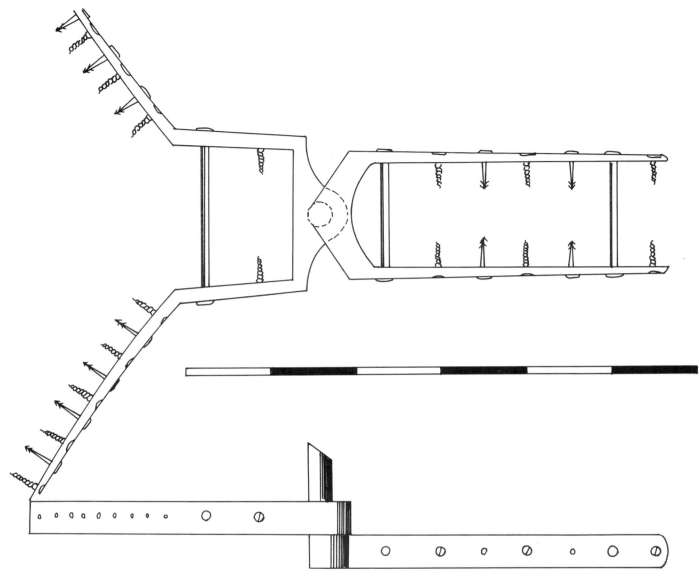

tiller to be fitted. By modern standards it did not extend far in a fore-and-aft direction, but its great depth compensated for that. In profile it tapered gradually as it rose, and then more sharply above the waterline, so that its head was almost square, and able to take the tiller. In early periods this tapering above the waterline was achieved by a series of steps, but in the nineteenth century it was done by a sharp curve, and this was known as the round-headed rudder. A system of gudgeons and pintles fixed the rudder to the sternpost: the pintles, which were bolted to the rudder itself, had a pin projecting downwards, which fitted into a hole in the gudgeons; these were bolted to the sternpost and to the planking of the stern.

Though the rudder itself remained largely unaltered throughout the ages, the means of moving it was forced to change as the ship of the line grew larger. The tiller alone was still satisfactory for a small merchant ship or warship, but the large man of war had long outgrown it. The tiller did not give enough leverage for steering a large ship, and on such a vessel the helmsman was likely to find himself buried beneath several decks, and unable to see the trim of the sails or any other point of reference. A partial answer was found in the whipstaff, first recorded at the end of the

sixteenth century. This was merely an extension upwards of the end of the tiller, allowing slightly more leverage and raising the steering position by one deck. The whipstaff itself was a wooden pole, vertical when the tiller was in the central position, and pivoted about a fixture on the upper deck (or middle deck on three-deckers). Its lower end was hinged to a metal bar at the end of the tiller, while the end above the pivot – about three-quarters of its total length – was held by the helmsman and pushed from side to side to move the rudder. It was not a wholly satisfactory solution. On a two-decker the helmsman might be able to see out through a specially fitted window, but on a three-decker he was below both the upper deck and the quarterdeck, and could see nothing. The extra moment given by the whipstaff was small, and moreover, the movement of the tiller from side to side was greatly restricted.

The situation was improved in the early 1700s, when ropes were led from the end of the tiller through blocks on the side of the ship, and then upwards to a windlass fitted athwartships on the quarterdeck. Several problems were thus solved at once: the helmsman could move up to the quarterdeck; much more force could be applied to the rudder; and the tiller could be moved further from side to

The first step towards the steering wheel *c*1703: the 'steering rowle' is fitted athwartships, and moved by handles on each side.

An early eighteenth century single wheel, with binnacle.

The break of the poop and the forecastle of one of the 70-gun ships of 1677. The helmsman's companion, which allowed the men at the whipstaff a view of the sails, can be seen in the upper drawing. Also to be seen are the heavy carved decorations which were fitted to these parts of Third Rates during the 1677 programme, the flag lockers on the poop, and the doors to the small cabins under the gangways.
National Maritime Museum

The double wheel of the *Victory*, as fitted at her launch in 1765. Forward of the wheel can be seen the binnacle, containing a compass and other navigational instruments, in a visible but protected position. Forward of that, the structure of the gratings over the hatches can be clearly seen.

side. It was a short step to the next improvement, the classic ship's steering wheel[5]. The windlass had to be moved to the fore-and-aft position instead of athwartships, and fitted with spokes and a rim instead of a pair of handles, and this seems to have been achieved on most ships by about 1710. Curiously, there is no sign of an Admiralty order to fit either the steering windlass or the wheel, though the evidence of models suggests that their use spread very quickly after 1700.

Early wheels were fitted aft of the mizzen mast, so that they could be directly above the end of the tiller, which obviously had to stop short before reaching the mast. It has been suggested that this was because the wheel had not yet been fitted with a sweep, a curved piece of timber which would regulate its travel from side to side, but in fact the sweep pre-dated the wheel by several years. Contracts show that it was common in the 1690s, though there is no evidence of the wheel being fitted before about 1703. The important point was not the introduction of the wheel itself, nor the sweep, but the discovery of a system of ropes and blocks which would allow the full use of the tiller, allowing it to move as far from side to side as its position in the hull would allow. It is probable that the early wheel allowed little more movement than the whipstaff, before the purchase of the ropes became ineffective. From about 1735[6] there was a tendency to move the wheel to a new position forward of the mizzen mast, and this suggests a slightly more sophisticated system of blocks, but is not conclusive. The earliest written evidence is in an Admiralty order of 1771, which demanded the fitting of 'Mr Pollard's system of sweeps and rowles'[7] to keep the tiller ropes taut. Possibly it was not until that time that the power of the rudder could be used to full effect.

The steering system was obviously of great importance to any ship, and several emergency procedures were available in case of damage to one of the components. If necessary the ship could be steered by a party of men handling ropes attached directly to the tiller. Though the tiller was fitted above the lower deck, the rudder head actually passed up through the deck above, so that another tiller could be fitted on that deck if the normal one was rendered unusable. As a last resort, chains were fitted to the aftermost edge of the rudder and led through the stern ports, and these could be pulled in an emergency to give some control over the rudder. After 1822 iron tillers were fitted to ships with round sterns, as the head of the rudder was left exposed by the new method of construction.

In wooden shipbuilding, keeping water out of the hull was a constant problem. In normal circumstances, the water's most common method of entry was through the spaces between the planks. In an attempt to prevent this, ships were caulked shortly after their completion, and at intervals during their service as occasion demanded. Pieces of oakum were forced between the seams in an attempt to make them more waterproof.

As ships ventured further from their home bases, and for longer periods, a new range of problems appeared. Of these, the most serious was the shipworm, found in tropical waters, and capable of destroying the whole strength of the underwater hull of a ship in a few months. Throughout the seventeenth century, and most of the eighteenth, there was

The *Bellona* on the launchway after coppering: the rudder is of the typical form, as broad as the sternpost, and tapering upwards by means of a series of steps. The run of the copper sheathing roughly follows that of the planking. The rail of the stern gallery is of a geometric pattern, not unusual in the third quarter of the eighteenth century, when there was some move away from the more common system of vertical pillars.
National Maritime Museum

no fully satisfactory answer to this. The commonest method of protection was by sheathing, whereby the underwater hull was coated with a mixture of tar and hair, and then covered over with a layer of thin planking. This may have been intended to protect the tar and hair, or merely to placate the shipworm, and reduce its incentive to penetrate the unpleasant inner coating; in either case it was of limited effect, and it was well known that ships which spent any length of time in the West Indies were likely to decay much faster than others.

By comparison, the problems encountered in cooler waters were less serious. Encrustation with weed and shellfish did not in itself seriously damage the structure of the ship, but it did impair its speed and sailing qualities. To counter this, hulls below the waterline were coated with a variety of compositions intended to deter marine life. Mostly these consisted of mixtures of resin, tar, turpentine, and other compounds. The result was often white or off-white, and this accounts for the finish to be found on the bottom of many ship models of the period. Numerous experiments were made with different compositions, and sometimes one side of the ship was coated in the standard way, the other with a new substance to be tested. Again, little was achieved, and ships continued to gather weed. Normally they had to be put into a dry-dock every four months while on active service, in order to retain their sailing qualities. This might have been acceptable in the mid-seventeenth century when ships were fitted out for summer campaigns only, but by the middle of the eighteenth, when continuous blockade was coming into use, it posed a serious problem of regularly reducing strength by sending ships back to port.

The answer, of course, was copper sheathing. This was not entirely a new idea (see Volume I, Chapter 10), and experiments with either copper or lead had gone on for over a century. The twin problems of expense and the electrolytic action of the copper with other metals had deterred real progress until, in the crisis of the American War, the Admiralty had been forced to adopt it. Even then the solution was not ideal, until it was realised that all the iron bolts of the underwater hull needed to be replaced with those made of copper alloy, and time and money were found for doing this. It was the verge of the French Revolutionary Wars before the British fleet could be said to be fully coppered.

The copper was fitted in the form of plates, 4 feet by 1 foot 2 inches on a ship of the line. Thick plates, 32 ounces per square foot, were used on the parts most vulnerable to wear, such as the bows; thinner plates of 28 ounces per square foot were used on the rest of the hull. The plates were bolted onto the wood with copper nails, in lines which generally

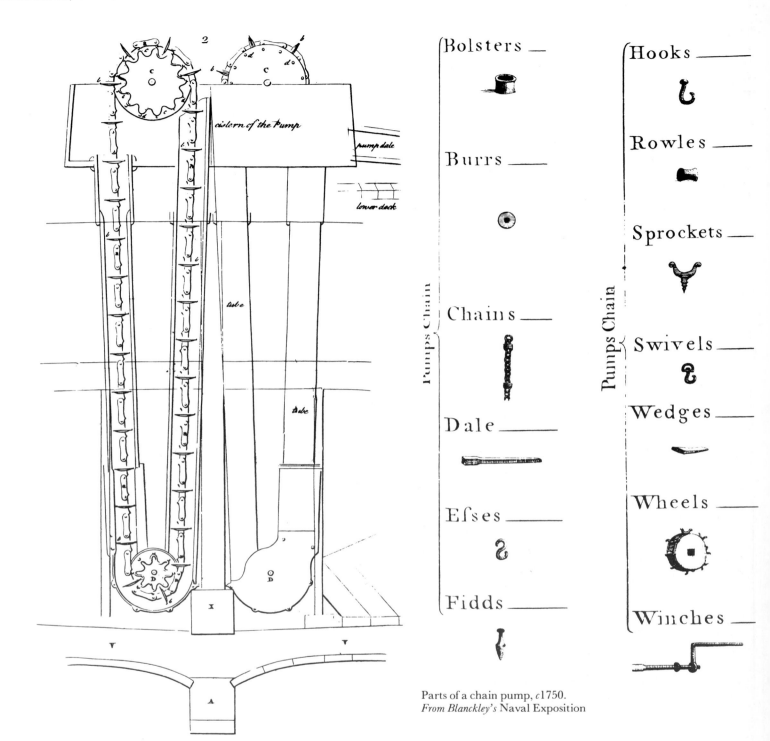

Section of a chain pump of about 1760.
From Falconer's Marine Dictionary

Parts of a chain pump, *c*1750.
From Blanckley's Naval Exposition

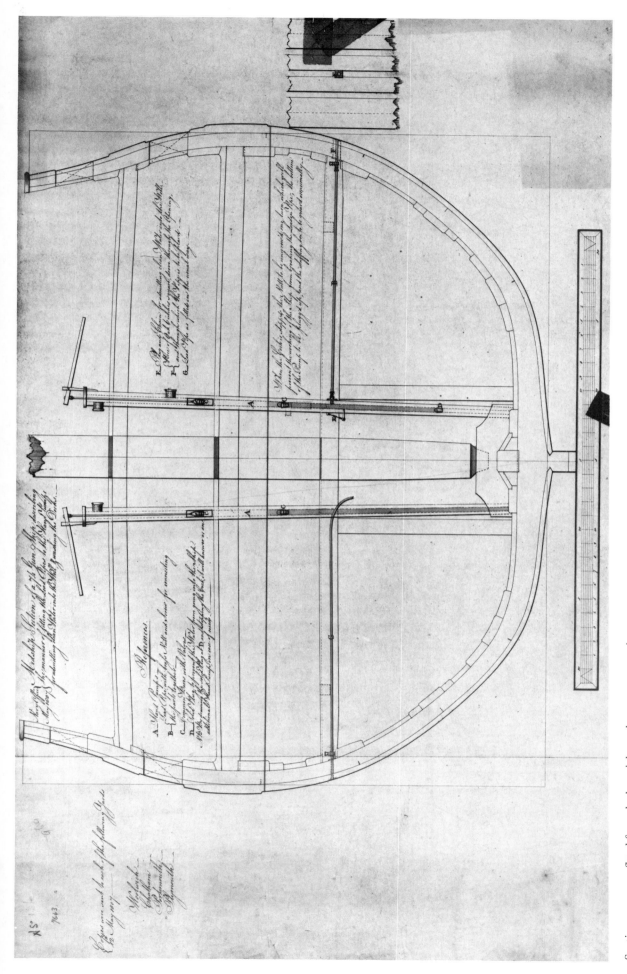

Suction pumps, as fitted from the late eighteenth century onwards, were used to provide water for washing the decks, and for firefighting. Seawater was allowed into the main pump system by means of pipes sited just under the waterline, and then pumped to the decks by means of the suction pumps. This drawing dates from 1807.
National Maritime Museum

GUN DECK STRUCTURE AND FITTINGS, ON THE *AJAX* OF 1767

1. Rudder head.
2. The base of a small cabin for a junior officer in the gunroom.
3. Transom knees.
4. Deck beam with carlines and ledges between.
5. Pillars to support the centres of the beams above. These could be removed when, for example, the capstans were in use.
6. The base of the main capstan, showing the pawls.
7. The pumps.
8. Pump dales, leading the water through the sides of the ship, and only rigged when the pumps were in use.
9. Pump handles, on each side of the pumps.
10. Curved deck beam, used, in this case, to avoid interfering with the main hatchway.
11. Fore jeer capstan.
12. The bitts, used for securing the anchor cables. The vertical supporters reached right down to the floor of the ship, to give extra rigidity.
13. The fore mast partners.
The Science Museum

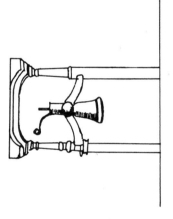

The belfry of the *Stirling Castle* of 1779: belfries took too many different forms for their variations to be adequately documented in a book of this nature.

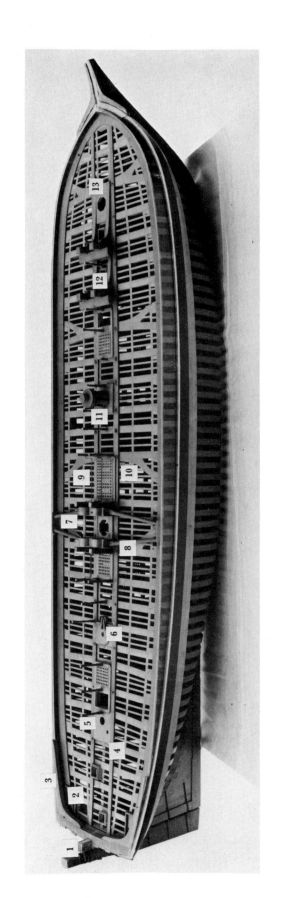

followed the run of the planking, and they stopped sharply at the level of the load waterline. There was some overlap between the plates, in order that the shipworm could not penetrate between them. Copper was successful because it formed a solid surface which could not be penetrated by the worm, and because it interacted with the water to form a slightly poisonous liquid which was enough to kill weeds. It was expensive, but, once the initial period of scepticism was over, most critics thought that it was well worth the cost.[8]

No wooden hull, however well constructed, caulked, and sheathed, was ever completely watertight, especially in a seagoing vessel which might be subjected to the stresses and strains of great waves, so that the hull might be worked out of position and the frames and planking distorted, leaving gaps. All ships needed pumps to remove water from the interior, to prevent the ship from foundering.

The first problem was to collect as much of the water as possible in a single place, where a pump could draw it out and jettison it overboard. Water which seeped through the outer planks would find itself in the spaces between the timbers of the frame, and, if it were given the chance, it would gravitate towards the midships, where the hull was deepest. Therefore holes were drilled in the timbers, to form a channel for the bilge water. Other water which found its way into the hold would also sink into the spaces between the frames, and be channelled towards the midships in the same way. The system was not absolutely efficient, for some stagnant water remained in the spaces below the levels of the holes, causing dampness and unpleasant smells. Nevertheless enough was removed to prevent the ship from sinking, or the stores in the hold from being too seriously damaged.

The fact that most of the bilge water found its way to midships dictated the position of the pump which was intended to remove it. In the seventeenth century two pumps were carried, situated aft of the main mast; in the eighteenth century, it was usually four, forming the corners of a square around the main mast. In the early period, suction pumps were fitted. These were operated by long handles which could be stowed away if the pumps were not in use, but as early as 1625 there is mention of the successor to the suction pump, the chain pump[9], and this was being fitted to ships of the line by 1680. It functioned by means of an endless belt made up of S-shaped links, which would carry water as they travelled upwards and discharge it into the pump dales before returning downwards to pick up more. The chain travelled through two wooden tubes, one leading downwards and the other upwards, and was turned around a wheel at the top and bottom. Motive power was supplied by the crew, who turned handles running fore and aft from the pumps. The pumps led water up to the level of the gun deck, where it was discharged into a large square cistern, and then into the dales – wooden tubes which led to the side of the ship – from whence the water was emptied overboard.

The British chain pump was regarded as highly efficient in comparison with the suction pump used on the majority of foreign warships, but it seems to have been subjected to more experiments and inventions than any other part of the ship; perhaps because it was useful both to the Navy and to the mining and civil engineering industries ashore, or because pumps were particularly important in British warships, which spent long periods at sea. As early as 1698 we hear of 'A new sort of pump (still reserving the use of the chain pump', which, it was claimed, would do three times as much work as the old.[10] In later years, inventions multiplied, and in the 1750s alone the ideas of Cooper, Rowe, Millay, Templar, Tuite, and Hudson were all considered and rejected by the Navy Board. By 1800 the Board was tired of experiments, and ordered that in future pumps should be standardised. There was, however, one version which was successful: this was the Coles pump, which was first noted in 1761, went out of favour in 1773, owing to the belief that it was too fragile, and was fitted as standard after 1774, when its teething troubles had been sorted out.[11] From the third quarter of the eighteenth century suction pumps were also fitted; these generally led to the upper deck rather than the gun deck, so that they could be used to supply water for cleaning the decks. Unlike chain pumps they forced water up under some pressure, and therefore they were useful for fire-fighting. They took in water via a small pipe leading through the side of the ship, just under the waterline.

The pumps were designed to remove water which found its way through the sides of the ship, but other water might be found on the decks, because of rain, spray, or heavy seas. To remove this, a simple drainage system was required. In profile the decks curved downwards towards the midships (very sharply in the seventeenth century, rather less so in later periods), and this sheer was partly designed to help the water drain away. In cross section the decks also curved upwards towards the centreline, allowing it to run down towards the sides. Efforts were made to stop the water from making direct contact with the sides, where it might contribute to rot and decay, and to this end the waterway, a particularly thick plank, was placed along the edges of the deck. It was pierced with holes which were fitted with lead scuppers, which allowed the water to drain overboard.

One place where water might enter was through the hawse holes in the bows. These could be stopped up with oakum when the ship was at sea, but this was not always possible when she was riding at anchor. The extreme forward part of the gun deck was therefore separated off by a partition which reached about halfway up to the next deck. The space forward of the partition was known as the manger, and, as its name implies, was sometimes used for keeping live animals. To prevent deck water from emptying down hatches to the deck below, and to avoid the danger of men falling down hatches in the dark, these openings were surrounded with coamings – thick pieces of timber approximately square in cross section.

Many different types of boats were carried by the ship of the line during its history. At different times we hear of longboats, launches, cutters, skiffs, pinnaces, barges, yawls, and several others. In fact there were three basic types of boat, according to the functions which they performed. Firstly, there was the heavy boat, for use in moving anchors and carrying large numbers of men and heavy stores, especially fresh water, which often had to be obtained from the nearest available creek. Secondly there were harbour boats, of light construction and designed for rowing, used mainly for ferrying the officers ashore or from ship to ship.

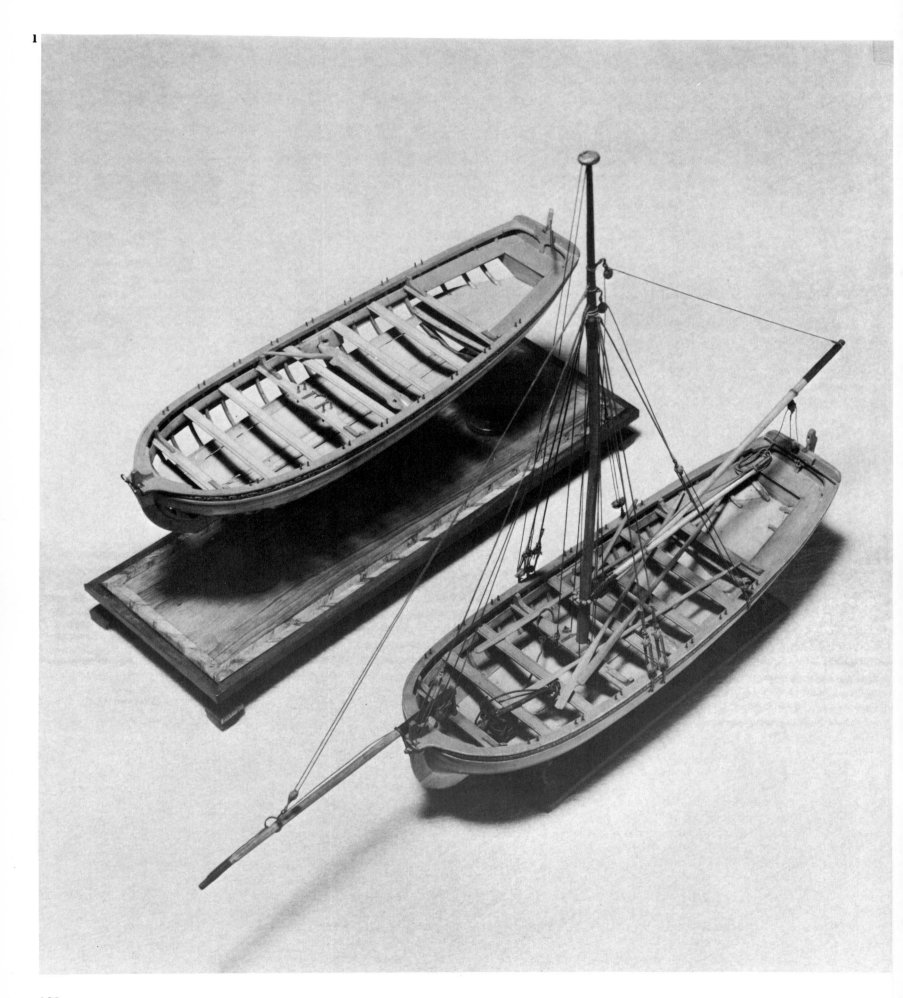

Thirdly there were light sailing boats, which could be used at sea when the larger boats were unnecessary.

The prime example of the first type was the longboat. Wide and of heavy construction, able to perform under both sails and oars, to carry a heavy load and to operate both at sea and in harbour, early longboats were very large – normally half the length of the ship's keel in 1618, so that the *Prince Royal* had a longboat 52 feet long.[12] After this there was a tendency for them to become shorter in relation to the length of the ship, and by 1719 the longboat of a First Rate was 36 feet long. In succeeding years she began to belie her name, and a ship's longboat was often shorter than her barge or pinnace.

A longboat was expected to perform in a wide variety of roles, and perhaps it was a natural corollary of this that she did none of them particularly well. Certainly there were many complaints about their suitability from the early 1700s onwards, and some captains began to suggest alternatives. One which was favoured by some was the launch, originally developed as a dockyard boat for use in towing and anchor work. Compared with the longboat it was 'longer, more flat bottomed, and by rowing a greater number of oars is better adapted for going up narrow and

shallow rivers.' It was less suited to the open sea than a longboat, but by the mid-eighteenth century other types of sea-boat were coming into use, so this quality was less necessary. The first suggestions for the replacement of the longboat were made as early as 1739, but met with a certain amount of resistance from the Navy Board. However, captains continued to ask for launches in individual cases over the next forty years – especially for amphibious expeditions where the capacity of the launch could be used for carrying troops – and sometimes the requests were granted. Finally, in 1780, it was made standard for all ships in place of the longboat, and continued in use as the main ship's heavy boat for the rest of the age of sail.

From the middle of the seventeenth century the main types of harbour boats were the pinnace and barge – lightly constructed, narrow, and designed mainly for the transport of officers within sheltered anchorages. The distinction between the two is not always clear, but the barge, intended for admirals and captains, was larger than the pinnace, which was mostly used by lieutenants. According to some definitions the barge had ten oars or more, and the pinnace had less, though this was not always adhered to. Both had high and narrow sterns, and the barge especially often had

1 Longboats, *c*1740: that in the foreground is rigged for sailing; the other is fitted with a windlass for lifting anchors and other heavy weights. *National Maritime Museum*

2 A ten-oared barge, *c*1750. *National Maritime Museum*

2

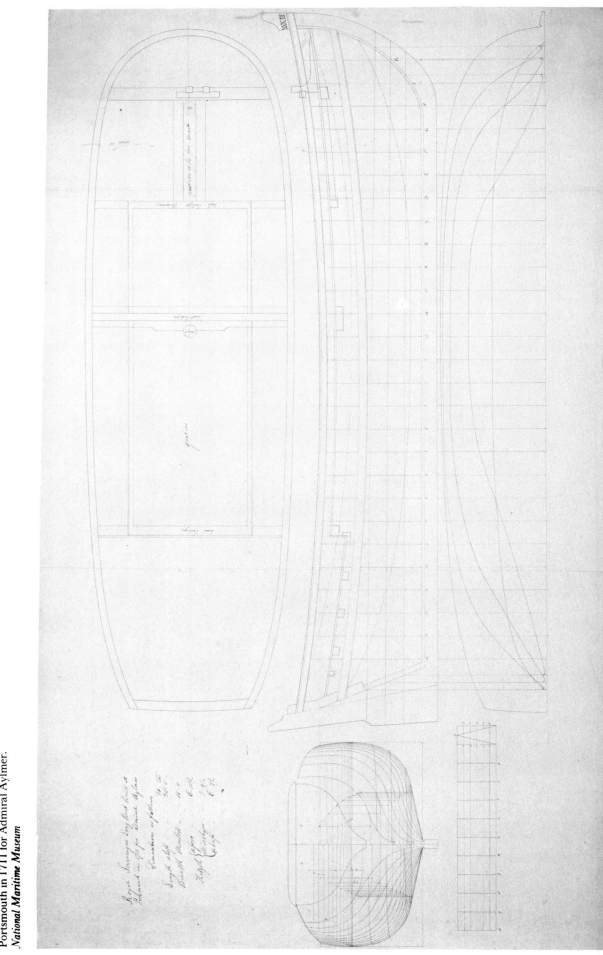

A 38-foot longboat for the *Royal Sovereign*: the boat was built at Portsmouth in 1711 for Admiral Aylmer. *National Maritime Museum*

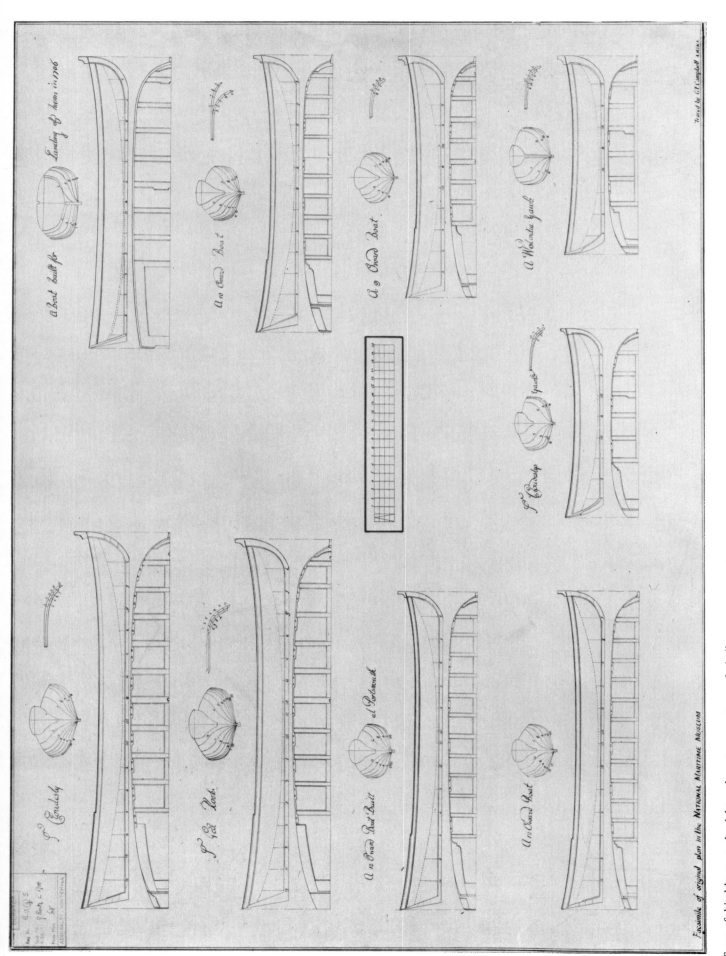

Types of ships' boats, early eighteenth century: most are admiral's personal barges, but two types of yawl are also shown.
National Maritime Museum

1

some decoration, elaborate painting schemes being common. Both barges and pinnaces were long and difficult to handle: on the 1719 establishment a pinnace was only marginally shorter than a longboat for the same rate, and the longest barge in 1817 was 37 feet long, more than the biggest launch. This sometimes caused inconvenience for captains who wanted their boats hoisted out quickly, and by the 1790s some were being replaced by cutters, which were lighter and better sailers, or by gigs, which were smaller than the pinnace or barge.

In the early days the longboat had to double both as a heavy-lifting boat and as the main sea-boat, but from the early seventeenth century, attempts were made to find a boat which was smaller, lighter, and more easy to handle than the longboat, but could nevertheless be used at sea and under sail. The first answer was the yawl, which became standard in 1701, though it had evidently been used forty years earlier. It may have been based on a Norwegian boat of a similar name, but in England it was first built at Deal, where clinker building was common, and the Navy's yawls had this form of construction. This made then unique among ships' boats, for all the others were carvel-built. The yawl was short and relatively broad-beamed, with finer lines and a sharper bow than either the longboat or launch. Early on it was apparently used by some admirals as their personal transport in cases where the barge was unsuitable.

The cutter had much in common with the yawl. It too was clinker-built, and had its origins in Deal. It had a relatively broad beam, and a particularly sharp bow by the standards of the time. It was generally larger than a yawl, and therefore more useful for various tasks at sea, including independent patrol in certain circumstances. Cutters were first issued as standard in 1740, when 25-foot ones of six oars were given to ships of the line for use in pressing men; but soon they were found to have many other uses, and became very popular with captains, and by 1771 a second cutter had been added to the establishment of ships of the line. Though successful as a sea and general purpose boat, the cutter did attract some adverse criticism, for its clinker building was lighter and more difficult to maintain than the carvel build of the other boats, and this sometimes caused problems in service.

The cutter introduced one new feature into the service. In the older boats, the oars had rested on the top strake of planking, being held in position by thole pins fixed in the strake. The cutter had holes cut in the top strake to hold the oars, thus allowing a slightly higher freeboard, and this feature eventually spread to other boats. The sharp bows of the cutter also had some influence, and to a certain extent was copied on other types.

All boats were fitted for sailing, even the barges and pinnaces which were 'very unfit for sea'.[13] In 1771 a 74-gun ship's longboat had a single mast, with a bowsprit, boom and gaff. The other boats had two masts. Barges, pinnaces and yawls were apparently spritsail rigged, with two masts of equal length. Cutters had a schooner or ketch rig, with two masts and gaff sails.[14] It had apparently been normal to pay boats with materials similar to those used on the sides of the ship, thus giving a natural wood finish, though of course some boats – especially those used by captains and admirals – were often painted in bright colours. In 1771 it was

Types of boat, *c*1800: the heavy angular lines of the launch can be clearly seen. The cutter, on the other hand, has particularly fine lines. *From Steel's* Naval Architecture

2 A two-decker entering harbour, late 1750s: a longboat and pinnace are being towed; the longboat, in which a man is stationed, is attached to the ship by two ropes, the boat rope and the guest (or gust) rope. *National Maritime Museum*

ordered that 'the bottoms of all ships' boats of every kind to be painted in future with white lead instead of resin or any other composition'[15], and thus they gained the white appearance that is now associated with ships' boats.

The number of boats carried by each ship tended to increase over the years, as fleets spent more and more time away from their home bases. In 1618 a large ship had three boats: the longboat, pinnace and skiff. This remained standard throughout the century, though the skiff was gradually replaced by the yawl, and Third Rates are sometimes listed as having only two boats instead of three. In 1701 an extra Deal yawl was added, giving three-deckers a total of four boats, while Third and Fourth Rates carried three. In 1740 a cutter was added to ships of the Third Rate and above, so that a three-decker now carried five boats, and a two-decker four. Another cutter was added in 1755, making the total up to six and five, and by 1771 a 74 also carried six boats – a longboat, pinnace, barge, yawl, and

two cutters of different lengths. These of course were the official figures; there would have been many variations in service, as officers carried private boats at their own expense, or picked up native boat-types on foreign service; as experimental types were fitted on occasion, or for special service; as boats were lost or replaced unofficially, or the dockyard ran out of supplies of the appropriate type.

The stowage of boats was always a problem on the crowded decks of a ship of the line. The enormous longboats of the early seventeenth century could not have been hoisted aboard at all, and were usually towed behind by the boat rope and the gust rope. By the middle of the century, as longboats became smaller, it became more common to hoist them aboard, by means of tackle stretched between the main and fore yards, and they were sited on booms or spare spars stretched lengthwise between the forecastle and the quarterdeck. Normally there would have been room for only one boat on the booms, and this left a problem of

A pinnace stowed on spare topmasts along the waist, early eighteenth century.
National Maritime Museum

stowing the others. Perhaps they were stowed inside the longboat, which may have had removeable thwarts for this between, or simply towed behind, though this would have caused a problem with the unseaworthy pinnaces and barges.

In the 1740s gangways were added, running along the sides of the waist between the forecastle and the quarterdeck. Between these, booms were stretched athwartships, and these could provide a considerable amount of space for boat storage. In later years the gangways became larger and more permanent, and the cross beams, instead of being fixed temporarily on top of the gangways, were fitted underneath them as a permanent part of the structure. They continued to support the boats, often three or four of them.

Though boat stowage was vastly improved in the second half of the eigtheenth century, the boats were still rather inaccessible in an emergency, and it must have taken a

large gang of men to hoist a longboat, for example, up from its position in the waist, over the gunwales, and down into the water. Even the rigging of the tackle preparatory to this operation must have taken a considerable amount of time, and there would have been little hope of launching a boat quickly if, for example, a man fell overboard. In the 1790s, therefore, davits were introduced on the quarter galleries and usually carried a cutter each, ready for immediate use.

A properly fitted ship of the line was intended to serve anywhere in the world, in any conditions of weather; to operate for long periods without the support of a main shore base; to survive the hazards of storm or enemy action, making her own repairs and often finding her own supplies as she went. Her fittings largely helped to make her self-contained, and ready for almost anything.

A barge on the cross beams between the gangways, 1765. *National Maritime Museum*

7. Accommodation

A SHIP OF THE LINE NEEDED A MUCH LARGER CREW THAN a merchant ship of comparable size. One of the smallest ships of the line, a 50 on the 1706 establishment, carried 280 men, while a large First Rate of the early nineteenth century could carry up to 875.[1] As well as being able to keep the sea in all weathers and in any part of the world, she had to be able to man all her guns in battle; finding living space for these men, as well as storage for water and victuals for several months at sea, was never easy, and it could only be achieved at considerable, if not intolerable, discomfort.

In the lowest part of the ship, below the orlop deck, was the hold, used for the bulk storage of provisions and ammunition. The stowage of the hold was more than merely a warehousing problem. The distribution of weight could decisively affect the trim, and therefore the sailing qualities, of the ship. The responsibility for it, therefore, rested with the master, whose duties were concerned with the sailing of the ship, rather than with the purser, who had responsibility for the goods themselves. At the very bottom layer, the hold was ballasted with iron and shingle. The actual amount of ballast for a particular ship was usually settled by her designer, and this was enforced by the orders of the Navy Board, though there were cases in which the captain altered the ship's ballast without permission. As to its distribution, the master was expected to look up the

records of previous commissions, or consult with the master shipwright in the case of a new ship. Iron ballast was laid first, then shingle, into which the casks which held the provisions could sink.

Apart from gunpowder and shot, which were stored separately in magazines sealed off from the rest of the hold, two basic types of provisions were carried. Wet goods, comprising drinking water, spirits, and beer when the ship was operating close to a home base, were kept in casks to prevent them from leaking out over the hold, and to avoid contact with the bilge water. Water was usually laid on the bottom tiers of the hold, for its weight could help the stability of the ship. Spirits, on the other hand, were kept in a separate compartment known as the spirit room, and secured against the desires of the crew. Dry provisions, including the basic ship's diet of beef, pork, biscuit, cheese, oatmeal and butter, were salted where appropriate and also stored in casks, partly to prevent natural decay, and also to protect them from the bilge water. From the early nineteenth century, metal water tanks were fitted on the lower tier of the hold, and means were provided to pump the water up to the deck.

The hold was stowed tier by tier, with wedges to hold the casks in position, and smaller casks to fill up some of the space around the edges. Along its length, the hold was

THE HOLD OF A 74-GUN SHIP IN 1778, SHOWING THE METHOD OF STOWING IRON BALLAST

A. The kelson.
B. Well.
C. Rising to the ceiling.
D. The riders.
E. Bulkhead of the fore hold.
F. After bulkhead.
'Eight tons left for shifting'.
Based on a drawing in the Public Records Office

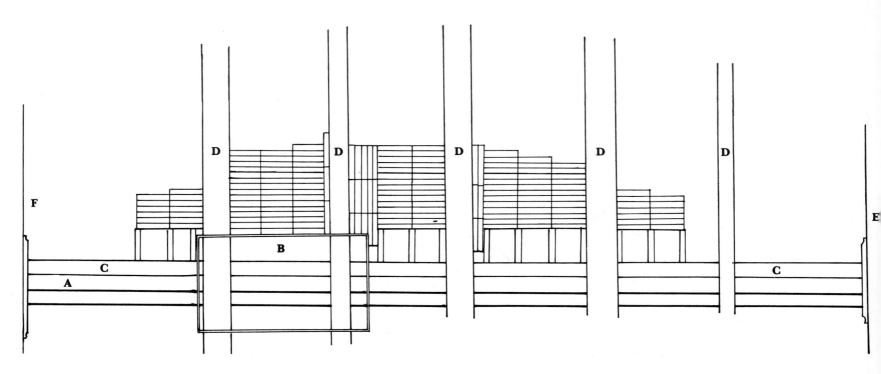

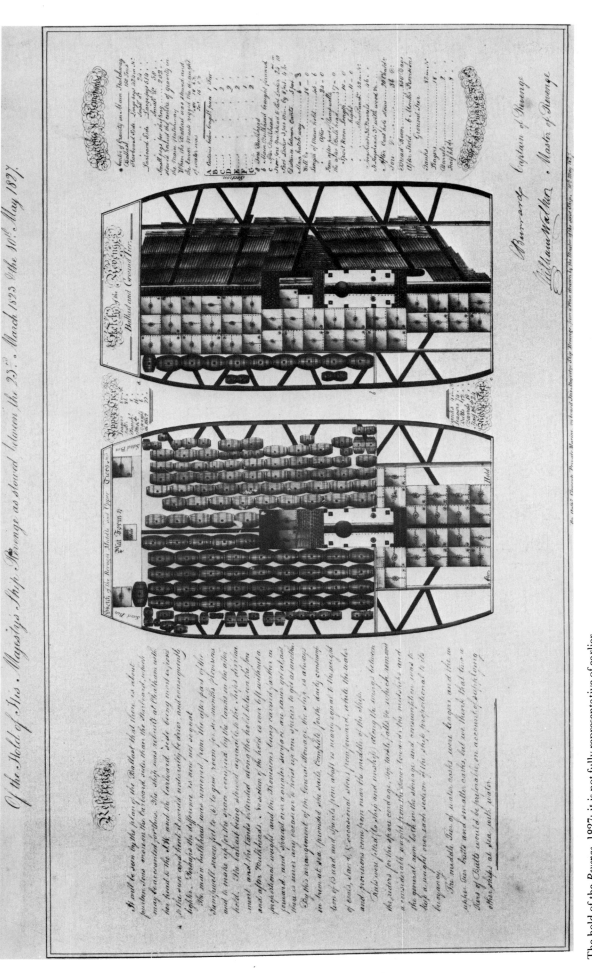

The hold of the *Revenge*, 1827: it is not fully representative of earlier years – the diagonal framing allows the iron ballast to be stowed diagonally, whereas in previous periods it would have been laid longitudinally, and by this time water was kept in metal tanks rather than wooden casks.
National Maritime Museum

1

1 The lower deck of a two-decker, *c*1800: hammocks are shown stretched between the deck beams, though they are not so crammed together as other evidence would suggest. Women were allowed on board when the ship was in port.
National Maritime Museum

2 A seaman's mess table, in this case suspended from the beams of the deck above. As usual in a ship of the line, it is fitted between two guns, with a rack for crockery in the space between the ports. In the background can be seen the bags for the seamen's personal belongings.
National Maritime Museum

2

divided into compartments by bulkheads. A typical ship of around 1800 had, in order from forward to aft: a fore-peak in the extreme bows, which, because of its awkward shape and the danger of leaks, carried no stores; the forward magazine, with filling rooms for cartridges and the gunner's store room; the main hold, reaching up to just forward of the main mast; the pump well, with shot lockers on either side; the after hold; the spirit room, situated where it could be entered only via the officers' cabins on the orlop; the after powder room; and the bread room, which extended up through the orlop deck, and was situated where the rise of the deadwood lifted it above the worst of the bilge water; in the extreme aft position was the lady's hole, as useless for stores as its counterpart in the bows.[2]

The sailing warship was not so independent of the shore as many believe, for, although it needed no fuel for its main propellant, it had to carry a vast crew, and had no effective means of preserving their food and drink, except to store them in watertight casks, salt the more perishable goods, and hope for the best. Nevertheless efforts were made to keep ships at sea for as long as possible. In the early seventeenth century it was considered adequate if a ship could carry provisions for four months. After the example of the French *Superbe* in 1672, efforts were made to increase this to six months, and this was generally achieved by the eighteenth century. A ship carrying provisions for six months would generally carry water for only half as long, because water would not keep for such a period in casks, and it was usually possible to replenish it from a river or stream, using the ship's longboat or launch.

A 74-gun ship of 1806 carried 640 men, of whom 7 where commissioned sea officers, 3 were marine officers, and 32 were warrant officers.[3] This left, if the ship was up to full strength, nearly 600 petty officers, able and ordinary seamen, landsmen, boys and marines. Traditionally the junior ranks were accommodated on the lower deck, though on a three-decker they would also find some space on the middle deck. The lower deck of a 74 at this time was about 175 feet long, and 50 feet broad, but all that space was not available to the crew, for it had to be shared with 28 or 30 large guns. Additionally, the fore part at the manger was unusable, as was the after section, known as the gunroom, because it was used to a certain extent for officers' cabins, but largely because it was unsuitable for slinging hammocks owing to the sweep of the tiller. Furthermore, large areas around the centreline were taken up by stairways and hatches, and in bad weather the space under the grating which covered the hatch would be uninhabitable. Yet space had to be found for eating and sleeping accommodation, and, optimistically, for recreation, of 600 men.

The answer to the sleeping problem was, quite simply, the hammock. These had been discovered by early English travellers to the West Indies, and had been introduced to the Navy by 1597. To a naval administration which was already encountering the problems of fitting out large ships for long voyages, they must have seemed like a godsend, and they were to remain the standard form of bed for a Royal Navy seaman until very recent times. As used in the late eighteenth century, they were described as follows: 'A piece of canvas, six feet long and three feet wide, gathered

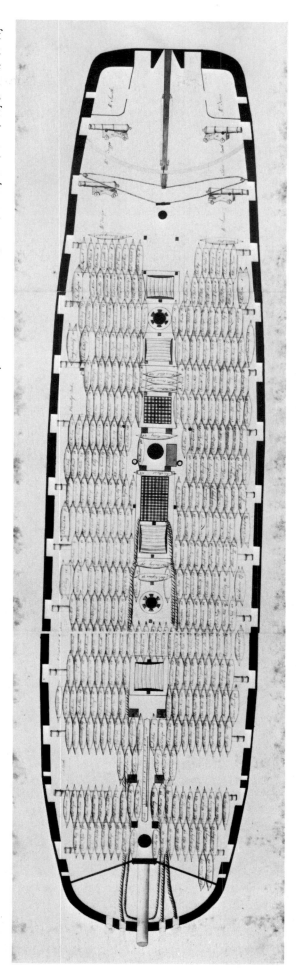

The hammock plan of a mid-eighteenth century two-decker, probably the *Torbay* (ex-*Neptune*) of 1730: the overcrowding of the lower deck is shown very clearly. Space is restricted by the fact that certain areas cannot be used – that below the hatchways and above the manger, around the ladderways and masts, and that allotted to the cabins and the gunroom. The petty officers have wider berths at the sides of the ship. In the gunroom, cabin space is severely restricted by the need to allow the tiller to swing from side to side. Permanent cabins are fitted against the transom, with four of lighter construction forward. Note that the sweep of the tiller is not used to direct the tiller rope. This arrangement, which would have made the tiller easier to move at extreme angles, was probably not introduced until the 1770s.
National Maritime Museum

1 Luxury at sea, c1690: the officers' quarters of a three-decker. W, on the lower deck, represents the sparsely furnished gunroom. T is the wardroom, 'allotted for volunteers and land officers'; this is the first known appearance of such an area. S is 'the state room out of which is made the bedchamber and other conveniences for the commander in chief'. Q is the captain's cabin, while R represents 'the cuddy, which is commonly divided for the master and officers' secretaries. 96 shows the trumpeters' cabins on the poop, which were later to develop into the topgallant roundhouse. The drawing also gives us the only clear picture of an English whipstaff (103), connected to the tiller (105) by means of the steering roll, at middle deck level.
National Maritime Museum

2 The Admiral's accommodation on the *Britannia* of 1719.
British Library

or drawn together at the two ends, and hung horizontally under the deck, lengthways for the sailor to sleep therein.'[4] A seaman was normally issued with two hammocks, so that one could be cleaned while the other was in use. Hammocks were slung fore and aft with each end fixed to a deck beam. A minimum of fourteen inches width was alloted to each man. This sounds impossible, but it was mitigated by the fact that, at sea, half the crew would be on duty at any given time. In harbour, congestion must have been barely tolerable, especially when 'wives' were invited on board. The petty officers, who were 'not to be pinched', were accommodated along the sides of the ship, and were given rather more space. During the day the hammocks were rolled and stowed in nets above the gunwales, where they offered some protection against enemy small arms fire.

The eating arrangements were equally spartan. One table was fitted between each pair of guns, hinged to the

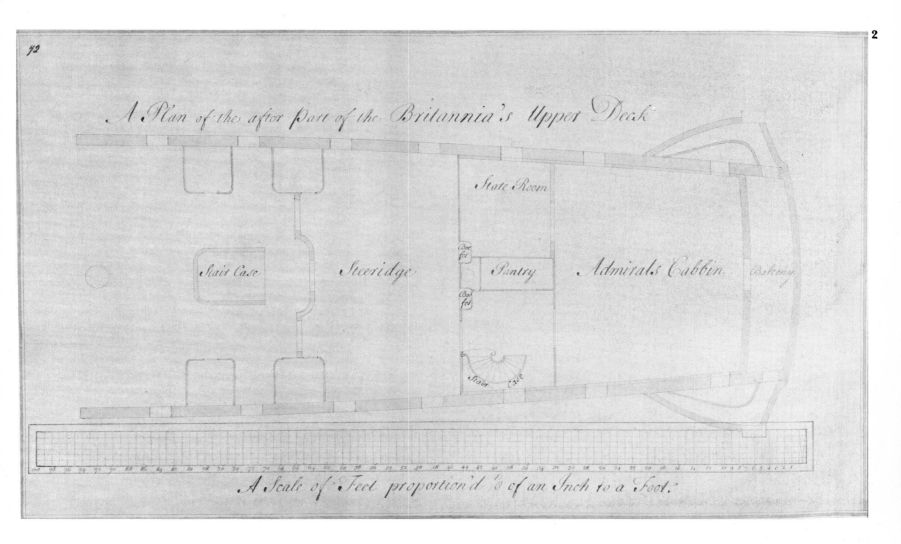

72

A Plan of the after Part of the Britannia's Upper Deck

State Room

Stair Case   Steeridge   Pantry   Admirals Cabbin   Balcony

Stair Case

A Scale of Feet proportion'd ⅛ of an Inch to a Foot.

side of the ship, and supported either by a folding leg or by ropes from the deck above. Benches were fitted on either side of the table, and perhaps upturned casks provided additional seating. Cutlery was kept in racks between the pairs of gunports. When not in use, the tables were either folded against the sides or raised and stowed between the beams of the deck above. The seaman had little space for any personal belongings: most kept a few items of clothing in a small bag which was stowed near the mess table; anyone with more valuable possessions was well advised to keep them about his person, or have them locked up for safe-keeping.

The toilet accommodation of the crew was no less basic. Two, four or six 'seats of ease' were placed on the gratings over the head of the ship, and these discharged directly into the sea. Petty officers were slightly more privileged, in that they had the use of the roundhouses – small semi-circular cabins which, from the early eighteenth century, were placed on either side of the beakhead bulkhead, giving some measure of privacy.[5]

The officers of a ship of the line might cover a wide range of social backgrounds, from scions of the highest aristocracy, and even royalty, to men who had risen from humble origins to warrant or even commissioned rank. They covered a similar range of service rank, from Admiral of the Fleet to Cook, and their accommodation reflected this difference in status, but all at least were entitled to something better than the common seaman with his 14

inches of hammock space.

By long tradition, the officers of the ship were housed in the stern, for that part was regarded as more comfortable, having larger space between the decks and easy access to the steering and conning positions, and to the stern and quarter galleries. By the early seventeenth century, several different apartments had been designed especially for the officers' use. The great cabin, on the upper deck, was for the senior officer, whether captain or admiral. Forward of this was the steerage (so called because it was located near the whipstaff), which was used as a dining room. Above the great cabin was the roundhouse on the quarterdeck, serving as the master's cabin, and forward of that was the coach, which originally had a roof raised above the normal level of the deck, and was sometimes used as a dining cabin for the captain in place of the steerage.[6] Many of these terms were to survive into the eighteenth century, but over the years there was to be a gradual rationalisation and standardisation of the officers' accommodation.

An admiral was usually to be found aboard a three-decker, where the after part of the upper deck was set aside and partitioned off for his use. He would probably be entitled to the private use of a stern gallery, and have several cabins all to himself, including the great cabin in the stern, taking up the whole width of the ship, and used as a sitting room and perhaps an office. Forward of this was the sleeping cabin to one side, a lobby with a staircase to the other side, and a pantry between. In addition, there were

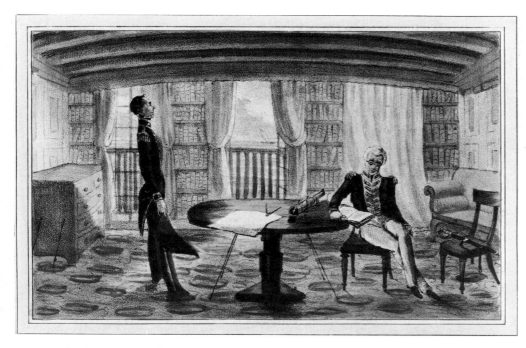

A well furnished captain's cabin, nineteenth century.
National Maritime Museum

As the years progressed, the quarterdeck accommodation became more desirable. In the 1670s it gained windows and stern galleries of its own, and retained the latter even when they died out on the upper deck, in the 1730s. It became wider as the tumblehome was slowly reduced. The fitting of the steering wheel meant that it, rather than the upper deck cabin, had immediate access to the conning position, and it had always been in a better position for observing the trim of the sails. Captains must have coveted the accommodation of their subordinates for some decades before, in 1745, they were officially allowed to use the quarterdeck cabins on 60- and 70-gun ships.[7] This was not immediately implemented, as some ships were unsuitable for conversion, but it became standard on new ships.

The captain's cabin was 'the sanctum sanctorum he inhabits; all mortals are excluded by a marine with a brandished sword.'[8] In layout and size it was similar to the admiral's cabin, if a little smaller, with a large day cabin with access to the stern gallery, and smaller sleeping and dining cabins forward. Of course captains often provided their own furnishings and fittings, and this led to great extremes of splendour or plainness, according to the wealth and inclination of the individual.

In the early days, the middle ranking officers were a disparate collection of men of very different backgrounds, from the master who performed a vital role and was appointed because of his great sea experience, to the gentlemen volunteers who were virtually 'along for the ride' and gained their places through the captain's influence. In the 1670s Pepys began to sort out the confusing heirarchy of land officers, reformadoes, volunteers, midshipmen and so-called servants who crammed the decks of some ships commanded by gentleman captains. These supernumeries had been in the habit of having their cabins erected along the sides of the ship between the gunports, or displacing more experienced and essential officers. By the orders of 1673,[9] accommodation aboard warships was regularised, and the first establishment of cabins was brought into force. The officers were still scattered around the ship, however, the small cabins being still found in odd corners, and between the gunports.

There was a gradual growth of a group of officers, of middling rank, who were eventually to get together to form the wardroom. Of these, the most established was the master, who had long been borne as a technical adviser to the captain, who might in the seventeenth century be a court appointee with little sea experience. The lieutenant was originally, as his title implies, the direct successor to the captain, who would take over in the event of his illness or death, but had no great responsibility until then, and might be as ignorant of the sea as his captain. After the Pepysian reforms of the 1670s, care was taken that the lieutenants should have at least some training in seamanship, and their real status began to increase as the old breed began to die out. Meanwhile, their numbers and duties began to increase. Even by the 1670s, a second lieutenant was often carried on Third Rates, and invariably on larger ships, and a third was added in 1720. By the middle of the eighteenth century a First Rate carried six lieutenants, and a Third

small cabins for servants and staff forward of the admiral's cabin. This was the standard form until about the middle of the eighteenth century. After that there was some re-arrangement and re-positioning of the different apartments, but few admirals on three-deckers had to put up with much less: after all, an admiral usually came from a high social class, and might be vested with a very grave responsibility, and the eighteenth century did not regard it as unfair that he should occupy as much room as a hundred ordinary seamen. On a two-decker, he might be a little more cramped, for no separate quarters had been set aside for him. He might share the captain's cabin, or, more likely, take over the cabin and move the captain into one of the lieutenant's cabins.

On a three-decker with an admiral aboard, the captain would be accommodated on the quarterdeck directly above the admiral. If the ship was not serving as a flagship, he would be entitled to take over the admiral's cabin and give his own to his senior officers, perhaps the master and first lieutenant. On a two-decker of the early period, he would normally be the most senior officer of the ship, and entitled to what was then regarded as the best site for his cabin. In the seventeenth century this was aft on the upper deck – this position was clear of the bilge water of the ship, and well ventilated, but the tumblehome had not narrowed the hull sufficiently to cause him inconvenience. Before the 1670s he had the exclusive use of the stern windows, which were only fitted on the upper deck, and he had immediate access to the steering in an emergency, for the whipstaff was operated from the upper deck. The cabin immediately above him on the quarterdeck was less comfortable in the seventeenth century, having no stern windows, and being narrower. It was usually divided into two halves, perhaps with a lobby between, and allocated to the two next most important officers, the master and the first lieutenant. Before this, in the area known as the coach were other cabins for more junior officers.

Rate four or five. They had taken over many duties, including the supervision of the watches and the general administration of the ship, and were now an essential part of the complement.

Other officers were also rising in real importance. Some, such as the purser, surgeon and chaplain, had qualifications which were essentially shore-based, but were nevertheless useful aboard ship. The marine officers first came under Admiralty control, and therefore became a regular part of the ship's complement, in 1755. All these officers had different qualifications and roles, but they were of similar status, and by the middle of the eighteenth century they began to group themselves together to form the wardroom.

The origin of the term wardroom is obscure, and two main theories have been advanced about its early meaning. One suggests that it was a room in which valuables taken from prizes could be stored, and which would naturally be empty at the beginning of a voyage, and might, if the ship was unlucky, still be empty at the end. It was therefore slowly taken over by the subordinate officers as a mess room. The other theory suggests that it was originally a room for the watch-keeping officers.[10] The two theories are mutually contradictory, for one would expect a store room for valuables to be in the bowels of the ship, where it could not easily be broken into, and a room for the watch-keepers to be on the upper works, where they could be ready to go on deck: the evidence suggests the latter explanation. The

earliest wardroom is to be found around 1690, and was for the use, not of the commissioned officers but of the 'volunteers and land officers'. Though well below decks, this position allowed immediate access to the whipstaff. It can be seen again in deck plans of ships from around 1710.[11] Its use is unspecified in this case, but it is sited on the quarterdeck of a two-decker, where the master and first lieutenant were normally berthed, and this would suggest that it was being used by these officers. Another drawing, undated but perhaps from around 1740,[12] shows it on the middle deck of a three-decker 80, again the normal site for the lieutenant's cabin, and round it are erected the cabins for three naval lieutenants and a lieutenant of marines. By 1745 the wardroom was clearly recognised in official orders, and the Norris committee recommended that 60- and 70-gun ships should have 'no other cabins but the following; two under the stern of the wardroom contrived so as to have only one window in each cabin, and that one of the quarter galleries be kept in common. Two cabins on the gun deck on the transom where there is room to put them, clear of the after gun.'[13] The other officers were to sleep in hammocks set up in the wardroom. The wardroom was now moved to the upper deck for the first time, for by the same orders the captain's cabin was to be put on the quarterdeck.

By orders of 1756, the officers' cabins were further regulated, and this order was to remain in force for most of the rest of the age of sail. On a three-decker, there were to be

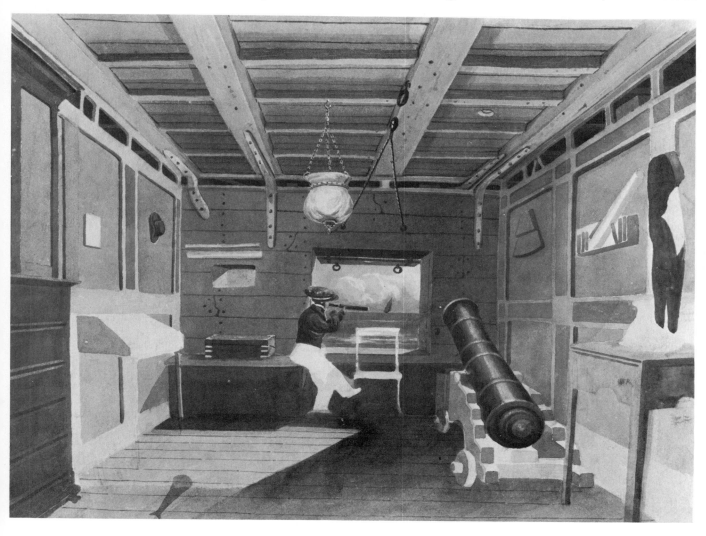

A master's cabin, early nineteenth century: the figure is far too small, and gives an unwarranted impression of spaciousness, but the stark utilitarianism of most officers' cabins is well emphasised. The gunport tackle can be seen, leading through two holes in the side above the port, and secured against a beam of the deck above, with a block and tackle to aid the lifting of the port lid. This cabin is probably the one on the quarterdeck forward of the captain's cabin, which was used by the master mainly for his work in connection with the navigation of the ship. He would also have had a sleeping cabin leading from the wardroom.
National Maritime Museum

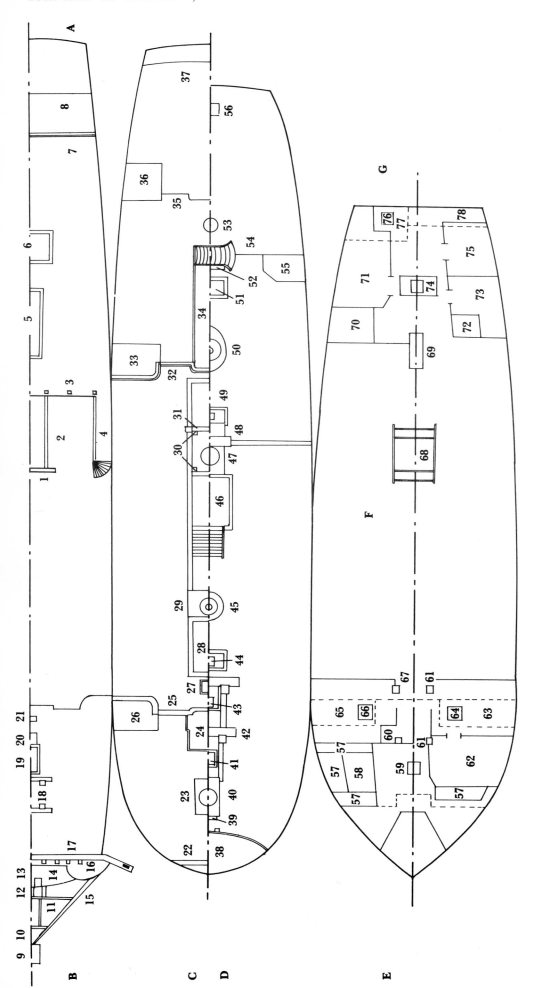

DECK PLANS OF THE RESOLUTION, 1708

A. The quarterdeck

1. Cross piece to the main topmast sheet or gallows bitts.
2. The carling from the quarterdeck to the gallows.
3. The breast works stanchions.
4. The gangway and ladder to the upper deck.
5. A grating.
6. A hatchway for the bell ladder to the upper deck.
7. The bulkhead to the roundhouse.
8. A lieutenant's cabin.

B. The forecastle and head on the flat

9. The lion.
10. The cross pieces.
11. The carlings.
12. The stem.

13. Cat tails and supporters.
14. Knight-heads or bollard timbers.
15. The main trestle-trees.
16. The bolsters for the main stays.
17. The fore jeer bitts.
18. Timber heads.
19. 20. 21.

21. A hole for the steam of the furnace.

C. Upper deck

22. The bulkhead or collar beam.
23. The partners for the fore mast.
24. The cook room.
25. The bulkhead of the forecastle.
26. The carpenter's cabin.
27. A scuttle.
28. The long coaming, carlings and head ledges.
29. The partners for the jeer capstan.
30. The main topsail sheet and jeer bitts.
31. The cross piece to the main jeer bitts.
32. The bulkhead of the steerage.
33. A lieutenant's cabin.
34. A grating.

40. The partners of the fore mast.
41. A scuttle to the powder room.
42. The main jeer bitts and their spars and cross pieces.
43. A hatch with a scuttle to the foremost platform.
44. The fore hatch with a scuttle.
45. The step for the jeer capstan.
46. The main hatch.
47. The partners for the main mast.
48. The pumps.
49. A hatch with a scuttle to the shot locker.
50. The partners for the main capstan.
51. A grating for light and air to the cockpit.
52. Steward room hatch.
53. The partners for the mizzen mast.

60. The light room.
61. The fore and main bitts.
62. The sailroom.
63. The boatswain's store room.
64. A scuttle into the boatswain's lower store room.
65. The carpenter's store room.
66. A scuttle into the carpenter's lower store room.
67. Doorways to the powder room.

F. Orlop

68. The well and shot lockers.
69. The step of the main capstan.

G. After platform

70. The surgeon's cabin.
71. The captain's store room.
72. The slop room.
73. The purser's cabin.
74. A hatch and scuttle into the fish room.

Note the spotted lines are bulkheads in the hold for the powder room, fish room, and carpenter's and boatswain's lower store rooms.

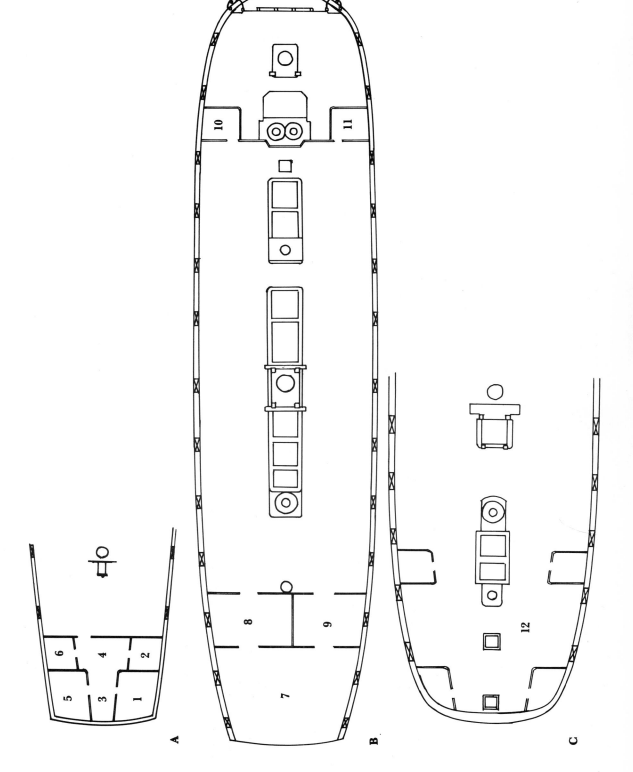

13. The knighthead.
14. The bulkhead.
15. The upper rail.
16. The house of easement.
17. The cathead.
18. The fore topsail sheet and jeer bitts with their cross pieces.
19. A grating.
20. The chimney hole.

35. The bulkhead of the great cabin.
36. The captain's dressing room.
37. The screen bulkhead.

D. Gun deck
38. The manger.
39. The pillars or step of the bowsprit.

54. The bulkhead of the gunroom.
55. A lieutenant's cabin.
56. The bread room scuttle.

E. Foremost platform
57. Powder chests.
58. The filling room.
59. A scuttle into the powder room.

75. The steward's room.
76. A scuttle into the after powder room.
77. A doorway to the after powder room.
78. Platform abaft the bulkhead.

THE CABIN ARRANGEMENTS OF AN OLD 50, AS DRAWN IN 1756

These show the captain's cabin still on the upper deck, with the roundhouse, on the quarterdeck, divided between several officers.

A. Quarterdeck
1. First lieutenant's cabin.
2. Second lieutenant's cabin.
3. Roundhouse.
4. Coach.
5. Master's cabin.
6. Captain's clerk's cabin.

B. Upper deck
7. Captain's cabin.
8. Coach.
9. Bed place.
10. Boatswain's cabin.
11. Carpenter's cabin.

C. Gun deck
12. Gunroom.

two cabins for the master and first lieutenant, if the ship was a private ship; the same space was to be used for the captain if a flagship. The great cabin was on the upper deck, to be used by the captain if a private ship, the admiral if a flagship. The wardroom was to be sited on the middle deck, parted off from the rest of the deck by a bulkhead, just before or abaft the mizzen mast. More officers were to be allowed some kind of rudimentary cabin: from the bulkhead to the stern there was to be 'a space enclosed on each side for three or four berths by canvas hanging loosely before it or laced above and below with a parting in the middle of each berth to go in and out and roll up in the daytime when not wanted.' The cabins could thus be removed easily in time of action. Two-deckers were to be similarly fitted, with the captain on the quarterdeck, and the wardroom on the upper deck, which was 'to be fitted as on three-decked ships'.

Not all wardroom officers lived in the wardroom itself, though they were entitled to use it for eating and recreation. The purser and surgeon normally slept in the cockpit on the orlop deck, for there the purser issued his stores, and the surgeon had his dispensary and operating theatre. Some of the more junior members of the wardroom, the junior lieutenants, the lieutenants of marines and the chaplain, might be accommodated in small cabins in the gunroom. The master would usually have a cabin in the wardroom, but might also have a small sea cabin on the quarterdeck, forward of the captain's cabin. The wardroom in its developed form was described as follows:

> It is usually in a line of battle ship, about 35 feet in length, and 16 or 18 feet wide. Within the walls, which are of painted canvas, are the cabins of six officers; the centre of the room is occupied by the mess table; and the extremity, under the stern windows, by a projection called the rudder head. The opposite end is so arranged as to do the office of a sideboard; with the door of entrance on one side of it; and a space to sling a quarter cask of wine, on the other.[14]

In the early nineteenth century there seems to have been a tendency for cabins to become more permanent, and for wood to replace canvas in their structure.

Below wardroom rank, there was a mixed collection of warrant officers who aspired to reach the wardroom one day, the largest group consisting of those who were hoping to gain commissions as lieutenants. The best known of these ranks was of course the midshipman, who was established in Pepysian times as an officer under training. But before even becoming a midshipman, it was ordered that a candidate should have several years sea experience, and this was usually gained in the rank of captain's servant or volunteer first class. The master's mates were originally experienced seamen who might expect eventually to reach the rank of master, but in the late eighteenth century there was a tendency for the post to be taken over by senior midshipmen, desiring an increase in pay and seniority while awaiting their commissions. All three of these groups were accommodated in the cockpit, in 'that infernal cell, the orlop'[15], where they slung their hammocks between the store rooms and cabins of the surgeon and purser. They shared the space with the surgeon's mates, who might one day enter the wardroom as fully fledged surgeons, and with

the captain's clerk, who might be promoted to purser. The master's mate had once been a relatively senior officer, with duties similar to that of an eighteenth century lieutenant and accommodation to match, but with the rise of the lieutenant proper he had declined in status.

In contrast to the warrant officers of wardroom and gunroom level, who were mostly of middle or upper class background and often had expectations of reaching the highest ranks, the standing warrant officers of a ship had usually risen from the ranks of the seamen, and were important to the ship because of their experience and specialised skills. These were the gunner, boatswain and carpenter, who were responsible respectively for the maintenance of the armament, the rigging, and the hull of the ship. In the early days of sea gunnery, good master gunners had been difficult to come by, and had been given high status aboard the ship. This was still reflected in the accommodation of an eighteenth century gunner, for 'no officer but the captain, is accommodated like him; he challengeth the gunroom, as his hereditary estate.'[16] The gunroom was the part of the lower deck directly below the wardroom or great cabin. Though spacious, it was not entirely useful to the gunner, for he probably had to share it with his numerous mates and assistants. Nor was it particularly suitable for accommodation, because the sweep of the tiller would make it impossible to either fit cabins or sling hammocks in it, though this was less of a problem in the days of the whipstaff, when the range of movement of the rudder was very small. Most gunrooms allowed space for only four small cabins, one on each side at the extreme stern, in the corners of the gun deck, and further forward, clear of the tiller. Three of these were usually given to the junior wardroom officers, the other to the gunner. By the nineteenth century, the gunroom was also being used for a variety of other tasks – as an office for the ship's clerks, or as a schoolroom for the midshipmen and ship's boys, for example. The naval cadets, the captain's servants and volunteers first class, eventually moved in there as their permanent accommodation, and were later followed by the midshipmen.

The other two standing officers, the boatswain and carpenter, were berthed in small cabins by the bulkhead of the forecastle. This situation had several advantages, and reflected their status aboard the ship. Since it was near to the cooking stove, it would be warm in Winter, but, being in an exposed position, it could be easily ventilated; it also gave easy access to the deck, and to the roundhouses for toilet facilities.

Captains, admirals, and wardroom officers had their toilets in the quarter galleries beside their respective cabins. Captains and admirals had two quarter galleries each, though it is possible that only one was actually fitted as a lavatory, and the other used as a store room or ante-room. The wardroom officers – twelve in number in a typical 74 of the late eighteenth century – had only two galleries between them, and one of these was normally allocated to the first lieutenant alone, and could be entered only through his cabin. The other officers, therefore, had to share a single gallery. Presumably the waste from the quarter galleries had originally discharged directly into the sea, and this must have formed a strange contrast with the

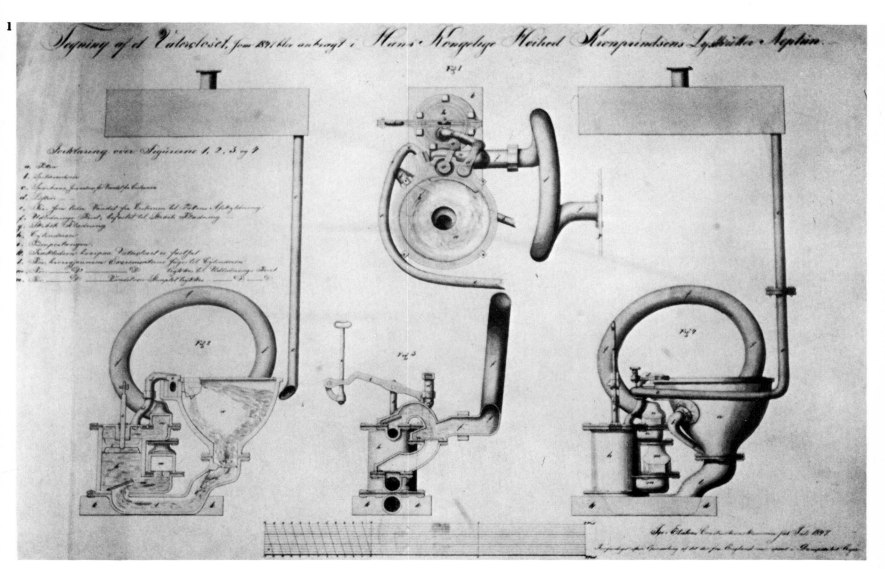

1 A flushing water closet of 1847: these were first fitted in the quarter galleries of British ships of the line in 1779.
Rigsarkivet, Copenhagen

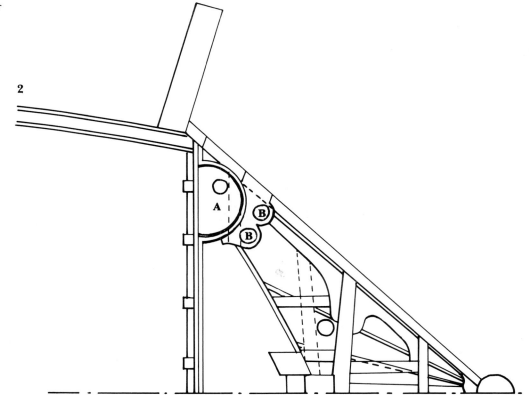

2 PLAN OF THE HEAD OF THE *SUFFOLK* OF 1765
A. The roundhouse for the use of petty officers.
B. Twin seats in the open for the common seamen.

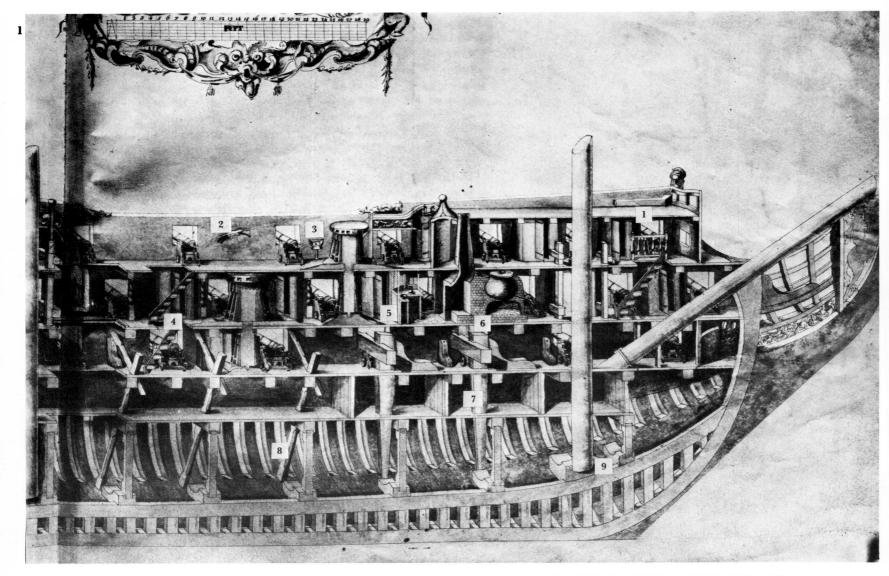

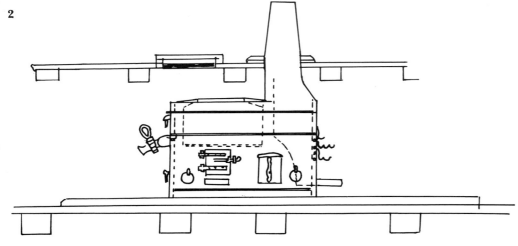

1 THE FORE PART OF A FIRST RATE, *c*1680

1. The arm of the cathead: in later years it would extend across the ship instead of longitudinally, just aft of the beakhead bulkhead.
2. A belaying cleat.
3. A piss-dale, for the crew to urinate in.
4. Small cabins for the junior officers are placed between the gunports of the middle deck.
5. The cook's working area, with a table for food preparation.
6. The copper kettle, enclosed in a brick furnace, with a chimney to carry the smoke clear of the decks. On a two-decker the galley would be on the upper deck, directly under the forecastle.
7. The bitts, used to secure the anchor cable; they lead down through two decks, and are anchored on the floor timbers.
8. The cross pillars in the hold.
9. The step of the fore mast.
The Science Museum

2 An early iron stove, on the *Dorsetshire* of 1757.

elaborate carvings of the gallery. From 1779, an early form of water closet was fitted. The junior officers were never so well provided: they had to share the roundhouses at the beakhead with the petty officers, and to travel a long way from their cabins in case of need.

Galley facilities on a ship of the line were never sophisticated or elaborate, but it had always been recognised that some form of cooked food was necessary to the seaman's diet. The main problem with siting the cookhouse was the danger that the fire might ignite the timbers around it, and in the days of wooden shipbuilding this was a very serious risk. In the early seventeenth century there were some who advocated that the stove should be sited in the hold,[17] but this could overheat the provisions stored there and cause their premature decay. Others advocated the orlop deck, where it was out of the way of the ordnance. The position under the forecastle was objected to on the grounds that 'a man of war ever carries much ordnance there, and therefore it is fit to avoid (as much as may be) any weight that may charge her foreship.'[18] Nevertheless this soon became the standard position on two-deckers, for the gradual abandonment of forward-firing armament left a suitably clear space for it. It allowed convenient venting of the smoke from the fire, and easy ventilation, and the danger of conflagration was minimised provided that the fire was put out as soon as an engagement was threatened. In three-deckers it was usually placed one deck lower, forward on the middle deck, thus allowing the forecastle to be used for other purposes.

A ship's cook was usually a partly disabled pensioner from Greenwich Hospital with no specific training for the task, and the ship's provisions, after several months salted in casks in the hold, were rarely very palatable, so there was no attempt at any sophisticated form of cooking. Two large 'copper kettles' were provided and in these the food was boiled. The kettles were placed on a furnace constructed of fire bricks, and heated as necessary. From the 1760s onwards, the advances in the metal-working and engineering industries allowed more modern stoves to be fitted, made entirely of iron.

Provisions were of course kept in the hold. They were issued via the steward's room, on the after end of the orlop deck, just forward of the bread room; casks for immediate use were brought up from the hold and stored there for a day or two until needed. The steward, chief assistant to the purser, also had a tiny bedplace there. The cook was generally berthed under the forecastle or on the middle deck, close to his galley.

A ship of the line had a large crew, and these were engaged in an unusually hazardous occupation, being subject not only to the dangers of enemy shot and shell but to accident, to rheumatism due to their damp environment, to various diseases caused by malnutrition or bad food, and to infections which might spread very quickly in the crowded quarters of the lower deck. The ship was therefore provided with a surgeon, two or three assistants who were also qualified in medicine, and several less skilled helpers. In action the surgeon took over the cockpit on the orlop deck, and used the midshipmen's mess table for amputations and other primitive operations. There the wounded men were at least safe from gunfire, though the ventilation and

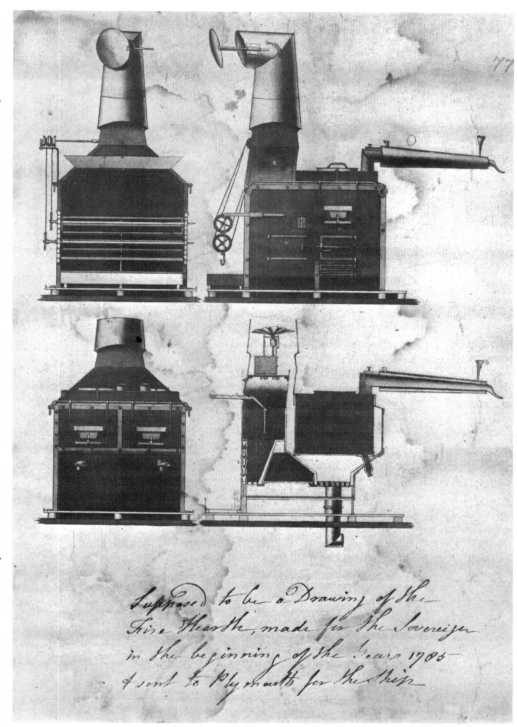

An iron fire hearth, of the type introduced in the 1770s.
National Maritime Museum

lighting must have left much to be desired. During less active times, the surgeon used the space under the forecastle which was not already occupied by galley and cabins, and set up a sick berth. It was suitable for convalescents, being easily ventilated or heated as necessary, but it had the disadvantage that the men often had to be removed to the orlop when action threatened.

Various store rooms were sited on the orlop deck. The carpenter had a store forward for spare pieces of timber, the boatswain one close by for ropes and blocks, and the gunner for gun tackles. The sailroom was sometimes sited well forward, and sometimes in midships among the cable tiers. Aft on the orlop were to be found other stores: one for the captain's personal effects, another for the lieutenants'; a 'slop room', where spare clothing for the crew was kept, to be sold by the purser; a similar room for marines' clothing; a compartment for the storage of the surgeon's medicines and instruments; and another for various small items to be issued or sold by the purser, such as candles. The steward's room was right aft, and contained food ready for issue to the cook. Along the sides of the orlop were passages known as wings. These could occasionally be used for light storage, but their main purpose was to allow the carpenter access to any shot holes just below the waterline.

There was no regular system of heating in a ship of the line, for the danger of combustion prevented the lighting of fires about the decks. The ship of the line had originally been designed for Summer use only, and in this respect there was no real means of adapting it to Winter. Officers sometimes had small stoves fitted in their cabins, or in the wardroom, but the common seamen had to rely on the effect of massed human bodies for their warmth when cruising in the Baltic or North Sea in Winter.

Ventilation of the lower deck was slightly better, even when the gunports were closed. The hatches which filled up much of the space along the centreline of the deck were intended primarily to give access for goods entering and leaving the hold, but they were covered with gratings which would allow the smoke of the guns to escape during an action, and air to enter at more normal times. Hammocks were not usually slung directly under the hatches, but even so the spaces near them must have been very damp and draughty in bad weather. As usual, the senior officers were better provided for. The quarterdeck cabin had a window which opened onto the deck above, and the gunports in the cabins were usually fitted with glass windows so that light could be admitted even when the weather did not permit the opening of them.

Movement from one deck to another was done by ladder. In the late seventeenth century elaborate staircases, sometimes winding, had been installed in the areas around the officers' cabins (especially on three-deckers), to allow the admiral immediate access to the quarterdeck from his cabin on the upper deck. In the early eighteenth century the Admiralty and Navy Board campaigned against these, on the grounds that they were expensive, and took up much valuable space. In general the Boards were successful, and ladderways became much plainer, though as late as 1757 it was ordered that all remaining winding staircases should be removed.[19]

The disparity between officers and men was enormous on a sailing warship. Perhaps the best that can be said about it is that all aboard were enduring greater hardships than they would do on shore. The admiral, who might be used to a spacious country house, had to confine himself to an apartment little bigger than a workman's cottage on shore. The seaman, cramped and uncomfortable as he was, was said to be used to the life, and was perhaps little worse off than he would be in a merchant ship, where the owner might attempt to cram in as much cargo as possible, at the expense of the crew. Complaints about the discomforts of accommodation rarely figure in the many mutinies that occurred around the end of the eighteenth century, but it is easy to understand how they helped seamen to become frustrated and desperate.

The deck plans of a 74, second half of the eighteenth century. The great cabin, coach and bed place on the quarterdeck are for the use of the captain. The two small cabins on the quarterdeck are for the master and the captain's clerk. The space aft of the bulkhead on the upper deck is the wardroom. No cabins are shown there, for at that time they were removeable and of very light construction. The cookroom is forward on the upper deck, screened off from the rest of the ship to prevent pilferage. The gun deck has no permanent bulkheads, but the gunroom was usually screened off in some way. Aft on the orlop deck are officers' cabins and store rooms. The space between these is the cockpit, used as the midshipmen's mess and the surgeon's operating theatre. The large open spaces on the orlop, on either side of the sailroom and pump well, were used for stowing cables. Forward are the store rooms for the maintenance of the hull, rigging and guns, under the care of the carpenter, boatswain and gunner.

A. Forecastle

B. Quarterdeck
1. Great cabin.
2. Coach.
3. Bed place.
4. Cabin.

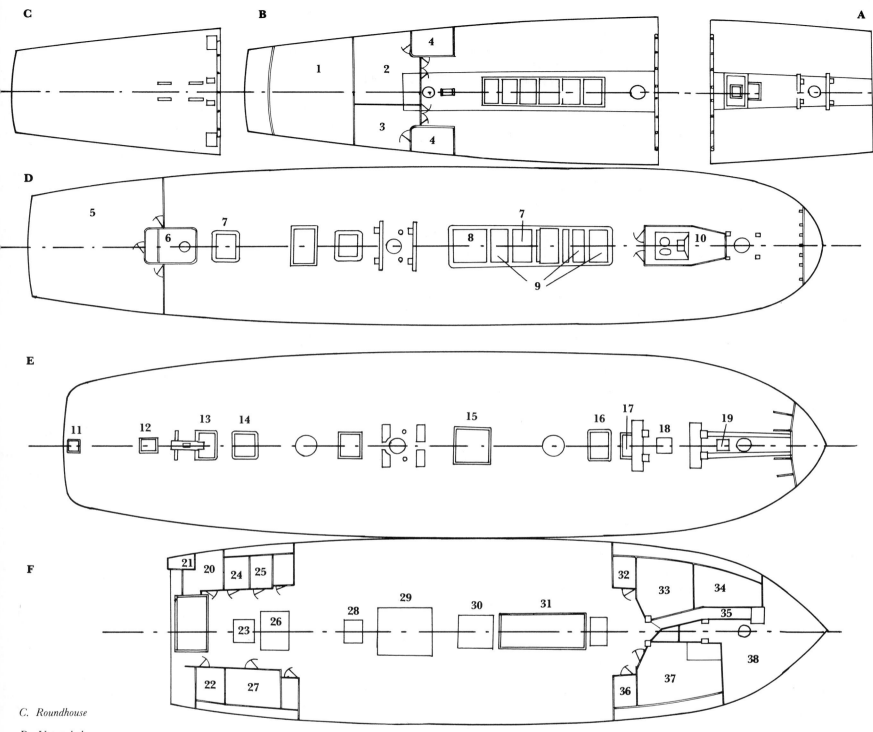

C. *Roundhouse*

D. *Upper deck*
5. Wardroom.
6. Pantry.
7. Ladderways.
8. Main hatch.
9. Gratings.
10. Galley.

E. *Gun deck*
11. Lady's hole.
12. Bread scuttle.
13. Steward's room hatch.
14. Fish room hatch.
15. Main hatch.
16. Fore hatch.
17. Ladderway.
18. Powder scuttle.
19. Gunner's store room scuttle.

F. *Orlop*
20. Steward's room.
21. Bed place.
22. Surgeon's cabin.
23. Fish room.
24. Purser's cabin.
25. Slop room.
26. Spiritous liquor store.
27. Captain's store room.
28. After hatch.

29. Well.
30. Main hatch.
31. Sailroom.
32. Block room.
33. Boatswain's store room.
34. Fore sailroom.
35. Passage to the light room.
36. Pitch room.
37. Carpenter's store room.
38. Gunner's store room.

8. Armament

THE GUNS WERE THE FINAL RAISON D'ÊTRE OF A SHIP OF the line, and the ultimate object of her existence was to bring them to bear on an enemy warship. In action or in gunnery practice they needed large numbers of men to serve them, and they were the chief reason why a warship required a very large crew. It is ironical, therefore, that the guns, with their mountings and tackles, were the only parts of the ship not under the full control of the Admiralty and Navy Board: they were provided by the Ordnance Board, which also had the duty of supplying guns and other equipment for the Army. This was an arrangement which often caused difficulty, and there were many conflicts between the Admiralty and the Ordnance Board over the allocation of money,[1] and the tardiness of the latter in providing suitable guns, but it was to continue until after the age of sail, when the introduction of new types of guns made it necessary to have a specialised department dealing with naval ordnance. It is possible that the division of responsibility between the Admiralty and the Ordnance Board held up development, for gunnery remained one of

the more conservative aspects of ship design until the nineteenth century. Its survival is partly attributable to the fact that guns were not an integral part of the ship, but were taken out and stored at the end of each commission, and possibly issued to different ships for their next period of use.

Once aboard a ship, the guns were under the care of the gunner, or master gunner as he was originally known. In the late sixteenth century, when the use of guns aboard ships was expanding rapidly, good master gunners were scarce, and were rewarded with good pay and high status. After that the gunner slowly declined: he ceased to be responsible for the actual firing and direction of the guns, and this task was taken over by the lieutenants and midshipmen, leaving the gunner in charge of the maintenance of the guns and their carriages, tackles, and ammunition; in action he supervised the supply of powder and shot to the guns. In status he was equal to the boatswain and the carpenter as a standing officer, kept on even when the ship was out of commission. His accommodation was a little superior to the other two, for until the nineteenth century he had the use of the gunroom, a large compartment aft on the lower deck, under the tiller. He was

assisted by a large crew, with several mates and one quarter gunner for each group of four guns.

In the late medieval period, when cannon were first fitted aboard ships, the most common type was the bombard, made up of strips of metal fitted together and bound by metal rings, as in the construction of a barrel. By our period, these had been entirely superseded by guns cast in one piece, in brass or iron. Many of the light guns aboard Tudor ships had been breech-loaders, with a removeable section at the rear of the weapon to allow rapid loading. Without a precision engineering industry to construct them, these were inevitably small, inefficient, and highly dangerous to their own crews, and by the seventeenth century they had fallen out of use.

The classic ship's gun, then, was a muzzle-loader, cast in one piece in iron or bronze. Essentially it was a long tube sealed at one end, so that the effects of the explosion of its charge would be forced in one direction. The metal was rather thicker towards the rear, for that area had to contain the main effect of the explosion; the outside of the gun was therefore tapered towards the muzzle. Internally, the bore was smooth, and retained the same diameter for most of its

The Ordnance Wharf at Portsmouth, late eighteenth century: in the centre foreground, a gun carriage is being painted; on the right, guns are stored in the open; in the middle distance, ships are being fitted with guns.
National Maritime Museum

THE DEVELOPMENT OF THE 32-POUNDER

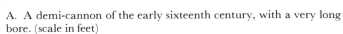

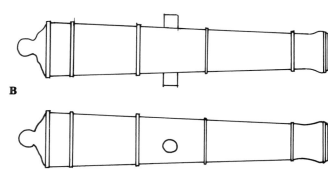

A. A demi-cannon of the early sixteenth century, with a very long bore. (scale in feet)

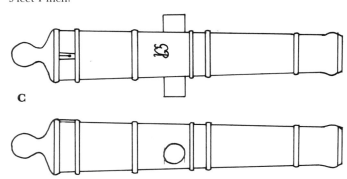

B. A brass demi-cannon recovered from the wreck of the *Edgar* of 1709: by this time the 32-pounder had settled down to the basic proportions which were to remain standard for over a century; length 9 feet 1 inch.

C. A brass gun recovered from the *Royal George*, lost in 1782, but probably made much earlier: weight 57 cwt, length 9 feet 6 inches.

D. A lighter type of 32-pounder, used for a time in the 1750s; length 9 feet 6 inches, weight 53 cwt.

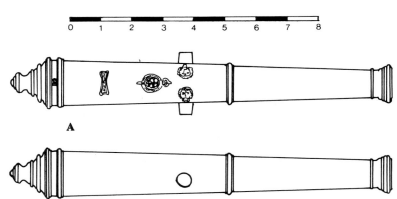

E. An upper deck gun from the 1830s, considerably shorter than the lower deck weapon.

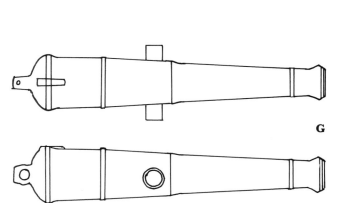

F and G. Two guns from the 1840s: F weighs 58 cwt, and G 50 cwt.

SMALLER GUNS

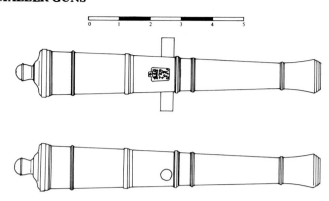

A

A. A 24-pounder from the lower deck of the *Maidstone*, a 50 of 1744, lost in 1747. (Scale in feet)

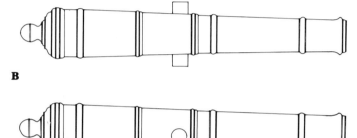

B

B. A 24-pounder, *c*1775.

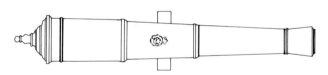

C

C. A culverin (18-pounder) of 1590: length, 8 feet 6 inches.

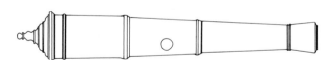

D

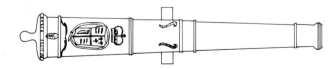

D. A brass 18-pounder, dated 1738, recovered from the *Royal George*: length 9 feet 0 inches.

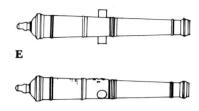

E

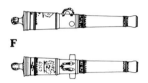

E. A bronze 4-pounder of 1638: length 3 feet 8 inches, weight 2½ cwt.

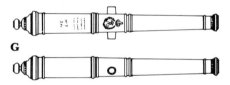

F

F. A Dutch cannon made in 1642: presumably captured during one of the Dutch Wars, and lost in one of the Third Rates which foundered on the Goodwin Sands in the Great Storm of 1703.

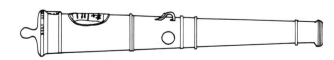

G

G. A minion of the late seventeenth century, with a relatively long bore: length 6 feet 0 inches, weight nearly 8 cwt.

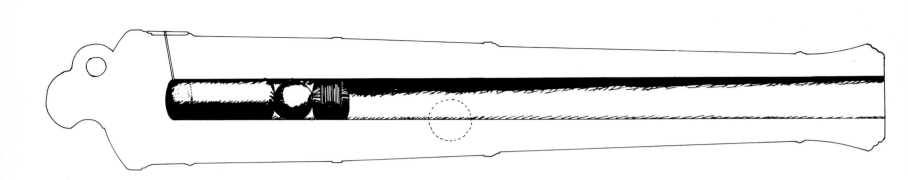

A cross section of a typical 32-pounder sea service gun of the Napoleonic Wars period: the cartridge is made of paper with the rear part of flannel. Note that the ball is significantly smaller than the bore, necessitating the use of a wad to hold it in place. (Scale in feet) *Based on a drawing in the Public Records Office*

length, though some guns had a bell-shaped compartment in the breech to hold the charge of powder. At the extreme rear of the gun was the cascabel, a ball-shaped piece which formed a mounting for the breeching tackle. On the sides, about halfway along the length, were the trunnions, cylindrical axles which jutted out on either side and allowed the gun to be attached to the carriage and elevated or depressed. Several rings were moulded round the barrel, to help reinforce it against the shock of the explosion, and the touch hole was drilled through the top of the breech, to permit the powder to be ignited. Many guns carried some kind of decoration – perhaps a royal coat of arms, a date, and the title of the king and the royal officials responsible for producing the gun, but this practice tended to decline as time went on.

The original shipboard guns were identical to land weapons, and it was not until the time of the Tudors, when guns were fitted to ships on a more regular and systematic basis, that any attempt was made to design guns specifically for sea service. Even so, many traces of land gunnery remained, and it was not until the eighteenth century that they were fully designed for shipboard use. In a crisis, any guns might be used, and at the outbreak of the First Dutch War the forts and arsenals of the Army were scoured for weapons that might be lent to the Navy.[2] Throughout the seventeenth century, the names of most types of gun were derived from their original use on shore.

One of the most popular guns of late Tudor times was the culverin, a long gun of medium calibre intended for long-range shooting. The culverin proper fired a ball of about 18 pounds weight, and it was supported by a family of guns of smaller size but similar proportions – the demi-culverin of 9 pounds, and the sakers, minions, and others of even lighter weight. In opposition to the culverin type was the cannon family: large heavy weapons of relatively short bore and range, intended for battering the sides of a heavy ship. The cannon proper was an enormous weapon, firing a ball of 60 pounds and weighing 6000 pounds. Apart from a few Tudor experiments, it was too heavy for use aboard ship; the heaviest weapon in normal use was the 'bastard cannon' or cannon-of-7, so called because of the width of its bore. It fired a ball of 42 pounds, and in general its use was confined to the lower decks of the largest ships. More common was the demi-cannon, eventually to develop into the 32-pounder, the standard heavy gun of the Navy.

Other guns had even shorter bores than the cannon. The perier was sometimes used on the upper decks of the Great Ships of the early seventeenth century, probably for bombarding an enemy's decks, but it found no permanent role. The mortar had even less purely naval application, for it was specifically intended for the reduction of fortifications on shore. Its only use at sea was on the specialised mortar vessels which developed at the end of the seventeenth century for shore bombardment duties. The mortar had no place aboard a ship of the line.

Alongside this classification of gun types, there were several possible variants: 'fortified' guns had especially thick metal, to take a heavier charge, while 'drakes' had lighter metal than usual; 'cutts' were shorter versions of particular guns (originally they may have been weapons which had been reduced because of some defect in the casting of the muzzle; later, they seem to have been specially cast to fulfil particular roles).[3]

Besides the 'great guns', intended to attack the hulls and rigging of an enemy, early warships had carried a large secondary armament of very light guns, intended to fire from the upper works onto the men on the enemy's decks. Falconets, port-pieces, fowlers and curtals were fitted in large numbers down to the time of the Armada campaign, but by the middle of the seventeenth century they had declined steeply in numbers, and were soon to fall out of use.

By the beginning of the seventeenth century, the different types of gun in naval use were beginning to converge. The Armada campaign had to a certain extent discredited the concept of the culverin, and very long range gunnery was found to be largely useless, so that culverins tended to become shorter. There was a gradual tendency for names to be associated with a particular calibre – the demi-cannon with 32 pounds, the culverin with 18 pounds, and the demi-culverin with 9 pounds, for example.

Gun founding may have become slightly more accurate during the seventeenth century, and the improvement may have contributed to the process. All the same, there were gaps in the range of guns available, and new guns, named after their weight of ball rather than some ancient concept of gunnery, were developed. In the second half of the seventeenth century the 24-pounder and the 12-pounder, for example, came into regular use. Nevertheless the old names continued in use throughout the century, and the number of types in use remained large. Around the end of the century, there were at least twelve types of whole-culverin, ten types of demi-culverin, and similar numbers for the other classes of gun. They varied according to length, weight, and sometimes by slight variations in the diameter of the bore.

The gun establishments of 1703 and 1716 made some steps towards standardisation. That of 1703 re-imposed some order on the fleet after the stresses of the war with France. That of 1716 was the first to impose the same gun arrangement on each class as a whole, rather than on sub-groups within the class, and it also reduced the number of variations prescribed for standard use. Moreover, it was the first establishment to list guns by calibre rather than type, and therefore to abolish the old names of culverin, saker, minion, etc. Most guns were now roughly proportioned on the cannon type, and the term cannon gradually came into use as the generic name for ship's guns, replacing 'great guns'. But the changes did not take place overnight, for it took a long time to replace all the guns of the fleet: the *Stirling Castle*, when lost in 1703, was carrying a Dutch gun cast in 1642, and presumably captured during one of the Dutch Wars.[4]

There were still many hangovers from the past, and many of the new types of guns retained features and proportions which had never been seriously thought out and planned. As Benjamin Robins was to show in 1747, most guns had too heavy a weight of metal for their calibre. Robins, taking the first rational and scientific look at gun design, showed that the smaller guns, below the 32-pounder, were far too heavy for the work they had to do, and advocated reductions in weight. His proposals may have had some affect; by 1753 new, lighter, guns were coming into use, though they did not fully match Robins' proposals in terms of lightness.[5]

It had long been believed that the best guns were made of 'brass' (actually an alloy which was closer in composition to bronze). Brass had been used for the great majority of heavy guns in Tudor times, because it was found to be stronger in proportion to its weight than iron, as then cast. By the second half of the seventeenth century, this situation had changed, and most of the smaller ships carried a large number of iron guns on their lower decks. In 1662, for example, the *Mary* had iron demi-cannon on her lower deck, and brass culverins, 12-pounders and 3-pounders on her upper deck and quarterdeck. In 1672 the *Fairfax* had iron 24-pounders on the lower deck, iron 12-pounders on the upper deck, and brass sakers on the quarterdeck, forecastle, and poop.[6] The larger ships, on the other hand, had brass throughout. The *Royal Charles* had 80 brass guns in 1660, the *Royal James* 68.[7] Brass was enormously expensive in comparison with iron; when planning the 1677 programme, Pepys found that to equip all the ships with brass guns would add £400,000 to the cost of the thirty ships.[8] Therefore it was reserved for the large prestige ships, and for some of the smaller, cheaper guns on the lesser ships.

The eighteenth century saw some notable improvements in iron-founding, and it would be surprising had these not had some effect on naval guns. There was a slowly growing confidence in iron and its ability to resist the pressures and dangers of a naval action: by the 1743 gun establishment, several types which had often been cast in brass were replaced with iron guns, and several other types were replaced in the 1750s. By the 1770s, it was reported that the fleet relied entirely on iron guns. By 1782 even 42-pounders were being made of iron.[9]

Early methods of gun-founding had been grossly inaccurate. Both the bore of the gun and the shot which was intended to fit into it, could vary considerably in size. Gunmakers therefore made the bore of the gun about a $\frac{1}{4}$ inch greater than the ball, to allow for any variation. This of course was very wasteful; between a quarter and a half of the force of the explosion was commonly lost because of this. By the 1770s, when the new iron industry of the industrial revolution was gaining strength, time was ripe for a change. It came, not surprisingly, from one of the most notable of the new ironworks, the Carron Works in Scotland. The carronade was an important innovation, not just because it used a more rational distribution of metal than the older guns; it also reduced windage, the gap between the size of the bore and that of the ball, by about one half, making the weapon much more efficient. It served only a specialised purpose, being of short range and useful only in close action, but this was the very type of action which was to be most favoured by the British Navy in the late eighteenth and early nineteenth centuries.

Surprisingly, the carronade had little immediate effect on the development of other naval guns. There is no sign of any attempt to reduce windage in the later years of the eighteenth century, and the weight of metal, which had tended to reduce down to 1753, began to increase slightly again. There was an enormous gap between the carronade and the normal cannon: the cannon was long, with a bore length of about 12 times the calibre; the carronade was shorter, with a bore of 4 or 5 calibres. A 32-pound cannon weighed over 55 hundredweight in 1800; a carronade of similar calibre, less than a third of that, 17 hundred-weight.[10] It should have been obvious that guns between the two extremes would have found many uses, especially in that they would have allowed heavier calibres to be mounted on the middle and upper decks of the line of battle – for much had changed in gunnery and tactics in the second half of the eighteenth century. The line of battle was no longer rigid, and medium-range gunnery had given place in importance to short-range firing. Many captains tended to give much more emphasis to gunnery practice, so that rate of fire was much increased. It was found to be dangerous to equip a ship entirely with carronades, for an enemy could bring her long guns to bear while keeping out of range of the return fire. The long 32-pounders on the lower deck of a ship of the line were still useful in the occasional bouts of long-range gunnery, but the guns between the lower deck 32-pounders and the carronades on the upper works had no real role; they were inferior in all respects to the lower deck guns, and could not match the carronades in penetrating power.

But the British Navy, victorious in every battle and on every sea, saw no need to change the system. It required a series of small-ship defeats, in the early stages of the War of 1812 with America, to cause some re-thinking. The big American frigates with their 24-pounder guns outclassed the British vessels, the largest of which carried 18-pounders. Until light 24-pounders could become available, some 18-pounders were bored out to take the heavier calibre in a lighter barrel. Experiments were also carried out on ships of the line, and by 1815 First Rates were carrying light 24-pounders on their upper decks. This policy was greatly extended in the 1820s, again under pressure from America; the new American ships of the line already carried a homogeneous armament of 32-pounders on every deck, and this forced the British Navy to come into line. By this time the shell gun was just around the corner, and rifling and breech-loading were not far behind; the new homogeneous armaments were never fully tested in action.

Many early ship's guns had been light and breech-loading, and so there was no need for them to recoil. They were fitted to a simple wooden bed, which was fixed to the deck. Heavier guns needed some system of recoil: they were invariably muzzle-loading, and this normally meant that they had to be run back to be reloaded. There is some

controversy about whether these early guns were in fact loaded from outboard, but it seems to be agreed that some kind of recoiling system was necessary to prevent a great strain on the sides of the ship. The truck carriage, based on the kind of mount used on a heavy fortress gun, was well established in the early seventeenth century. It took its name from the four wheels (trucks) which supported the carriage. The wheels themselves were small, their axles relatively large, and this provided a force which tended to slow down the recoil. Seventeenth century carriages were based on a solid wooden bed, which rested on the axles and supported the sides of the carriages. In the eighteenth century the bed was abandoned, and the sides rested directly on the axles. The sides in turn supported the gun by its trunnions, with a semi-circular hole recessed at the top of each side to take the trunnion. Over this was placed a piece

The typical seventeenth century gun carriage: it is based on a solid wooden bed, which supports the sides of the carriage, and the quoins.
National Maritime Museum

152

of metal known as the cap-square, which was hinged at its rear end, and bolted down on its forward end, to hold the trunnion firmly in place. Each side of the carriage had a system of steps towards its rear, to provide points of varying heights from which handspikes might be used to lever the gun into position. The bed, or the rear axle in the later type of gun, provided a base from which wedges (or quoins) were fitted, to allow the breech of the gun to be raised to varying heights for aiming. Ring-bolts were fitted to the carriage to hold or guide the various items of breeching tackle.

This type of carriage had many disadvantages. Because it was mounted on wheels, it could be highly dangerous if it broke loose. There was no effective way of bringing it slowly to a halt, and it tended to stop with a sharp jerk when the breech ropes were fully extended. The direction of its recoil was unpredictable, especially on a rolling and heaving deck, and this could be dangerous to the unwary seaman. It was not very efficient mechanically, for it was restrained too

near its rear, and this probably caused it to jerk violently near the end of its recoil. Nevertheless the truck carriage survived throughout the age of sail. It did have some advantages[11]: it was simple and required little maintenance; it allowed guns to be moved easily from one position to another, provided the seas were calm; it also reflected the division between the Admiralty and the Ordnance Board – any other type of carriage would have been a permanent fitting in the ship, but the truck carriage was easily removeable, and could be taken into the Ordnance stores when the ship paid off. Perhaps it is not safe to make too much of this last advantage, for other naval powers used the truck carriage as much as the British, and only in Sweden, where the innovating genius of Chapman was applied to the task, was there any real movement towards its replacement on the main deck guns of ships of war.

Impetus for improvement came, not for the first time,

The eighteenth century gun carriage: the bed has been abolished, so that the sides rest directly on the axle; the tops of the sides have also been made wider.
National Maritime Museum

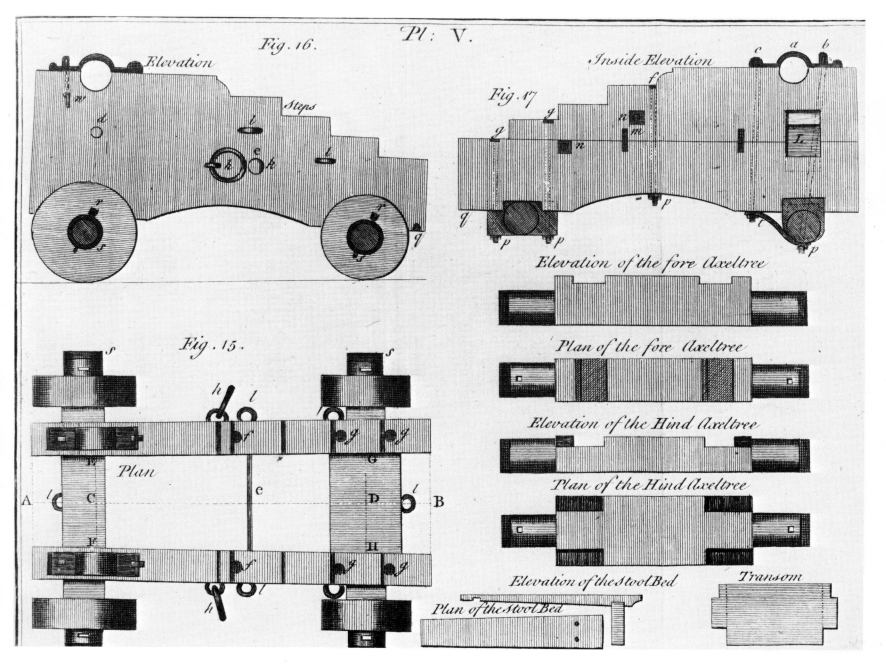

153

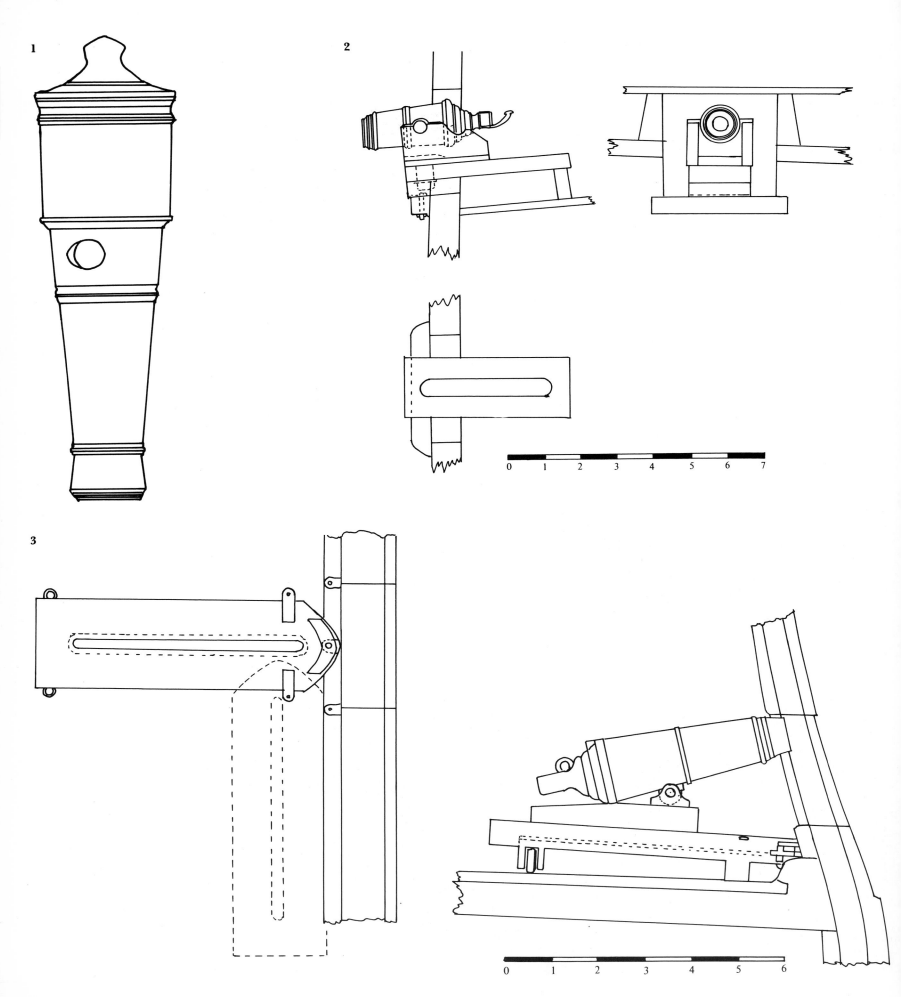

1 A distant ancestor of the carronade: this gun, dated 1672, is probably 'Punchinello', a short fat gun invented by Sir Anthony Deane and demonstrated to Samuel Pepys.

2 An early carronade, showing a mounting 'on the outside principle', with the pivot outside the ship's side. (Scale in feet)

3 A carronade fitted 'on the inside principle', with its pivot inside the hull. (Scale in feet)

4 A model of an early nineteenth century carronade, mounted 'on the inside principle'.
The Science Museum

from outside the Navy. Almost from the first, carronades were fitted on carriages which were radically different from those used for the rest of the Navy's guns. Firstly, the carriage itself did not recoil with the gun. Instead, the gun was mounted on a slide which could move backwards over the bed of the carriage, thus allowing the direction of the recoil to be controlled. Secondly, most carronades had no trunnions, but instead had a mounting underneath the gun which allowed elevation and depression. Thirdly, the elevation and depression was controlled, not by wedges and quoins which might fly out under the impact of the explosion, but by a screw at the rear of the weapon, thus presumably allowing more accurate aiming. Fourthly, the rear wheels of the carriage were arranged to allow the whole mounting to traverse, rather than to recoil, making it much easier to swing the gun round in action. There were many variations in the carronade carriage, as the Carron Company, and some individual naval officers, continued to experiment to find improvements; but essentially it was a rational, scientific, development of the old truck carriage.

Yet it never entirely replaced its antiquated rival during the age of sail. It was fully exploited with the carronades on the quarterdecks, forecastles and poops of the ship of the line, but it was never seriously applied to the long guns of the main armament. Perhaps this was pure conservatism; or perhaps experience showed that there were some real snags with the carronade carriage. There is some evidence

4

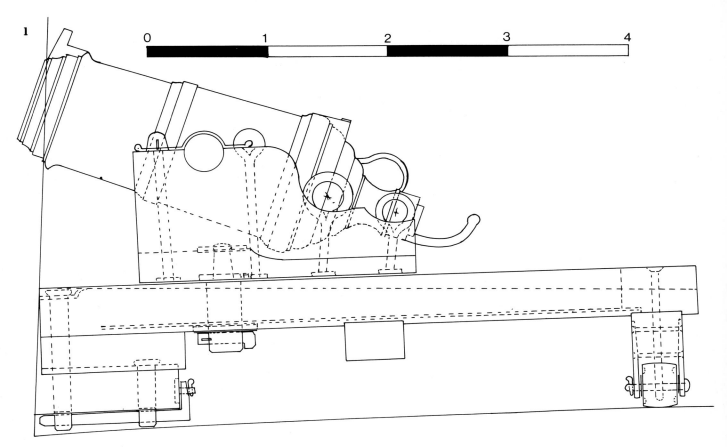

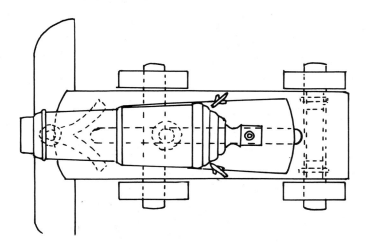

1 An 18-pounder carronade: unlike previous examples, it has trunnions on each side of the gun, instead of a single pivot below. (Scale in feet)

2 A carronade of 1808 on a truck carriage: these carriages were useful in that they allowed the guns to be moved to chase ports in the bow and stern when necessary.

3 A model of guns in position on a three-decker, *c*1750: the quarterdeck gun is run in for loading; the upper and middle deck guns are run out ready for firing, with the gun tackles pulled tight. The gun on the lower deck is stowed, with the port closed and the barrel raised to maximum elevation so that the muzzle is above the port; the gun tackle is pulled tight, and the gun and breeching tackles are bound together. Another tackle was often used to secure the muzzle to the deck above.
National Maritime Museum

QUARTER DECK

UPPER DECK

MIDDLE DECK

GUN DECK

that the slides tended to crack and fracture after continued and regular exposure to the recoil of the gun. If this happened with the relatively light blast of the carronade, would it not be even worse with the greater force of a long gun? The elevating screw was a great advance in its way, but it had a serious disadvantage, in that it made it much more difficult to change the elevation quickly. For good reason or bad, the Navy preferred the old reliable method, and it was not until the very end of the age of sail that the truck carriage began to be replaced.

The gun pointed out of the ship's side through a gunport. Normally this was a rectangular hole, slightly broader than it was high, though round ports were used for some of the smaller guns in the mid-seventeenth century. Gunports tended to increase slightly in size throughout the seventeenth century, to allow the guns more room to elevate and traverse. Until the late seventeenth century port lids were fitted to all ports on the lower, middle, and upper decks, and also to many on the quarterdeck, but it was found that some of these were unnecessary, for example on the upper deck at the waist, where the deck was uncovered in any case. Around 1700 ports were occasionally fitted with two lids, opening sideways, but the standard port lid for nearly all our period opened upwards in one piece. It was fitted with two hinges, which reached down over most of the surface of the port, and was opened by two ropes, which were fitted to the bottom of the lid and passed through a hole above the port, allowing the crew to heave up the port lid by pulling on the ropes. Gunports

served several purposes. Especially on the lower decks, they kept out the water when the ship was heeling, or in a heavy sea, and it is believed that the *Royal George* was lost in 1782 because she was heeled with her lower ports open.[12] Ports were sometimes caulked to increase this protection, particularly when the ship was regarded as crank (unstable). Port lids also helped keep the crew warm and dry; as a corollary of this, they shut out much of the light from the decks, though from the late eighteenth century ports were fitted with small glass panels known as deadlights. The port lids also helped protect the gun crews against enemy fire during reloading.

Several types of tackle were used to hold the gun in its place, restrain its recoil, and for running it out after reloading. The breeching tackle was a thick rope – 7 inches in circumference on a 32-pounder of the early nineteenth century[13] which passed round the cascabel of the gun, with its ends secured to a ring-bolt on each side of the gunport. It defined the limit of the gun's recoil. In 1824 the *Victory*'s 24-pounders had breeching tackles 34 feet long, which meant that the guns could recoil a little less than 17 feet, allowing part of the length of the rope for fixing to the cascabel and the ring-bolts. The smallest guns, the 6-pounders, had breeching tackles of 23 feet, allowing a recoil of perhaps 10 or 11 feet. Since the guns themselves would have been about 7 feet long, this would have allowed ample room for reloading. The gun tackle itself was much lighter and longer – 3 inches in diameter and 54 feet long in the case of the *Victory*'s 32-pounders.[14] One was fitted to each side,

Making snot at Woolwich Arsenal, 1750.
National Maritime Museum

being led through two blocks, one fixed to the side of the gun carriage, the other at the side of the gunport. This allowed the crews purchase for hauling the gun back into the firing position after reloading. Even so, hauling out the guns was a very labour-intensive process, and most of the 13 men allocated to a 32-pounder were there mainly for that purpose. The third part of the gun's 'rigging' was the train tackle, one of which was allocated to each gun. Again, it passed through two blocks, one at the rear of the gun carriage, the other fixed to a ringbolt on the deck near the centreline. Its main purpose was to hold the gun in position during reloading, preventing it from rolling outwards and perhaps crushing the loaders. Finally, tackles were provided for securing the gun when not in use; in which case it was raised to its maximum elevation, and the muzzle pressed against the side of the ship above the gunport; the gun tackles were drawn tight, and the securing tackle entwined around them to help hold the gun in place. In some cases another tackle was used to hold the muzzle against the side of the ship.

With the traditional truck carriage, aiming was a crude and laborious process, but there was no great impetus for change, for the limitations of the gun itself made any sort of accurate fire impossible. Elevation was controlled by a wedge or quoin, which rested either on the bed or on the rear axle of the carriage. By moving this in or out, the breech could be raised or lowered to the desired position, though it seems unlikely that many gunners made much use of this; it would have been easier to allow the roll of the ship to carry the gun into a suitable position. Traversing was much more difficult, for the wheels of the carriage were intended to carry it back and forwards, rather than from side to side. Gunners therefore used levers, known as handspikes, to push the carriage to one side or the other. It was an extremely cumbersome process, and survived only because there was little call for anything better: while ships fought in a rigid line of battle, in the early eighteenth century, the enemy's line was too big a target to miss; when the line was largely abandoned later in the century, captains were expected to take their ships so close to their opposite numbers on the enemy side that aiming was almost unnecessary.

British seamen believed in firing into the hulls of an enemy ship, to disable her, dismount her guns, and kill and injure their crews. The best projectile for this purpose was the round shot, cast in solid iron, and of a weight which gave each type of gun its designation on the armament lists. Originally the shot had been left unpainted, but it was found that this allowed it to rust while in storage, thus affecting its size. When carronades came into use, they demanded a shot which would fit much more tightly into the gun, and the custom of painting shot black began. Though the round shot was the basis of British naval gunnery, other types were used for different purposes. For firing into the rigging, there was chain shot, which consisted of two balls linked together by a chain, or a hollow ball which could open up on firing, and contained a chain; bar shot, a strip of iron with a heavy cylinder or hemisphere at each end; and expanding shot, in which the bar telescoped out to give a greater spread. For killing or injuring the men about an enemy's decks, several forms of grape and canister

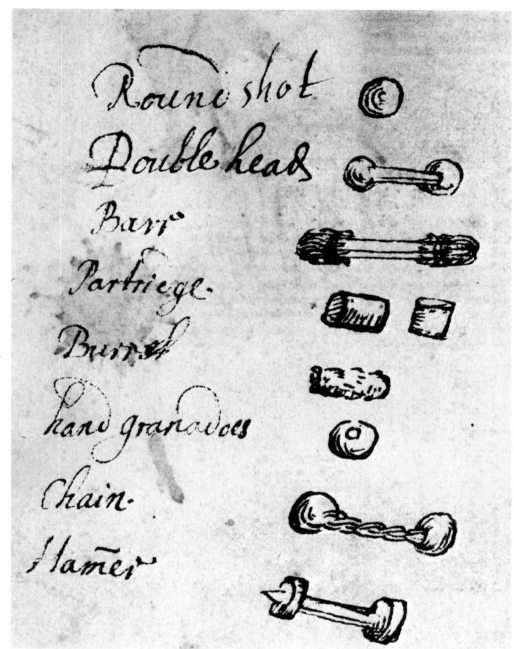

shot could be used: small balls could be held together in a canvas bag, in a thin metal case, or by metal plates.

For long-term storage, shot was kept in lockers fore and aft of the main mast. For ready use, it was placed on racks beside each gun. In the late eighteenth century, holes were drilled in the coamings of the deck gratings, to hold round shot.

Shot, whether round, grape, case or chain, was easy to store, and posed no danger at all to the ship and its crew. Powder, on the other hand, was by far the most difficult and volatile of a ship's provisions. It had to be kept dry, to preserve its effectiveness; it had to be stored well away from the danger of fire, or the whole ship was lost; it had to be regularly aired and kept in condition. The magazine, therefore, was placed in the hold of the ship, with a single entrance which could be locked and easily guarded. The walls and floors were lined with felt to prevent any accidental spark, and anyone entering it had to wear

Types of shot, c1660: from the top they are round shot, double headed, bar, partridge, burrel [grape], hand grenade, chain and hammer.
British Library

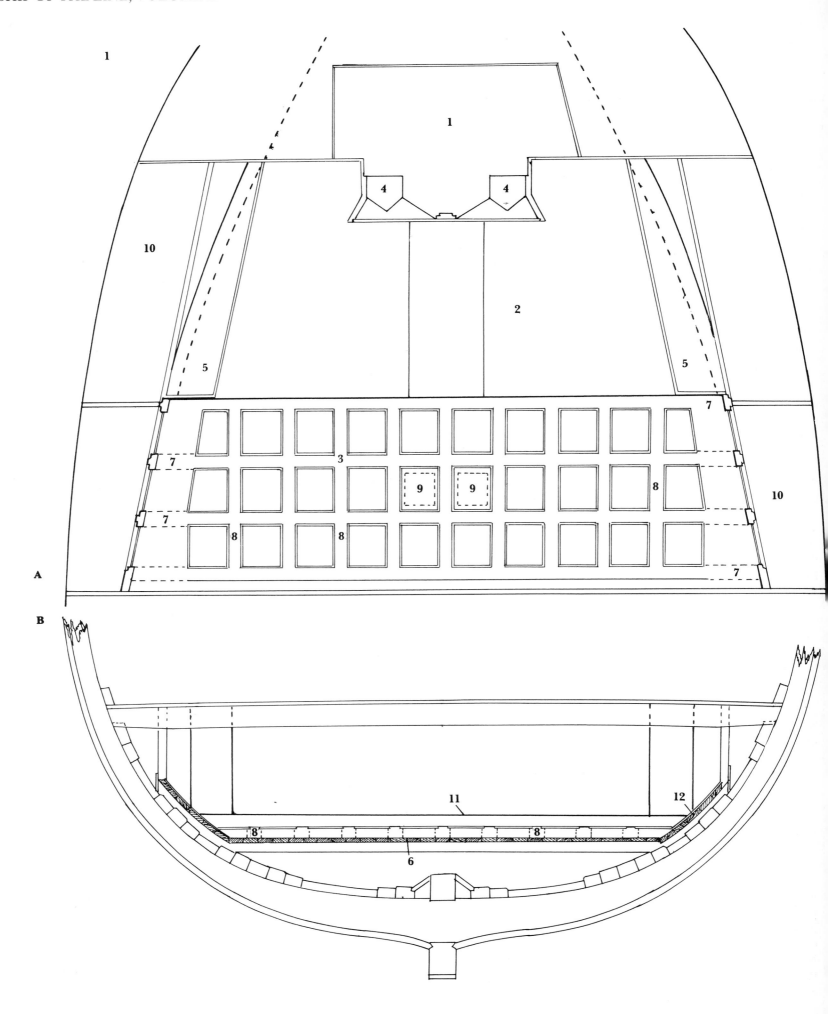

1 THE MAGAZINE OF THE *COURAGEUX* OF 1797

A. Plan view

B. Cross section of the after part, looking forward

1. Light room.
2. Filling room.
3. Magazine.
4. Lights.
5. Filling room shelves.
6. Three-inch plank below the magazine pallating.
7. Cross beams of the pallating in the magazine.
8. Fore-and-aft beams.
9. Hatches below, for access to the hull for repairs.
10. The wings.
11. Deck of filling room.
12. Plank of magazine continued up sides to help keep water out.

2 THE AFTER POWDER ROOM OF A 74-GUN SHIP, 1808

1. Racks for filled cartridges.
2. Powder room.
3. Pillar.
4. Light room.
5. Passage to the powder room.

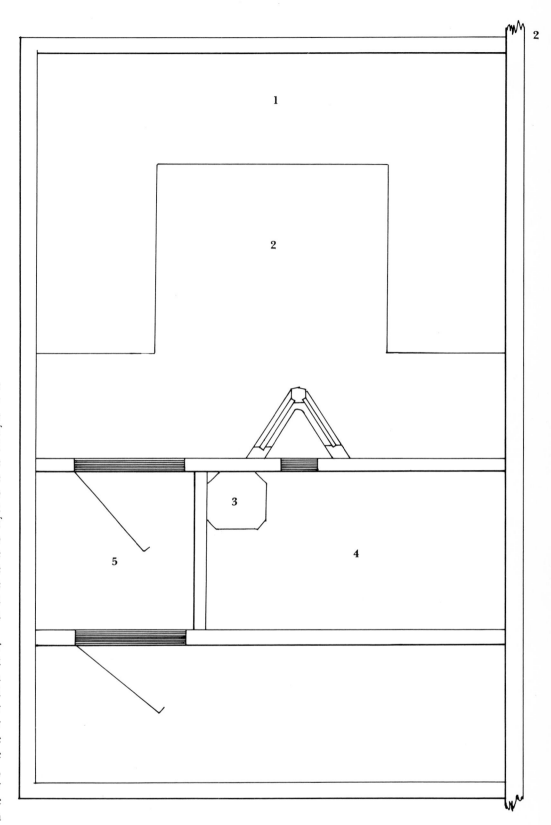

special slippers for the same reason. Of course the magazine had to be illuminated in some fashion. This was done by means of the 'light room', actually a compartment separate from the magazine itself, and sealed off from it by a pane of glass. The light room contained a candle, which provided illumination for the rest of the magazine. Ships of the line generally had their magazine well forward, below the warrant officers' store rooms on the orlop. In contrast to other parts of the hold, the contents of the magazine did not rest directly on the floor timbers and internal planking of the hold. The magazine had a short deck underneath it, to prevent the powder coming into contact with the bilge water. By the mid-eighteenth century, as ships became larger, a powder room was added in the after part of the hold, to provide supplies for the after guns. It was fitted with racks to hold cartridges, and eventually developed into a separate magazine.

Next to the magazine was the filling room. The powder was normally stored in barrels, which were suitable for bulk storage, and were reasonably watertight, but for use in action they were put into cartridges. Originally these had been made of paper, but in the late eighteenth century flannel was substituted, for it was found that it was totally consumed by the explosion, whereas paper might leave burning traces which could ignite the next charge prematurely. Cartridges could not be stored indefinitely, because they were not watertight, and there were too many possible variations of size according to the type of gun, the desired range, and so on. Therefore they were made up in the filling room as needed. The filling room was equipped with shelves to store the cartridges as they awaited use.

Traditionally guns had been fired by applying a lighted match to the touch hole. This method had many dangers and disadvantages. It took a little time for the resultant flame to reach the charge of powder, and in the interval the motion of the ship might have carried the gun off target. Moreover, a lighted match had to be kept in the vicinity of the gun, and there was a severe danger that it might

1 GUN CREWS' INSTRUMENTS, *c*1760

6, 9. Two types of worm, for removing charges.
7. A ladle, for inserting powder.
8. A wooden handled sponge.
10. A flexible sponge and rammer, made of thick rope, so that it would not stick out through the port when in action.

Types of shot
11. Bar.
12. Chain.
13. Grape.
14. Case or canister.
From Falconer's Marine Dictionary

2 A cross section of a 70-gun ship of the 1690s, showing the gun crews in action.
The Earl of Pembroke.

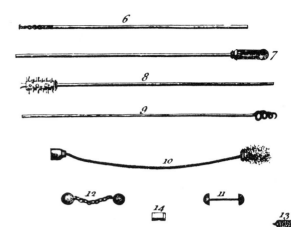

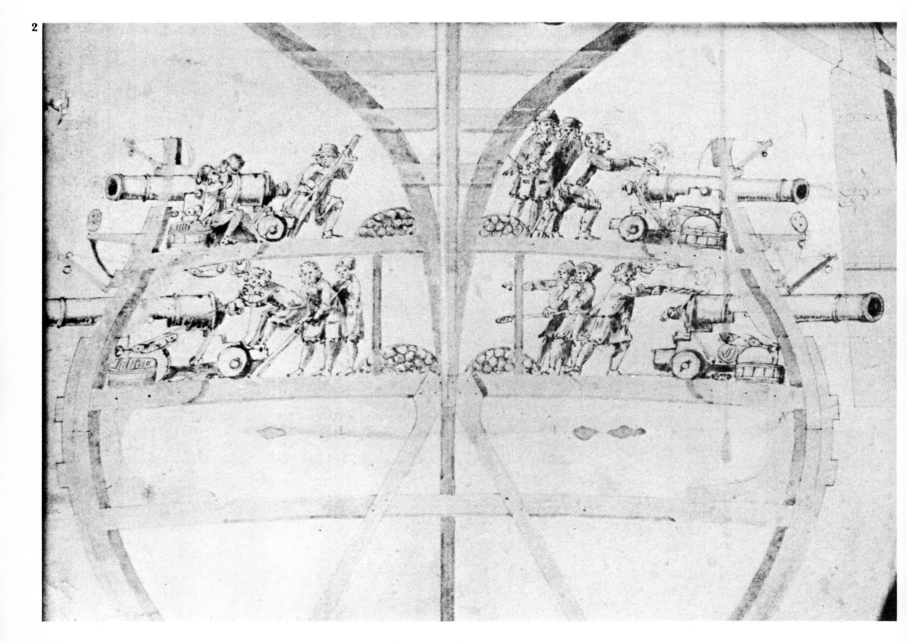

accidentally be brought into contact with a charge being taken to the gun. In the Seven Years War experiments were made with flintlocks similar to those used on muskets of the time. Initially they met with some resistance among officers and gun crews, but they became standard during the American War. From then on, the gun captain fired his weapon by pulling on a lanyard, allowing him to stand clear of the recoil.

The gun crew's implements were stored near the gun, usually suspended from the deck above. A ladle was used for inserting powder when cartridges were not in use. A sponge was used to clean out the barrel before loading, for there was great danger from burning fragments of the previous charge. The sponge had a handle made of thick rope, so that the seaman using it did not have to move too far in front of the gun, thus exposing himself to enemy fire. A rammer was used to force the charge of powder home, and also to push down the shot ahead of it. A circular wad of rope was placed between the powder and shot, and another in front of the shot, to prevent them moving because of the motion of the ship.

The operation of a ship's cannon demanded a great deal of physical effort, and a large number of men. Indeed, the main reason why a warship demanded such a large crew (about ten times that of a cargo ship of similar size) was the need to man the guns in action. This of course had profound effects: it caused the vast overcrowding of the ship's decks; it created the need for the press gangs, quotas and bounty systems which were found necessary to man the fleet; but the seamen, however unwilling to enter the Navy, seemed to have been trained into increasingly effective gun crews. No precise details are available about the rate of fire of ship's guns in the age of sail; but it would seem that it took four or five minutes to load a gun in early Stuart times; by the time of Nelson the rate of fire may have approached one round per minute. Until the technological revolution of the mid-nineteenth century, the naval gun remained a clumsy and inaccurate weapon, and much of its increasing effectiveness was due to the skill of the men who served them.

Appendix I
(see Chapter I)

Although it was standard practice to send both a model and a draught of any new ship to be built to the Admiralty, comments on them are extremely rare among the Admiralty papers, especially in the eighteenth century. The letters below are among the few to be found.

Appendix Ia:
Letter concerning several 60-gun ships (PRO Adm 106/3297)

Rt Honourable,

In obedience to your honour's commands to us of the 26th ulto, we have viewed and considered both the solids the Master Shipwright of his Majesty's yard at Deptford proposeth as the shape of the *Nottingham* ordered to be rebuilt there, one of them with a square tuck and the other with a round buttock. We are of the opinion that the round buttock is the strongest, best in the sea, or in riding at anchor, being little subject to draw dead water in great ships, but in small ships we think a square tuck may be serviceable.

We judge it would be proper to make the *Nottingham* eight or nine inches deeper in hold than the dimensions established for 60-gun ships, from which we know no ill conveniency but drawing more water, and not lying so easy on the ground. We approve of the shape of the said solids. We have also viewed the solid prepared for rebuilding the *Revenge* at Woolwich, and approve of the same as Mr Hayward proposes to finish it; are of the opinion that the great cabin of the *Revenge* and the 60-gun ships may be commodiously placed on the quarterdeck. The 60-gun ship may have a cabin 15 feet long, and a small coach of 12 feet if that accommodation be thought fit, and by means thereof the upper deck may be made flush for men and guns, the quarterdeck of the *Revenge* to be lowered 4 feet abaft, and that of the 60-gun ships 3 feet aft. All which is most humbly submitted to your honour's better judgement

Woolwich, 1 July 1717   Richard Stacey, John Naish,
                                                                John Hayward

APPENDIX Ib:
Letter relating to the design of the *Exeter* (PRO Adm 91/2)

Mr Lock, 21 December 1739

Sir,

...as to the draught you design for the *Exeter*, though the body is not strictly agreeable to my sentiments, it may do very well, but had the ship more rake afore the body would have less resistance, sheer better, and look much pleasanter to the eye, and the head may undoubtedly be greatly amended. The sheer of the ship is very well, but the stern too far aft, and the taffrail much too high, the gallery too much fore and aft, and the top of it, and upper lights, much too high. 'Tis pity we can't build these 60-gun ships snugger abaft. However, we should build them as snug as possible, and advance no one part of their finishing that can be kept down, and nothing of the gallery seen above the planksheer of the after drift. However, now I have said all this, I only mention it for your consideration, and desire you will forthwith lay down a body and send a draught and solid to the board.

And assure yourself that I am,
Your faithfuly servant,

J[acob] A[ckworth]

Appendix II

(see Chapter 2)

The contract for the *Yarmouth*, a Third Rate of 70 guns, launched on 7 January 1695. The dimensions and scantlings are probably identical to those used for the Third Rates of 1677, and basically similar to all 70s built up to the 1706 establishment. In fact the ship seems to have been fitted with 26 gunports on the upper deck, instead of 24, as demanded by the contract. (See Appendix VIIId)

Appendix II:
Contract for the *Yarmouth* (PRO Adm 106/3071)

This indenture, made on the three and twentieth day of January in the year of our lord one thousand six hundred and ninety between the Principal Officers and Commissioners of their Majesties' Navy (for and on behalf of their Majesties') of the one part, and Mr Nicholas Barret of Wapping in the county of Middlesex of the other part, witnesseth that the said Nicholas Barret, in considerations hereafter expressed, doth covenant, promise and grant to and with the said Principal Officers and Commissioners (for and on behalf of their Majesties) that he, the said Nicholas Barret, his executors, administrators, servants or assignees shall and will at their own proper cost and charges well and workmanlike erect and build off the stocks, for the use of their Majesties at Harwich, one good and substantial new ship or frigate of good and well seasoned timber, and plank of English oak and elm. And that the said ship or frigate shall contain in length upon the gun deck from the rabbet of the post to the rabbet of the stem, one hundred and fifty feet; breadth from outside to outside of the plank, thirty-nine feet eight inches; depth in hold from the top of the ceiling to the upper edge of the gun deck beam, sixteen feet nine inches; breadth at transom, twenty-five feet six inches; the rake forward at the harpin to be reckoned at three fifths part of the main breadth; the rake aft, five feet nine inches to the main transom; the keel not to be made of more than four pieces, to be sixteen and a half inches broad in the midships, and fifteen inches and a half up and down. To be sheathed with a four-inch plank well fastened for a false keel. To have four feet six inches scarph tabled in the keel, and to be well bolted with eight bolts of inch and half quarter inch auger. To have a firm substantial stem of sixteen inches thwartships and seventeen inches fore and aft, with a sufficient false stem of nine inches thick, and two feet six inches broad, with scarphs one foot long to the false stem, and not less than four feet to the main stem. To have a substantial sternpost of two feet two inches broad at the head and two feet six inches below on the keel fore and aft, and another post within it, to be fastened to the main post of sixteen inches fore and aft, and as broad as the main post, unto which shall be joined the rising woods sufficient for the run of the said ship, and also a long armed knee, of six feet long at the least, each arm to be well bolted with an inch, quarter and a half quarter auger fastening the same to the keel and to the sternpost at every twenty-two inches length at furthest. The space of timber and room to be no more than two feet three inches. The floor timbers of the said ship to be thirteen inches and one quarter of an inch fore and aft, and sixteen inches and one half inch up and down upon the keel, and twelve inches and one quarter of an inch in and out at the wrongheads [rungheads], or twelve inches full when wrought, and to be twenty-three feet long in the midships. The navel timbers to fill the rooms, being at least thirteen inches and one half inch fore and aft, and to have at least six feet nine inches scarph. The middle futtocks to have six feet six inches scarph. The timbers on the gun deck to be ten inches in and out, and twelve inches fore and aft, and to have at least six feet scarph. To have a substantial kelson of not more than five pieces, to be sixteen inches up and down and eighteen inches broad in the midships, and to end at the stem and sternpost in proportion to run fore and aft, each scarph to be three feet long at the least, and to be well bolted with inch, quarter and half quarter auger through every other timber, and to bolt every other

floor timber through the keel, and one bolt through the stem. The toptimbers to be sided alow twelve inches, at the head eight inches, and to be in and out at the gunwale or top of the ship's side four inches and a half inch. To put in one strake of four-inch plank next the limber board, and seven strakes of sleepers in hold on each side the wrongheads, three of them eight inches, two of seven inches and a half inches, and the other two of five inches thick and fifteen inches broad, and to run fore and aft. To have two strakes of clamps on each side fore and aft under the beams of the gun deck, of eight inches and one quarter of an inch thick, and seventeen inches broad each, and to be hooked one into the other to prevent reaching. To have an opening of six inches under the clamps for air. All the rest of the footwaling of ceiling in the hold to be good four-inch English oak plank. To put in ten beams for the orlop, to be sixteen inches fore and aft, and fifteen inches up and down, five of them to be placed before the mast and the other five abaft. To have five bends of floor and futtock riders, the futtock riders to be of fifteen inches, the floor riders to be of eighteen inches fore and aft, and twelve inches deep at the kelson, fifteen inches deep at the wrongheads. The floor riders to be bolted with nine bolts of inch, quarter and half quarter of an inch auger each rider, and to have seven feet scarph upwards and downwards, and to make platforms upon the orlop beams for stowing cables and other stores, and to lie five feet nine inches from the gun deck between plank and plank. To have one knee and one rider at each end of the beams, or double kneed, but if riders then the riders to be thirteen feet long, twelve inches sided, and sixteen inches deep at the beam, fayed into the beam, and to be well bolted with eight bolts of inch, quarter and half quarter of an inch auger, in and out, and two into the beams, with one knee fore and aft at each end of every beam, the shortest arm to be three feet in length, and to be ten inches sided, bolted with six bolts to each knee, of inch and three eights auger. To have a saddle for the step of the main mast, of two feet seven inches fore and aft, and depth sufficient for the same. To have a pillar in hold under every beam of the gun deck and orlop, eight inches square. The gun deck beams to be sixteen inches and one quarter of an inch broad, and fifteen inches up and down, and to be placed one beam under each port of the gun deck, excepting in the main hatchway, which must be eight feet asunder, and to be kneed with two knees at each end of the beams, one lodging, the other hanging, where the beams fall under the ports, of not less than three feet long each arm, and ten inches sided, to be bolted with six bolts of inch and one quarter of an inch auger. The beams that fall between the ports to be in like manner double kneed at each end, if knees can be procured; but if so many knees cannot be had, then to hang one knee at each end of the beams, and of the bigness of the other knees before mentioned, and one rider at each end of the said beams, to be thirteen feet long, thirteen inches broad, and twenty inches depth at the beams, to be bolted with eight bolts of inch and three eights auger. To have five pairs of cross pillars in hold, of ten inches square, and to be well bolted to the beams and riders, and to be kneed at the upper ends well bolted, and to have a double line of carlines on each side fore and aft of oak, to be nine inches thick and ten inches broad, and the ledges to lie within nine inches one of another, and six inches broad, five deep. The waterways to be six inches in the chine in thickness, and fourteen inches broad. All the rest of the gun deck as far as the hatchways from the side to be good four-inch English oak plank, well seasoned and cut of good lengths, the said plank and waterways to be trenailed, spiked with two good spikes in each beam, and two trenails in each ledge. To put out nine leaden scuppers on each side of the gun deck. To make as many hatches in the hatchways as shall be convenient, of two-inch plank, with the hatchway abaft the mast for the stowing of provisions, and hatchway to the steward's room and for boatswain's and gunner's store rooms, and powder rooms, which said store rooms and powder rooms are to be built of ordinary deals of such bigness and continuance as equals any of their Majesties' ships of like burthen. To make a manger on the lower deck, to have four scuppers in it of lead, two whereof to be four inches diameter, and to put in four hawse pieces not less than two feet three inches broad each, and to cut out four hawse holes in them. To place two pairs of conic bitts, eighteen inches square the aftermost, and sixteen inches square the foremost pair, with cross pieces to the same of equal bigness, and two pair of knees suitable to the said bitts, and to bolt them with five bolts in each knee, of inch and a half quarter auger. To have four breasthooks in hold, fourteen inches deep and fourteen feet long each, and seven bolts in each breasthook of inch and three eights auger. To have a step for the fore mast two feet four inches broad, and sufficient depth and length, bolted with eight bolts of inch and quarter auger. To have two strakes of spirket wales on the lower edge, of six inches thick form the waterway unto the lower edge of the ports fore and aft. To cut out thirteen ports on each side the same deck, three feet six inches broad and two feet four inches deep, with four ports abaft between the transoms, and to make and hang port lids with hooks and hinges, and to fit and drive two ringbolts and two eyebolts to each port, of inch and quarter auger for the guns. To place partners for the main and fore mast of ten inches thick and a pillar for the main capstan, to be iron bound, for the end of the spindle to stand on in the hold. A step for the mizzen mast on the kelson. To have three-inch plank upon the gun deck between the bitts and the main partners in the wake of the hatchways, and to raise the hatches above the deck, and to have turned pillars under the beams on the upper deck, as shall be found convenient, and placed upon four-inch plank for the pillar to rest upon the gun deck. To make a staircase up into the quarterdeck, and stairs and ladders to all the companionways. To bring on two breasthooks between decks, fourteen feet long, fourteen inches deep, and to fasten them with seven bolts in each hook, of inch and three eights auger. To have as many transoms abaft below the ports as may lie within eighteen inches of one another, the wing transom to be fourteen inches thick, and the rest not less than twelve inches thick, and one transom at the upper edge of the ports under the helm port to take hold of the sternpost. All the said transoms to be well kneed with long armed knees as is usual, fastened with six bolts in each knee by inch and three eights auger. To make twenty-four ports on the upper deck (that is to say) twelve on each side, two chase ports forward, and four right aft, to be two feet eight inches broad and two feet five inches deep, and to garnish them with carved works fore and aft. To bring on clamps fore and aft, of six inches thick and fifteen inches broad under the beams of the upper deck, and to shut up between decks with four-inch oak plank, fore and aft. The beams of the said deck to be eleven inches up and down and thirteen inches broad fore and aft, to lie between and under each port and not to exceed five feet asunder, excepting in the wake of the hatchways, and the beams over the main capstan. And under the said deck between plank and plank seven feet three inches in the midships. The beams to round ten inches, to go flush fore and aft, all the said beams to be double kneed with four knees to each beam, of seven inches and half an inch sided, the shortest arm three feet long, the hanging arm to come down to the spirketting under the port, and to be well bolted with three bolts in each arm, with bolts of inch and a half quarter auger. To have two tier of carlines on each side fore and aft, to be twelve inches square, the long carlines and the other short carlines eight inches broad and six inches up and down, with sufficient ledges of four inches square, to lie not more than nine inches asunder. To lay the said deck with good three-inch oak plank in the wake of the guns, the rest with the like plank or with good dry Prutia [Prussia] deals, to answer the said plank in thickness. To have a waterway five inches thick, fourteen inches broad. The spirketting to be of four-inch oak plank fore and aft. To have a string of English oak of six inches deep and ten inches thick, to be pricked home to the outside plank, and to make the lower sill of the upper ports to be well spiked and trenailed through and between the timbers. To have coamings, head ledges and grating hatches before and abaft the mast to vent the smoke of the ordnance. To fit topsail sheet bits, jeer bitts or knightheads, cats and supporters, a davit and clasp of iron, to fit partners

for the main and jeer capstan and partners for all the masts, and to put out nine scuppers on each side of the upper deck. To make a main capstan (drum fashion) thirty inches diameter in the barrel, and a jeer capstan (drum fashion) of twenty-two inches diameter in the barrel, with capstan bars and iron pauls sufficient for the said capstans. To make a large quarterdeck and a large forecastle, the beams of the same to be eight inches fore and aft, and six inches and a half up and down, and to lie within two feet one of another, and each other beam to be kneed with one up and down knee at each end of good length and six inches sided, and bolted with five bolts in each knee by a three quarter of an inch auger. To have round bulkheads in the bulkheads of the said forecastle and quarterdeck, for four cabins next the side and in the midships of the bulkhead of the forecastle. To place the cookroom for roasting and boiling, and to set all the bulkheads, upon oaken plank fayed on the deck at the foot of the stanchions, of ten inches broad and four inches thick, laid with tar and hair, and the seams leaded. To have two ports in the bulkhead of the forecastle, and two in the bulkhead of the steerage, and twelve ports on the quarterdeck, six ports on each side, of two feet four inches wide and two feet deep. The beams in the wake of the bulkheads to be double kneed at each end. To have three pair of standards on the upper deck, in each individual bulkhead one pair, to be nine inches sided and not less than three feet and a half foot long, each arm, and to have one pair in the bulkhead of the coach, to be bolted with six bolts with inch and half quarter auger. The quarterdeck to be laid with two-inch oak plank well seasoned next the side, and the rest with Prutia deal of like thickness. To have a rising of elm under the beam of the great cabin, of eight inches thick and ten inches deep, the beams to be dovetailed and bolted into the same. To make and hang with port lids about the whole ship, with substantial hooks and hinges. To have a transom abaft under the windows in the cabin, and one under the ports, and the same to be kneed and bolted with six bolts in each knee, and to have an open balcony abaft out of the great cabin, with rails and bannisters, and to have as large a roundhouse and coach as the works with conveniency will bear, to be completely fitted with bulkheads, joiner's work and doors to the same. To make all platforms in hold with bulkheads and partitions, viz. for the powder room and gunner's store room, sailroom, boatswain's, carpenter's and steward's store rooms, and steward's room, a fish room and a store room for the captain's provisions, and as many cabins for lodging as shall be convenient. To make a large bread room and sheath the same with lead or tin plate, the lead or plate thereof to be at their Majesties' charge. Without board the ship is to be planked up from the keel ten feet in height with elm, oak or beech plank of four inches thick, and from thence up to the chainwales with four-inch oak plank, excepting six strakes which is to be six inches thick and fourteen inches broad in the midships, and to lessen in thickness in proportion towards the stem and stern as is usual, ending at the stem and stern in four-inch plank, viz two strakes below the wale, two between the wales, and two above the wales. To have two formed wales of fourteen inches up and down and nine inches and a half of an inch thick, and to have two chainwales for the conveniency of the chain plates and bolts, to go fore and aft, both to be six inches thick and ten inches broad, to be chocked between the timbers with oak in the wake of the chain bolt. To have one strake of three-inch oak plank between the chainwales, ten inches broad, and the work upwards so high as the waist from the upper chainwale to be wrought up with three-inch English oak plank, and the quarter with well seasoned Prutia deals of two inches thick. To have a fair head with a firm and substantial knee, to have catheads and supporters under them. To have a fair lower counter with rails and brackets and open galleries, garnished with carved works. To have a house of office in the gallery windows, and casements unto the cabin. To have a fair upright, and to put in it a complete pair of King's arms or other ornament of like value, maskheads, pilasters and terms. To have a pair of chesstrees, fore, main and mizzen chainwales, well bolted, chain bolts and chain plates sufficient for the shrouds and backstays of all the masts. To have a sufficient gripe, well bolted, stirruped and dovetailed, and a stirrup on the skeg, well bolted. To make and hang on a complete rudder, with six pair of braces, gudgeons and pintles, a muzzle for the head and a tiller thereto. To gunwale and planksheer the said ship fore and aft, and to put on brackets, hancing pieces, and to garnish them complete. They are likewise to do and perform all the carved work, painting and gilding, answerable to their Majesties' ships of the like bigness in the Navy, the gilding work being intended to be only the lion in the head and the King's arms in the stern. The head, stern and galleries in carved work not inferior to those of the thirty ships formerly built, and to find and provide all materials for the same. Likewise to do and perform all the joiner's works, finding deals, locks, iron bars, hinges, for store rooms, steward's room's doors, settle beds and cabins, the cabins to be as many and as well adorned in all respects as any of their Majesties' ships of the like burthen, and to equal them in all respects both within board and without. They are to find all plumber's work, lead and leaden scuppers, and all glazier's work stone ground glass, with sash lights, scuttles for cabin windows, and all painter's work for painting and gilding as aforesaid, within and without board, and to do and perform whatsoever belongs to the carpenters to do for the finishing and completing the hull (without masts and yards) in like manner as is usually done and performed in like ships built in their Majesties' own yards, and to set the masts at his or their own charges with the help of the boatswain (that is to say) heel the masts, wedge them, and shut them in. And the said Nicholas Barret, for himself, his executors and assignees, doth covenant and grant to and with the Principal Officers and Commissioners of the Navy that he will at his or their own cost and charges find and provide all manner of iron work of the best Spanish iron, or what shall be equal to the same in goodness, and all spikes, nails, brasses, likewise all timber, planks, boards and trenails of Sussex, well fastened, which are to be all mooted from Prutia deals above the chainwale down to the keel. To find white and black oakum, pitch, tar, rosin, hair oil, brimstone and all other materials that shall be needful to be used or spent in or about the work and premises aforesaid, for the complete finishing of the said ship, and in like manner to discharge and pay all manner of workmanship touching all and every part of the work herein expressed and hereinafter expressed, or to be done and performed, and to finish, complete and launch the said ship or frigate, and to deliver her safe on float in the river of Harwich unto such person or persons as shall be duly and sufficiently authorised by the said Principal Officers and Commissioners to receive her for the use of their Majesties, by the last day of December next coming after the date herein.

[followed by several pages detailing the conditions for payment of the builder, the rights of the Navy Board to inspect the work, the penalties for late delivery, etc.]

Appendix III

(see Chapter 3)

Two documents relating to ship decoration: a list of carved works for the *Defiance*, 1666 (IIIa); and a contract for painting ships, 1676. Unfortunately the latter does not give much detail about the colours used, but it does suggest that the decks and insides of the hull were painted with red lead for protection against decay, rather than to hide the blood in action, as the popular myth would have us believe.

Appendix IIIa:
Particulars of carved works of the *Defiance*

(PRO SP 29/153 f73)

Mr Leadman,
this is the carved work on several places of the new ship that Mr Castle built are as followeth – 32 brackets on each gallery; 4 figures on each gallery; carved work to go round four lights on each gallery; 2 small hollow pieces on each gallery; one supporter carved under each gallery, with 16 brackets in the stern; 4 great brackets in the lower counter; 6 brackets in the bulkhead of the steerage; 6 brackets on the bulkhead of the quarterdeck; 8 hances with 8 dolphins lying on the top of the gunwale; 4 carved ports for the ladder going up the half deck.

One pair of King's arms carved in the great cabin, carved round the rail in the great cabin; carved round two lights, on each quarter, and chesstree carved on each side. 5 brackets on each side of the head. One supporter carved on each side under the cat. 2 term pieces carved, and 2 quarter pieces. One taffrail; one pair of King's arms on the stern; 40 round ports to be carved on the upper tier, quarterdeck; one lion and trailboard for the head; six knightheads.

10 April 1666   Jonas Shish

Appendix IIIb:
Contract for painting ships

(PRO ADM 106/3069)

Portsmouth
10 April 1676

Contracted the day and year above said with the Principal Officers and Commissioners of His Majesty's Navy by me, Mary Harrison, widow of Thomas Harrison, late master painter of His Majesty's yard at Portsmouth, and I do hereby oblige myself to do and perform or cause to be done and performed unto any of His Majesty's ships or vessels, or in His Majesty's yard at Portsmouth, such of the several painted works hereafter mentioned, as shall at any time within one year from and after the first of January last be directed by the said Principal Officers and Commissioners or by the Master Shipwright at the said yard, at the prices against each particular expressed, with the addition only of twelve pence to every twenty shillings that the several works done by me (the flat works only excepted, to the price of which there is not anything to be allowed more than what is expressed in this contract) shall amount to in consideration trouble and charges in the carriage of my oil and colours from London to Portsmouth.

For new work on ships of the

	1st Rate	2nd Rate	3rd Rate	4th Rate	5th Rate	6th Rate	
I will three times prime and once paint of a fair colour the head, stern and gallery of each ship for pounds	twenty	sixteen	ten	six	four	two	per ship
I will three times prime and once paint of a fair colour each carved port for pence	eighteen	sixteen	ten	eight	six	four	per port
I will twice prime and twice colour with red lead the inside of each port for pence	eight	eight	eight	eight	six	four	per port
I will three times prime and once paint of a fair colour all hancing pieces and terms on the sides, and all bulkhead brackets, for	1 shilling sixpence	1 shilling fourpence	ten pence	eight pence	six pence	four pence	per each
I will three times prime and once paint of a fair colour the rails for	two pence ob†	two pence ob	two pence	one penny ob	one penny	one penny	per yard

I will three times prime and once paint of a fair colour all other carved works on the bulkheads and sides according to the rates allowed for carved ports in ships of the same rate.

For new flat work

I will three times prime and once paint of a fair stone colour at –	ten pence ob	per yard
I will three times prime and once paint and grain all sorts of wood at –	ten pence ob	per yard
I will twice prime and twice black the said works at –	eight pence	per yard
I will three times prime and once paint plain timber plain timber colour on lead colour at –	eight pence	per yard

I will prime and paint all barges, pinnaces, waterboats, jollyots*, in the manner and for the prices following, viz:

	PAINTING Once	Twice	Thrice
All barges and pinnaces, I will prime and paint all withinside to the floor, and also the ceiling if any be, and the outboard strake, together with the rails if any – All waterboats and jollyatts* I will prime and paint all their timbers to the floor, all their gunwales and stern sheets, their upper strakes withinboard to their risings and their upper strakes withoutboard, for such barges, pinnaces, waterboats or jollyat* at –	five shillings	eight shillings	ten shillings
I will paint oars all over for pence –	six	eight	ten
I will paint all the plater's work of all lanterns for, per foot in height –	eight pence	one shilling	

For refreshing old work upon ships of the

	1st Rate	2nd Rate	3rd Rate	4th Rate	5th Rate	6th Rate	
I will paint the head, stern and gallery of each ship of a fair colour for pounds	nine	seven	five	three	two	one	per ship
I will paint each carved port of a fair colour for pence	nine	eight	five	four	three	two	per port
I will paint of a fair colour the rails for pence	one penny farthing	one penny farthing	one penny	three farthings	one half penny	one half penny	per yard
I will once lay with red lead of a fair colour the inside of each port for pence	four	four	four	three	three	three	per port
I will paint of a fair colour all hancing pieces and terms on the sides, and all bulkhead brackets for pence	eight	seven	four	three and a half	three	two	each

I will once paint of a fair colour all other carved works on the bulkheads and sides according to the rates allowed for carved ports in ships of the same rates.

For refreshing old flat work, I am to be allowed as followeth, viz:

Stone colour varnished and evailed [?]	Five	
Walnut tree – grained and evailed [?]	Five	
Plain timber colour	Three	
Lead colour	Three	Pence per yard
Black work	Three	
Painting rails, per yard square	Four	

To be paid one fourth part of the value of each work upon my going in hand therewith, and the rest in course after the passing of my bills for the same, which bills are to be passed without delay upon the finishing of the works. That the several colours used shall be good, and shall be all

ground and laid in linseed oil. And I do hereby oblige myself that all the aforesaid works shall be done in as good and workmanlike manner as such works ought to be, or have at any time heretofore been done in the Navy.

And it's further agreed that if the remainder to be paid in course shall happen not to be paid within the space of six months next after my bills shall be brought and entered in the Navy Office then to be allowed interest after the rate of six per cent per annum for so long time as the said bills shall remain unpaid more than the said six months. Witness my hand the day and year as abovementioned.

Signed in the presence of us

Mary Harrison
Danll Furzer
Nicho Belbin

*So spelt in the manuscript
†ob = obolus, meaning one halfpenny

Appendix IV

(see Chapter 4)

The contract for New England masts (IVa) is the earliest known contract for the import of masts, though there are references to their import from New England as early as 1670. The masts were to be cut roughly to shape ('sixteen squared') so that they would be easier to transport; the final finishing was presumably to be done by the dockyards.

The document on the making of masts (IVb) is undated, but is probably from around 1720. It is rather obscure in some of its wording, but it suggests that the practice of mastmaking from several pieces of timber was not entirely novel when it gained prominence during the American War.

Appendix IVa:
Contract for New England masts 1692 (PRO Adm 106/3069)

Contracted this 27 January 1691/2 with the Principal Officers and Commissioners of their Majesties' Navy, for and on behalf of their Majesties by me, Jno Taylor of London, merchant. And I do hereby bargain and sell, and do oblige myself to deliver into their Majesties' stores at Deptford, Chatham and Portsmouth, as the said Principal Officers and Commissioners shall direct, free of all charge to their Majesties (damage of the seas, fire, enemies and restraint of Princes and states excepted) and the said Principal Officers and Commissioners do on behalf of their Majesties oblige to cause to be received into their Majesties' said stores, two ships' loading a year for two years, to come of New England. Masts, bowsprits and yards, one or two each year after for three years more, as shall be directed by the said Principal Officers and Commissioners, at the prices following, for peace and war, viz.

Masts (ins diam)	(yds long)	Price of each in war	Price of each in peace
36	35	156.2.0	142.2.0
35	34	139.14.0	127.0.0
34	33½	124.6.0	113.0.0
33	33	110.0.0	100.0.0
32	32	96.16.0	88.0.0
31	31	84.14.0	77.0.0
30	30	73.14.0	67.0.0
29	29	63.16.0	58.0.0
28	28	55.0.0	50.0.0
Bowsprits			
36	26½	104.2.8	94.13.4
35	25	93.2.8	84.13.4
34	24½	82.17.4	75.6.8
33	24½	73.6.8	66.13.4
32	24	64.10.8	58.13.4
31	23½	56.9.4	51.6.8
30	23½	49.2.8	44.13.4
29	23	42.10.0	38.13.4
28	22½	36.13.4	33.6.8
Yards			
22	28⅔	49.14.0	39.2.0
21	28	35.3.0	31.9.0
20	27⅓	30.12.0	26.8.0
18½	25½	25.5.6	22.12.6
18	25½	25.5.6	22.12.6
17	23½	21.17.0	19.11.0

Yards		
22	28⅔	Six yards for each, one of
21	28	each size, and not having
20	27⅓	the said sizes above half
19	25½	one inch in the diameter nor
18	25½	27 inches in the length, nor
17	23½	to import two of the same size

The loadings of all the other ships to be such as shall be directed by the said Principal Officers and Commissioners, of which timely notice is to be yearly given for enabling me to provide the same.

All the said masts, bowsprits and yards to be fresh, good, sound, merchantable, well and workmanlike wrought into sixteen squares, having most of their sap taken out. To be two thirds in bigness at the hounds of what they are in the partners, and in all other respects fitting for the service of their Majesties' Navy.

It is further agreed that if any accident happening in the felling, or by any other cause, any of the aforementioned masts shall want two feet of the said length, there shall be abated five pounds from me in the price of each mast so defective in length, provided the number of such masts shall not exceed two in any one ship's loading, and that none shall want more than two feet of the said lengths. And in case, for the conveniency of stowage, I shall bring square oaken knees, and oaken stuff of any thickness from 5 inches to 8 inches, increasing by inches, the same to be sound, well conditioned white wood piece under 28 foot long of the thick stuff, fitting for the service of their Majesties' Navy, or any ash rafters or other stowage goods fit and wanting for the service of the Navy, the said Principal Officers and Commissioners on behalf of their Majesties do hereby oblige themselves to receive the said knees, thick stuff and other goods into their Majesties' stores and allow such rated for the same as upon view by their Majesties' officers upon the place, or by persons indifferently chosen by the said Principal Officers and Commissioners and myself, they be judged to be worth.

And it is further agreed that the said Principal Officers and Commissioners shall protect the masters and companies of the ships that shall be employed in fetching the said masts from being impressed outwards and homewards bound, and during the unlivery of the ships in which they come, and also that they shall have convoy (during the war) such as the Rt Hon the Commissioners of the Admiralty shall judge fitting.

And it is also further agreed and concluded between the said Principal Officers and Commissioners and me, the contractor, that I shall have the use of their Majesties' lighters, slings and winding tackle at their Majesties' yards where the masts shall be delivered, to help out and bear up the ends of them while they are delivering out of the ships, and carrying the stowage goods on shore, as hath been usual in such cases.

The said masts, bowsprits, yards and other goods to be received, such of them for the use of the 27 new ships appointed by act of Parliament to be built for their Majesties as shall be fitting and wanting for that service, and the rest for repair and current service of the Navy, and bills to be made out accordingly, to be paid in course according to the rules of the Navy, those for the new ships out of the money appropriated for that service, and those for repairs out of such funds as shall be allotted for that service. But if by the said course of payments, my bills shall not be paid me within 6 months time after they are entered and numbered in the Navy office, then I am to be allowed interest after the rate of 6 pounds per cent per annum from and after the said 6 months, until my money shall be paid me.

It is further agreed that I shall have a bill of imprests for £800 at the sailing forth of each ship, which bills are to take their course of payment according to the rules of the office, and to be abated at the return of the ship out of my perfect bill for the said loadings, as is usual.

And lastly, if any yards for necessary stowage come over of somewhat larger or lesser dimensions than those contracted for as before, and shall nonetheless be fit and wanting for the service of the Navy, there shall be allowed a reasonable rate for the same, provided none of the masts and bowsprits contracted for be left out to make room for the yards or stowage of such as are not in the contract. And no bowsprit to be allowed for more than that of 35 inches in diameter.

With half inches in the medium, and length answerable. If any masts, bowsprits or yards shall come over of larger dimensions than is here expressed, I am to be allowed such rates as shall be reasonable for the same. I do oblige myself that two of the said ships shall be made ready to proceed to New England in a months time from the date hereof, and that they shall bring home (danger of the seas, fire, enemies and restraint of Princes and states excepted as before) the masts, bowsprits and yards undermentioned, and deliver the same at Chatham and Portsmouth by or before the last of October next ensuing the date hereof, viz:

Masts (ins diam)	(yds long)	Chatham	Portsmouth
36	35	1	1
35	34	2	1
34	33½	2	1
33	33	1	3
32	32	3	4
31	31	3	2
30	30	2	3
29	29	1	1
28	28	3	2
38	37	3	
37	36	1	
		–	–
		20	18

Bowsprits		Chatham	Portsmouth
35	25	2	
34	24½	2	2
33	24½	3	
32	24	3	2
31	23½	2	
30	23½		1
29	23		3
28	22½		4
		–	–
		12	12

Appendix IVb: **A Made Mast** <small>(NMM SPB/37a)</small>

The spindle to be in two pieces, that's two mast of 22 hands each, the top ends scarphed ⅓ the length of the mast, or at least 36 feet long, tabled and bolted with bolts 3 sqr. Observe to leave the tabling whole the length of two tablings at the end of the scarph. Let the spindle be half the mast in the partners, and set off the heel of the mast so far as the fishes run as another mast, and below the fishes with the tree will hold what's wanting, eak out with fir. Let the spindle at the hounds be one inch more of each side, than ⅔rds of the partners. To line the tongue, set off ⅓ the head of the mast the fore and aft way, which must be the bigness of the topmast, and 2 inches more athwartships. Lay a ruler over the spindle at the lower end of the sheets, and set out the bigness the mast should be in that place. Strike a straight line from that to the thickness of the tongue, which will allow 1½ inches stop for the six fishes, and should butt at the lower end of the hounds. Leave them an inch above the spindle in the middle of the cheeks, but nothing at the edges. You may flush away the butt in the spindle for the two side fishes. Your side fishes to be of three 21 hands, and the two fore and aft, 22 hand mast, and if long enough to run up to the top of the mast or at least ½ the head. Coak all the fishes with 4 or 5 coaks in each, and fasten them with ragged spikes almost as long again as your fish is thick, a yard asunder. Let the scarph be the fore and aft way. Lay the mast straight on the blocks, and be very try with the 8 square inches both spindles and fishes, the latter bevel from a circle.

Keep the hoops clear of the wedges.

Appendix V

(see Chapter 5)

The rigging list (Va) is dated 1720 in the catalogue, but it is far more likely to be associated with the 1677 programme. Bonnets are listed, whereas these were abolished around 1680. On the other hand, there is no bobstay, though this appeared in the 1690s. Moreover, any later list would be likely to divide the Third Rates into two groups. The list includes exactly the same ropes as were used to fit the *Lennox* of 1678 (Pepysian Library, ms no 1339) but the sizes vary somewhat, with some ropes being larger, and some smaller.

In the list of sails of 1790 (Vb), there is no mention of royals, perhaps because these were made by the ship's sailmaker rather than issued by the dockyard. The lining was not a separate sail, but was used to strengthen the topsails.

Appendix Va: **A proportion of rigging for His Majesty's ships of the First, Second and Third Rates** <small>(BL Cup 651e, 28-31)</small>

	FIRST		SECOND		THIRD			FIRST		SECOND		THIRD	
	Ins	Fath	Ins	Fath	Ins	Fath		Ins	Fath	Ins	Fath	Ins	Fath
Bowsprit							**Spritsail Topmast**						
Sheets	4	72	4	75	4	68	Shrouds	3	20	2½	18	2½	17
Pendants	4½	7	3½	10	–	–	Lanyards	1½	13	1½	12	1½	9
Clew lines	2½	40	3	38	3	32	Lifts	2	26	1½	21	1½	18
Buntlines	2½	38	2½	32	2½	30	Braces	2	46	1½	40	1½	38
Lifts	3½	58	3	55	3	50	Pendants	2½	3½	2	3	2	3
Standing lifts	3½	8	3½	7	3½	6	Tie	3	4	3	3½	3	3
Lanyards	2	6	2	5	2	5	Halyards	2	15	2	14	2	13
Slings	6	5	6	5	6	5	Clew lines	2	40	2	40	2	36
Tie	–	–	–	–	–	–	Parrel ropes	2	4	2½	3	2	3
Halyards	3½	32	3½	34	3½	30	Pendants of backstays	2½	11	2½	9	3	6
Braces	2½	70	2½	70	2½	66	Falls of backstays	2	26	1½	20	2	18
Pendants	3	3	3½	4	3½	4							
Garnet	2½	55	2½	50	3	48	**Fore mast**						
Horses in the head	4	8	4	8	4	8	Pendants of tackles	8	22	7½	19	7½	18
Horses for the bowsprit	4	8	4	9	3½	8	Runners of tackles	6½	32	6	30	5½	26
Wolding for the bowsprit	7	100	7	100	6	75	Falls of tackles	4	180	3½	160	3½	142

Fore mast

	FIRST Ins	FIRST Fath	SECOND Ins	SECOND Fath	THIRD Ins	THIRD Fath
Shrouds	8	225	7½	170	7½	160
Lanyards	4	72	4	64	4	62
Stay	16	16	14	13½	13½	13½
Collar	12	4	11	4	11	3
Lanyard	5	15	4½	12	4½	10
Lifts	4	72	3½	60	3½	60
Sheets	6	83	5½	76	5	70
Tacks	8	44	7½	44	7½	38
Braces	3	60	3	54	2½	50
Pendants	4	6	3½	6	3½	6
Bowlines	4	60	4	60	4	52
Bridles	4	7	4	60	3½	7
Buntlines	3	124	2½	128	2½	120
Leech lines	2½	80	2½	76	2½	44
Clew garnets	3½	72	3	66	3	60
Parrel ropes	5	20	5	16	4½	14
Jeers	6½	110	6½	100	6	90
Futtock shrouds	4½	36	4	30	4½	28
Catharpin legs	3½	20	3	20	2	28
Catharpin falls	3	20	2	26	2	26
Knave line for the parrel	2½	32	2½	30	2	26
Luffhook rope	5	15	5½	12	5	12
Horses for the yard	5	15	5½	14	5	11
Stoppers for the topsail sheet bitts	6	6	6	4	–	–
Lanyards	3	3	2	3	–	–
Lashers for jeer blocks	4	45	4	40	–	–

Fore topmast

	FIRST Ins	FIRST Fath	SECOND Ins	SECOND Fath	THIRD Ins	THIRD Fath
Pendant of the top rope	8	30	7½	28	7½	14
Fall of the top rope	4½	100	4	90	4	41
Pendants of burton tackles	3½	7	3½	6	3½	5
Falls of burton tackles	2½	36	2	36	2	38
Shrouds	4½	82	4	66	4	80
Lanyards	2½	30	2	30	2	26
Standing backstays	4½	80	4½	74	4½	64
Lanyards	2½	26	2½	12	2½	12
Stay	6	18	5½	16	5	15½
Lanyard	3	10	3	10	3	8
Lifts	2½	66	2½	64	2½	56
Sheets	7	60	6½	58	6	54
Braces	2½	60	2½	68	2½	64
Pendants	3	5	3	4	3	4
Bowlines	2½	60	2½	70	2½	68
Bridles	2	10	2½	70	2½	68
Clew lines	3	80	3	80	3	72
Tie of jeers / Runner of jeers / Halyards of jeers	4	100	3½	100	3½	80
Buntlines	2½	40	2½	40	2½	34
Leech lines	2½	20	2½	46	2	15
Parrel ropes	3½	10	3½	9	3	7½
Lashers for jeer blocks	3	20	3	20	–	–

Fore topgallant mast

	FIRST Ins	FIRST Fath	SECOND Ins	SECOND Fath	THIRD Ins	THIRD Fath
Shrouds	2½	20	2½	20	2	17
Lanyards	1½	10	1½	10	1½	8
Stay	3	22	2½	22	2	20
Lifts	1½	24	1½	20	1½	20
Braces	1½	70	1½	66	1½	63
Pendants	2	4	2	3	2	3
Bowlines	1½	74	1	60	1	56
Bridles	1½	74	1	60	1	56
Clew lines	2	64	1½	60	1½	55
Tie	3	4	3	4	2½	3½
Halyards	2	34	2	34	1½	32
Parrel ropes	2	3	2	3	2	2½
Backstays	2½	48	2½	48	–	–
Lanyards	1½	4	1½	7	–	–

Main mast

	FIRST Ins	FIRST Fath	SECOND Ins	SECOND Fath	THIRD Ins	THIRD Fath
Pendants of tackles	8	22	8	20	7½	20
Runners of tackles	6	32	6	30	6	28
Falls of tackles	4	180	3½	160	3½	68
Pendant of the garnet	8½	13	8	12	8	12
Guy of the garnet	6	12	5	12	5	12
Fall of the garnet	4½	40	4	40	4	32
Shrouds	8½	260	8	236	8	198
Lanyards	4½	90	4	80	4	72
Stay	18	22	17	20	16	18
Collar	15	10	14	10	14	8
Lanyard	6	15	5½	15	5	12
Lifts	4	80	3½	80	3½	70
Sheets cablett	6½	90	6	80	5	78
Tacks taper and cable laid	9	42	8½	42	8	36
Braces	3½	82	3	80	3	66
Pendants	4½	10	4	10	4	8
Bowlines	4½	52	4½	52	4	48
Bridles	4	20	3½	16	3½	12
Buntlines	3	150	3	160	3	128
Leech lines	3	120	3	86	3	54
Clew garnets	3½	70	3½	70	3	64
Parrel ropes	5½	20	5½	20	4½	16
Jeers	7½	120	7	120	6½	100
Futtock shrouds	5	40	4½	40	5	36
Catharpin legs	2½	62	2½	45	2	24
Catharpin falls	2½	62	2½	45	1½	20
Bowline tackle	3	15	3	12	2½	12
Luff tackle	3½	15	3	14	3	11
Knave line for the parrel	2½	32	2½	30	2	28
Horses for the yard	5	16	5	15	5	13
Stoppers for the topsail sheets	6	5	6	5	–	–
Lashers for the jeer blocks	4½	36	4½	36	–	–
Running backstays	–	–	5½	34	–	–
Falls	–	–	3	16	–	–

Main topmast

	FIRST Ins	FIRST Fath	SECOND Ins	SECOND Fath	THIRD Ins	THIRD Fath
Pendant of the top rope	8½	35	8	32	8	26
Fall of the top rope	4½	100	4	96	4	90
Pendants of burton tackles	4	8	4	8	4	7½
Falls of burton tackles	2½	40	2½	40	2	38
Shrouds	5	110	4½	105	4½	88
Lanyards	2½	36	2½	36	2½	36
Standing backstays	5	86	5	92	4	78
Lanyards	2½	14	2½	15	2½	12
Stay	7½	24	7	23	6½	24
Lanyard	3½	14	3	12	3	11
Lifts	3½	80	2½	76	2½	64
Sheets	7½	68	7	65	6	60
Braces	2½	82	2½	70	2½	62
Pendants	3	6	3	6	3½	6
Bowlines	4	66	3½	76	3½	68
Bridles	3½	18	3	15	3	10
Clew lines	3½	94	3½	88	3½	82
Tie of jeers / Runner of jeers / Halyards of jeers	4	120	3½	110	3½	88
Buntlines	3	62	2½	54	2½	48
Leech lines	2½	30	2½	54	2½	18
Parrel ropes	3½	11	3½	10	3½	8½
Lashers for jeer blocks	3	20	3	16	–	–

Main topgallant mast

	FIRST Ins	FIRST Fath	SECOND Ins	SECOND Fath	THIRD Ins	THIRD Fath
Shrouds	3	28	3	26	2½	21
Lanyards	1½	12	1½	12	1½	8
Stay	3	25	3	24	3	22
Lifts	2	28	1½	28	1½	22
Braces	2	70	1½	70	1½	66
Pendant	2½	5	2	4	2	3½
Bowlines	2	80	2	80	1½	60

	FIRST Ins	FIRST Fath	SECOND Ins	SECOND Fath	THIRD Ins	THIRD Fath
Main topgallant mast						
Bridles	2	80	2	80	1	5
Clew lines	2	64	2	60	1½	58
Tie	3½	5	3	4	3	4
Halyards	2	36	2	38	2	34
Parrel ropes	2	4	2	3	2	3
Standing backstays	2½	54	2	50	–	–
Lanyards	1½	6	1½	6	–	–
Flagstaff stay	1½	27	2	24	–	–
Mizzen mast						
Shrouds	5½	110	5½	96	5	88
Lanyards	2½	36	2½	36	2½	35
Stay	6	15	6	14	5	13
Lanyards	3	6	3	4	2½	4
Futtock shrouds	3	14	2½	12	3	10
Pendants of burton tackles	5	7	5	6	4	5½
Falls of burton tackles	2½	48	2½	46	2½	46
Halyards	–	–	–	–	4½	38
Truss	3	20	2½	26	2½	22
Sheet	4	30	3½	25	3½	23
Tack	3½	5	3½	4	3½	4½
Bowlines	3½	16	3	12	3	14
Brails	2½	160	2½	140	2	120
Jeer	5	50	5	50	–	–
Parrel ropes	4½	7	4	5	4	4
Lashers for jeer blocks	3	16	3	16	–	–
Crossjack yard						
Standing lifts	3½	10	3	9	2½	8
Lanyards	2	6	1½	6	1½	4
Braces	2½	50	2	48	2½	45
Slings	4	7	4	7	3	4
Mizzen topmast						
Shrouds	3	32	3	30	2½	26
Lanyards	1½	14	1½	14	1½	9
Standing backstays	3	30	3	26	–	–
Lanyards	2	6	1½	5	–	–
Stay	3	12	3	10	3	9
Lifts	2	40	2	35	2	3
Braces	2	50	1½	44	1½	36
Pendants	2	50	2	3	2½	2
Bowlines	2½	50	2	38	2	38
Bridles	2	54	1½	6	1½	3
Clew lines	3	6	2	46	1½	36
Tie	2½	35	3	5	3	5
Halyards	2½	4	2	30	2	26
Parrel ropes	4	50	2	4	2	2½
Sheets	4	41	3	42	3	42
Cat ropes	6	70	5½	75	4½	64
Pendant of the fish tackle	8	9	8	9	7½	8
Fall of the fish tackle	4½	40	4	40	4	32

	FIRST Ins	FIRST Fath	SECOND Ins	SECOND Fath	THIRD Ins	THIRD Fath
Mizzen topmast						
Stoppers at the bow	8½	30	7	34	6	28
Shank painters	7½	36	6½	30	6	22
Stoppers at the bitts	12	17	10	17	10	14
Lanyards	3½	20	3½	20	3	12
Viol cable	12	42	10	40	10	34
Pendant of the winding tackle	11	12	10	12	19	11
Fall of the winding tackle	6½	55	6	55	6	53
Buoy ropes cablett	8½	80	8	70	7½	70
Boat rope cablett	8	32	7	30	7	30
Guest rope cablett	5	34	4	34	4	30
Pinnace rope cablett	6	35	5	30	6	30
Guest rope cablett	4	30	3	30	3	30
Butt slings	5	9	5	9	5	9
Gun slings	8	7	8	7	7	7
Hogshead slings	4	7	4½	7	4	7
Ratline of shrouds	1½	400	1½	500		
	1	400	1	350		
Robands and earrings of sails	1½	300	1½	300		
	1	200	1	200		

BOATSWAIN'S STORES (EXTRACTS)

	First	Second	Third
Canvas			
French (yds)	100	100	80
Ipswich (bolts)	6	5	3
Noyals great			
Old			
Vittery (yds)	100	30	40
Sails			
Spritsail courses	2	2	2
Spritsail topsail	1	1	1
Fore courses	2	2	2
Fore bonnet	1	1	1
Fore topsails	2	2	2
Fore topgallant sails	1	1	1
Main courses	2	2	2
Main bonnet	1	1	1
Main topsails	2	2	2
Main topgallant sails	1	1	1
Mizzen course	2	2	2
Mizzen bonnet	1	1	1
Mizzen topsails	2	2	2
Main staysails	1	1	1
Mizzen staysails	1	1	1
Main topmast staysails	1	1	1
Fore topmast staysails	1	1	1
Main studding sails	2	2	2
Topsail studding sails	2	2	2
Longboat	1	1	1
Pinnace	1	1	1
Skiff	1	1	1

Appendix Vb: **List of sails, July 1790** (BL Stowe 436, f73)

Species of sails for a ship of 74 guns		Cloth Head	Foot	Yards deep		Sort of canvas	Yds in each sail	value of workmanship
Spritsail	Course	31	31	8		2	261	4.17.10½
	Topsail	18½	29½	9		6	216	3.3.0
Flying jib			26	25		6	327	4.15.4½
Fore	Course	41	41	13		1	579¼	10.17.2½
	Topsail	27	42	17½		2	637¼	14.8.9½
	Lining					5	46	
	Gallant	18½	26½	8¾		6	196¾	2.17.4½
Main	Course	50	50	15¾		1	865¾	16.4.8
	Topsail	30	48	19¾		2	817¼	16.7.5½
	Lining					5	56	
	Gallant	21½	30½	10		6	260	3.15.10½
Mizzen	Course	16	17	21		2	284	5.6.8¼
	Topsail	21	30½	14½		4	391½	7.7.8½
	Lining					6	34½	
	Gallant	16	21	7		7	129½	1.16.11½
Staysails	Fore		22	13		2	145	2.14.4½
	Main		31	15¾		2	246	4.12.4
	Mizzen	20½	22½	9	13½	2	246	4.12.3
	Maintop	25	27	9½	24	6	436¼	6.7.3
	Foretop		21	17½		6	185¾	2.14.2
	Main topgallant	21	21	6	15½	7	231¾	3.7.7
	Mizzen top	19	20	6½	14½	6	209¼	3.1.0½
	Middle	24	24	7½	16½	6	295	4.6.0½
Stunsails	Main	16	20	18½		6	335¾	4.17.11
	Top	14	17	21		6	328	4.15.8
	Gallant	10	13	10½		7	240¾	1.15.3¼
	Fore	15	19	15		6	255	3.11.10½
	Top	13	16	18½		6	268¼	3.18.4
	Gallant	9	12	9¼		7	97¼	1.8.4½
	Driver	19	27	21		6	483	7.0.10½

Appendix VI

(see Chapter 6)

The method of sheathing, 1728 (VIa), was one of the systems used on ships going to the tropics, before the introduction of coppering.

The list of boats (VIb) is undated, but was probably connected with the 1719 establishment. The dimensions are detailed enough to allow one to reconstruct the exact shape of the boats, using the system of whole moulding (see Chapter 1).

Appendix VIa:
Method of sheathing ships, 24 January 1727/8

(PRO Adm 106/2507)

To cover the bottom all over with thick brown paper, and for preserving the sheathing from the worm, to fill the same with filling boards or nails, first taking care that all the iron work be examined and secured, and the seams and butts of the bottom are well shored up and caulked and payed with common tempered stuff as usual, and the bottoms all over with a good coat of soft tempered stuff, the seams and butts listed with spun hair, and that to cover the bottom with strong bag cap paper made out of old cordage, and not of the sort made of woollen rag, each sheet open to be about 22 inches by 18¾ inches, and each ream to weigh at least 45 pounds, scarphed with an inch over each other, and touched out at each corner, then, taking care that the sheathing board is sawed to a thickness, fayed, regularly edged, and to have two rows of holes bored in each butt to prevent splitting, and well dried with fire, and paid thick with boiling tar, and that covered with hair well beat, laid very smooth, and a good quality of tar on the hair, and then fastened to the side with sheathing nail about 2- inches asunder. And when the sheathing is caulked, to take down the edges and butts as smooth as possible, and then fill it with filling heads, or nails of 1¼ inches long, or so as not to have more than - inches in the plank, the heads to be about ⅜ inches asunder, taking great care the nails and bradds are regularly drove and well soaked up that so the bottom may be as smooth as the nature of the work will admit, and then be well breamed and graved.

Appendix VIb:
List of boats (NMM SPB/37a)

The established lengths and breadths of pinnaces and yawls for each rate, as is allowed by the board. Yawls allowed to First, Third and Fourth Rates, pinnace fashion. The Sixth Rates are allowed a yawl of 17 feet long and 6 feet broad and 2 feet 4 inches deep, Deal fashion, for weighing the anchor in the midships, but the yawls of 18 feet are built for sloops, and are sometimes deals and sometimes pinnaces.

	FIRST (ft ins)	THIRD (ft ins)	FOURTH (ft ins)	YAWLS First & Third (ft ins)	Fourth (ft ins)
PINNACES AND YAWLS					
Lengths from the fore side of the stem to the aft side of the post	35.0	31.0	30.0	24.0	23.0
Rake at the post at the top of the keel for pinnaces from 13 to 10ins; ditto yawls, 9½ to 7½					
No of oars	12	10	10	6	6
Breadths	6.3	6.2	6.2	5.8	5.7
A general rule for the rake of the stem the same as the depth–depth	2.9	2.7½	2.6½	2.5½	2.5
⊕ before the middle	1.10	1.10	1.0	1.4	1.4
Room and space	1.5	1.4	1.4	1.2	1.2
⊕ rising	0.2	0.2	0.1-	0.1-	0.1½
Transom broad	2.3	2.2	2.2	2.2	2.1½
Height of rising aft		2.1½	2.0	2.0	1.10
Height of rising afore		2.2	1.9	1.9	1.9
Fore side of the fore thwart from the fore side of the stem		2.2½			
Narrow of the bow 3 feet from the fore side of the stem		0.6½	0.7½	0.6	0.6
from the perpendicular aft		0.10½	0.9	0.9	0.9
Sheer in general ½ inch to every foot of the length of the boat, abating that to add, for the pinnaces at the stem, 4 inches less, but for yawls 2 inches less, or as discretion shall direct. A general rule for the height of the tuck – ½ between the height of the sheer and the bottom of the keel, and if deal fashion, 2 feet, from the top keel for 17 or 18 foot yawls					
Middle of the mainmast before the middle		1.5½			1.1
LONGBOATS					
Established length and breadth of longboats – length from the fore side of the stem to the aft side of the transom	100–36.0 90–35.0	80–32.0 70–31.0	60,50– 30.0		
Breadth	10.4	9.4	8.8		
Depth	4.1	3.11	3.8		
Sheers abaft	1.3	1.2	1.1		
afore	1.6	1.3	1.2		
Stems in general 2½ broader than the keel					
⊕ before the middle	1.6½	1.2	0.6		
Rake of the stem	4.0	3.3	3.0		
Rake of the post at the top of the keel	1.2	1.2	1.1		
Height of the tuck at the top of the keel	2.4	2.2	2.2		
Transom, at the aft side of the post	—	—	—		
Breadth of the post at the lower end	1.6	1.5	1.3		
at the tuck	0.11½	0.10	0.8½		
at the upper end	0.3½	0.3	0.2½		
Keel deep	0.8	0.7½	0.6½		
athwartships	0.4½	0.4	0.3¾		
Transom broad	5.4	4.6	3.9		
thick	0.3	0.2½	0.2		

	FIRST (ft ins)	THIRD (ft ins)	FOURTH (ft ins)
Half breadth of the floor in general at one third of the breadth			
No of thwarts	11	10	8
⊕ Rising	0.1½	0.1½	0.1½
aft	2.8	2.6	2.6
afore	2.6	2.1	2.0
Height of breadth at ⊕	2.9	2.6½	2.6
aft	4.6	4.3	4.2½
afore	4.6	4.4	3.11
Room and space	1.4	1.4½	1.5½
Narrowing of the bow at 2 feet 6 inches from the foreside of the stem	1.6	1.1½	1.2½
at 5 feet from the perpendicular aft	1.4	1.1	1.2½
Sweeps under the breadth at ⊕	2.3½	2.1½	2.1
at the transom	1.3	1.3	1.2
To sail with one mast, place the centre of the diameter abaft one third, or let the middle of the thwart be at the third			
Diameter of the mast hole (mast to rake 2 feet 4 inches)	0.7½	0.7	0.6
Breadth of the main thwart at the middle	1.2	1.1½	1.0
at the side	0.11	0.10½	0.9½
Fore side of the fore thwart from the fore side of the stem	3.9	3.1	2.10
Breadth of ditto	0.9	0.8	0.8
Aft side of the after thwart from the transom	6.7	6.1	6.0
Breadth at ditto	0.9½	0.8½	0.8

Appendix VII

(see Chapter 7)

The cabins of the *Victory*, 1642 (VIIa): 56 cabins are listed in all, far more than would be needed for the officers of a ship which at that time carried 260 men. It must therefore be presumed that many were used for petty officers, supernumeries and volunteers. In any case, it is clear that ships of this time were over-provided with cabins, and the scale of the problem faced by Pepys in 1673 is clear.

Appendix VIIb is the establishment of cabins, 1757. These rules remained broadly in force until well into the nineteenth century, though the very light structures of most of the cabins gradually became more permanent. The establishment confirmed that the captain's cabin should be on the quarterdeck, and the wardroom on the upper deck.

Appendix VIIa:
Cabins of the *Victory*, 1642 (BL Addit Mss 9297, f395)

6 cabins in the cuddy, complete.
The great cabin, complete.
1 standing cabin in the coach, complete.
4 standing cabins on the deck, complete.
6 cabins with shutters upon the poop, complete.
The store rooms alow, complete.
The cookroom, complete.
The gunroom complete, only no locks to the doors.
8 standing cabins under the half deck, complete.
3 hanging cabins and 3 lockers under the chief deck, complete.
9 standing cabins on the lower deck, complete, only 1 key wanting.
18 hanging cabins on the lower deck, complete.

Appendix VIIb:
The establishment of cabins, 1757 (PRO Adm 106/2508)

Accommodation proposed for officers on board ships of war in the Royal Navy, 24 June 1757

1. That all three-deck ships of 100, 90 and 80 guns be fitted with a great cabin, bedplace and steerage under the quarterdeck for the use of an admiral if a flagship, and for a captain when a private ship of war.
2. That there be parted off upon the quarterdeck two cabins, one for the first and the other for the second lieutenants, with a coach common to both before them, that may be extended forward as far as the mizzen mast if the ports will admit, which apartments are to be appropriated to the captain when a flagship, with the addition of an office for the secretary.
3. That there be a cabin for the carpenter and one for the boatswain under the forecastle, and cabin on the after platform for the purser and surgeon, and no other cabins to be on board any three-deck ship than those herein mentioned. And for the accommodation of such other officers as may by their rank be entitled thereto, the wardroom is to be parted off by a bulkhead across the ship, either just before or just abaft the mizzen mast as the ports will best admit, and from hence to the stern a space enclosed on each side (for three of four berths) by canvas hanging loosely before it like a curtain, or laced above and below with a parting in the middle of each berth to go in and out, and to roll up in the daytime when not wanted. And for such officers as were allowed cabins in the gunroom there is to be provided for them instead thereof canvas berths on each side of the gunroom, fitted in the same manner as proposed to be done in the wardroom above-mentioned, except that there is to be no deal bulkhead.
4. That the 74-, 70- and 60- gun ships be fitted with a great cabin, bedplace and coach upon the quarterdeck, or disposed that the bulkhead may be as far as possible from the sides of the ports, and that the said apartments do not extend beyond the mizzen masts.
5. That the carpenter and boatswain have a cabin provided for each of them under the forecastle, and one for the purser and one for the surgeon on each side as usual on the after platform. That no other cabins be allowed in either of these classes, and such as by their rank are entitled thereto, the wardroom and gunroom are to be fitted for their accommodation in the same manner as has been proposed on board the three-deck ships.
6. That ships of 50-guns built by the establishment of 1745 or of dimensions equal thereto, to be fitted with a great cabin, bedplace and coach for the captain upon the quarterdeck, cabins for the carpenter and boatswain under the forecastle, for the purser and surgeon on the after platform, and to have their wardroom and gunner's room prepared for the accommodation of such other officers as are entitled to cabins, in the same manner as is directed for the 74-, 70- and 60-gun ships.
7. And for such ships of 50-guns as are of inferior dimensions, or may be already fitted with a great cabin, bedplace and coach for the captain under the quarterdeck, they are to be continued as such, but as their main capstans are now made with a double barrell to heave on the upper deck, the foremost bulkhead of the coach is to be disposed of at

such a distance abaft as to give sufficient room for the sweep of the bars thereof, and to have no other bulkheads before it.
8. And as most of this class of ships, though small, have a roundhouse, there is to be parted off under the same a cabin for the first and second lieutenants (or master) with a passage in the middle between them to the stern lights, one cabin on each side before those for two other officers, and a small coach between them, to be common to all, and for such officers as were allowed cabins upon the gun deck, the gunroom is to be fitted with canvas berths for their accommodation, as directed on board of the foregoing classes.
9 & 10. [ships of 44 and 40 guns]
11 & 12. [ships of 36 to 20 guns]
13. [sloops]
14. That all bulkheads made use of in the several classes of ships before mentioned for parting off the great cabins, bed places, coaches, wardroom, and such other cabins and apartments therein proposed, with the cants prepared for receiving them, be fitted in such a manner that they may be taken down or disposed of out of the way of fighting the guns, or doing mischief by the enemy's shot, in the shortest time possible. That the said bulkheads be framed of deal panels, wrought strong, light and plain, and for the more convenient stowing of them out of the way when taken down, and the better to enable the panel part to bear the shock of the guns when they fire, none of them with the framing should exceed three feet from out to out, and those of them which are to form the bulkheads to be fitted with hinges and shifting pins through the joints thereof on the upper part, and below to fall on a rabbet prepared to receive them in the cant, with a batten before them, or small bolts, for their confinement in their places, from which state the said bulkheads may be taken quite away, or turned up under the beams, as shall be found most suitable to the service.

And as screen bulkheads are in general fitted with double sashes and double shutters, by which the whole bulkhead requires to be $7\frac{1}{2}$ or 8 inches thickness, is troublesome to take out, heavy and cumbersome to stow away when preparing for action, and with difficulty restored to their places again after it is over, that in future all screen bulkheads be fitted with a single sash and single shutter; that the height be so divided that the depth of the sash may be equal to the panel below, that both sash and shutter may be buried therein when down, by which the quantity of glass will be reduced, the cabin made warmer in winter, the panels, by being reduced more than a third, will become more portable, prepared at less expense and easier taken in and out.

That great care be taken that the cants for the several bulkheads herein allowed be placed as far as can be from the sides of the ports, and do not exceed 3 inches in thickness; that they be fitted in three parts, each side part of which to extend within 6 inches of the midship side of each door of the bulkhead to which they belong, that they may be taken away on any occasion of traversing the guns, caulking the decks & co, in the least time possible without affecting the middle parts.

Appendix VIII

(see Chapter 8)

Appendix VIIIa lists guns and gunner's stores for some of the ships of Sandwich's squadron at the bombardment of Algiers, 1661-62; it is a very complete list, with the figures added in manuscript on a printed form. Only the items which were actually carried have been copied – there are many others on the printed list which are not relevant to the actual ships listed. Some items (here enclosed in parentheses) were not for the use of the ships which carried them, but for the smaller ships of the squadron, which had small holds and were often unable to carry their full complement of shot and other items. The ships are fitted with their light, overseas armament.

Appendix VIIIb gives the weights of guns carried by the *Edgar*, 1679. This list is unusual in giving the exact weight of each individual weapon.

Appendix VIIIc is a list of gun types, weights and lengths, undated but presumably from 1692-93. This is linked to the list of ships' armaments in Appendix V of Volume I. It is a much more theoretical list than that in the next appendix, but it shows how much variation there could be, despite some efforts at standardisation.

Appendix VIIId is a list of ships' guns – undated, but, from internal evidence, from the years 1699-1702. It would appear that the returns were collect by the captains of the individual ships, which explains some of the discrepancies in the methods of listing. The second half of the list is a compilation from the first. The number of types of saker is particularly remarkable, but all other types show a considerable variety, before the establishment of 1703 began to enforce standardisation. This list confirms that the establishment of 1685, previously thought never to have been implemented, was actually put into practice; the *Vanguard* and *Suffolk* carry exactly the ordnance proposed in 1685, and that of the *Tiger* is similar but not identical.

Appendix VIIIe gives a list of iron guns, 1782. These guns are a little heavier than those listed by Falconer in 1753. When compared with the previous list, the effect of the eighteenth century policy of standardisation is evident.

Appendix, VIIIa:

List of guns and stores, 1661-62 (PRO WO 55/1650)

An account of all ordnance, carriages, powder, shot, match, muskets and other munition and habiliaments of war delivered out of the stores of His Majesty's Office of Ordnance, for the supply and furnishing of thirteen of His Majesty's ships, frigates and other vessels hereafter particularly named; with the remain and expense of the said provisions, together with the value of the said expense, viz:

		Royal James	*Swiftsure*	*Fairfax*	*Mary*	*Montague*
		brass	brass			
Brass and iron ordnance mounted for, viz.	Demi-cannon	23 f	20	20 incl 12 brass	20 iron	20 iron
	Culverin	25 f	28	4 brass	4 brass	4 brass
	Demi-culverin	22 incl 6 cutts	12	22incl 16 brass		26 incl 14 brass
	Saker			6 brass		
	Falcon					2 brass
	12-pound bullet				30 brass	
	3-pound bullet		2	2 bases & 4 chambers	2 brass	
Ship carriages, viz.	Demi-cannon	23	20	20	20	20
	Culverin	25	28	4	4	4
	Demi-culverin	22	14	22		26
	Saker		6			
	Falcon					2
	12-pound bullet				30	
	3-pound bullet		2		2	
Round shot for	Demi-cannon	1300	1150	1060	1070	1142
	Culverin	1560	1750	430	1120	285
	Demi-culverin	1000	1300	1530	(1300)	1262
	Saker			300		
	Falcon					60
	12-pound bullet	(160)			1660	
	8-pound bullet	(280)				
	3-pound bullet		100		100	

		Royal James	Swiftsure	Fairfax	Mary	Montague
Double headed shot for	Culverin	200	200	150	120	128
	Demi-culverin	130	150	150	150	146
	Saker			30		
The cases filled with musket shot for [other ammunition]	Demi-culverin	50	60	70	90	100
	Saker			20		
	Bace and bur	4 cwt	4 cwt	3cwt	3 cwt	5 cwt
	Bars of iron	400	300	250	250	270
	Hand granadoes		200	70	200	100

		Royal James la	Royal James sp	Swiftsure la	Swiftsure sp	Fairfax la	Fairfax sp	Mary la	Mary sp	Montague la	Montague sp
Ladles and sponges for	Demi-cannon	5	10	5	10	5	10	5	10	7	18
	Culverin	6	12	6	12	2	2	2	2	4	4
	Demi-culverin	5	9	4	8	6	10			8	18
	Saker					2	2				
	Falcon									1	1
	12-pound bullet							5	10		
	3-pound bullet			1	1			1	1		

		Royal James	Swiftsure	Fairfax	Mary	Montague
	Ladle staves	18	18	12	27	24
Cases of wood for cartridges for	Demi-cannon	35	30	30	30	30
	Culverin	38	40	6	50	10
	Demi-culverin	27	20	34		54
	Saker			10		
	Falcon					2
	3-pound bullet		3		3	
	Funnels of plate	3	3	3	3	4
[Small arms and ancillary equipment]	Corn powder (barrels)	480	478-55	250	280	280
	Match	31 lbs	20 lbs	16 lbs	16½ lbs	24 lbs 4 oz
	Matchlock muskets	50	50	40	40	45
	Snaphance muskets	30	30	30	30	32
	Musket rods	3 doz	3 doz	2 doz	2 doz	
	Bandoliers (rolls)	80	80	70	70	100
	Halberds	6	6			
	Blunderbusses	12	12	8	6	8
	Pistols (pairs)	20	20	15	12	15
	Pistol bullet (cwt)	1	1	1	1	1
	Long pikes	40	40	30	30	30
	Short pikes	40	40	30	30	40
	Bills	20	20	12	12	12
	Hatchets	40	40	30	30	40
	Swords	40	40	40	30	100
	Hangers	40	40	30	40	
	Musket shot (cwt)	7	7	6	16	10
	Sheet lead (cwt. lbs)	3.18	3.0	1.40	1.50	2.52
	Crows of iron	80	70	52	56	56
	Tackle hooks (pairs)	80	12	60	15	22
	Ladle hooks (pairs)	40	40	30	30	50
	Linch pins (pairs)	60	60	40	40	170
	Spikes	200	200	150	150	290
	Forelockeys (pairs)	100	100	100	40	100
	Sledges	3	2	1	1	1
	Great melt ladle	2	2	1	1	1
	Small	4	4	3	3	3
	Nails of sorts	8000	8000	8000	5000	9000
	Beds	82	84	60	66	78
	Coins	146	140	120	126	154
	Trucks (pairs)	8	8	6	6	8
	Axletrees	10	10	12	8	8
	Tompions	700	600	500	500	1000
	Pulleys great (pairs)	80	24	84	15	24
	Pulleys small (pairs)	12	40	54	30	30
	Heads and rammers (pairs)	12	12	12	12	12
	Formers	10	10	8	8	8
	Budge barrels	4	3	3	2	4
	Tanned hides	8	9	6	6	8
	Sheep skins	36	60	30	24	36
	Baskets	24	36	30	18	32
	Spare hoops	4	3	400	3	
	Canvas	1327	1790	943	700	500
	Paper royal (sheets)	10	31	9	11	6
	Oil (gallons)	4	6	3	3	6

	Royal James	Swiftsure	Fairfax	Mary	Montague
Tallow (cwt)	1	1	1	1	2
Starch (lbs)	8	32	12	16	12
Needles (dozen)	18	46	14	27	12
Thread (lbs)	18	74	16	27	12
Lanterns ordinary	8	8	6	6	12
Dark	2	2	1	1	1
Moscovia lights	4	4	3	4	5
Wad hooks	9	10	17	8	11
Hand crow levers	70	60	50	50	50
Rope sponges	70	60	52	50	56
Gunner's horns	62	64	52	54	52
Priming irons	40	40	20	20	52
Linstocks	50	40	20	20	40
Marlin (lbs)	50	150	36	136	72
Twine (lbs)	20	54	14	37	12
Wire (lbs)	8	29	15	21	6
Handscrews	2	2	1	1	1
Tarred rope for (cwt.lbs):					
Breeching	4.37	2.68	3.30	1.50	2.52
Tackles	10.72	4.130	6.52	3.100	4.100
Port ropes			1.0		3.0
Port tackles	1.4	2.0	2.0	2.0	2.0
Junk (lbs)		12			12
Trunks		24	8	24	12
Pikes		15	5	12	7
Cork		50 lbs	40 lbs	8 bails	

Appendix VIIIb:
Edgar's guns, 1679 (PRO WO 55/1715)

The length and weight of the ships' guns laid up in the month of July [1679]

Edgar
(cwt.qr.lbs)

Demi-cannon of 10 feet, fortified	Culverin of 10 feet, fortified	Demi-culverin of 10 feet, fortified
50.3.14	44.2.12	32.1.0
50.2.7	44.1.22	31.0.7
51.2.25	44.2.2	*of 8½ feet*
51.3.3	44.2.24	24.2.6
of 9½ feet	*of 9 feet*	25.1.20
50.0.12	37.0.0	25.1.18
46.2.22	36.2.7	21.1.16
46.0.22	35.0.0	26.2.2
of 9 feet	37.0.7	26.2.6
46.0.12	38.1.7	*of 8 feet*
44.3.27	36.2.0	20.1.21
46.0.5	36.3.4	23.3.14
45.3.22	37.2.26	24.1.0
46.0.22	36.2.25	21.1.14
46.1.12	36.3.25	21.1.0
44.3.12	38.0.7	24.0.4
46.0.12	36.2.4	19.2.21
46.0.12	37.1.18	21.0.1
46.2.8	36.2.7	*of 6 feet cutts*
45.1.12	36.3.2	17.0.8
46.0.1	37.1.7	16.1.14
43.3.14	37.3.18	14.1.25
46.3.16	36.2.27	14.2.21
46.1.4	37.3.7	Demi-cannon - 24 fortified
48.0.15	39.1.0	Culverin – 28 fortified
of 8½ feet	*of 8½ feet*	Demi-culverin – 20 incl 4 cutts
41.0.14	36.2.7	
	34.3.7	
	of 8 feet	
	34.2.6	
	33.1.0	

Appendix VIIIc:

List of gun types *c*1692 (BL Addit Mss 9289)

A compilation of the weights of iron ordnance according to their several natures and lengths hereafter mentioned.

	11	10½	10	9½	9	8½	8	7½	7	6½	6	5½	5	4½	4
Cannon-of-7	67	64	63	62	60										
Demi-cannon	59	57	55	53	49	46									
24-pounder	54	51	48	46	42	40									
Culverin		52	48	45	41	39	36	32							
12-pounder		40	38	36	34	32	30	28							
Demi-culverin			33	32	29	28	26	24	21	20	17	15½	13	11	
8-pounder						25	22	20	18						
6-pounder			29	27	26	24	21	18	17	14	13				
Saker			28	25	23	22	19	18	16	12	11	9	8		
Minion				21	20	18	16	14	10	9		7	6	5	
3-pounder									7		6	5	4	3½	

[The headings give the gun lengths in feet; the figures in the table are for gun weights in cwt.]

Appendix VIIId:

List of ships' guns c1699-1702 (BL Addit Mss 9303, ff40-43,35)

Establishment of the number, nature, wt and co of the guns lately employed on the respective ships hereafter named.

SHIPS' NAMES	ORDNANCE On what deck placed	Names of	No of	Wt of ore of the nature of (cwt.qrs.lbs)	Length (ft. ins)	Shot diam (ins)	wt (lbs. ozs)
SECOND RATES							
Association (1697)	Gun deck	Demi-cannon	22	54.1.8	10.6	6⅛	32
	Gun deck	Culverin	2	52.0.0	11.6	5⅛	18
	Middle deck	Whole cutt	26	43.0.0	10.0	5⅛	18
	Quarterdeck & forecastle	Saker	12	16.1.2	7.6	3⅜	5¼
	Upper deck	Saker	24	25.0.0	9.0	3⅜	5¼
	Poop	Saker	2	8.13.12	6.6	2⅞	3
			90				
Namur	Gun deck	Demi-cannon	24	55.0.5	9.6		32
	Gun deck	Whole cutt	2	53.1.20	9.0		18
	Middle deck	Whole cutt	26	53.1.20	9.0		18
	Upper deck	Saker	22	30.0.7	8.6		5.11
	Forecastle & quarterdeck	Saker	12	30.0.7	8.6		5.11
	Poop	Saker	4	30.0.7	8.6		5.11
			90				
Vanguard	Gundeck	Demi-cannon	22	from 50 to 56	9.6	6¼	32
	Middle deck	Culverin	30	38 to 43	9.6	5¼	18
	Upper deck, quarterdeck & forecastle	Saker	38	16 to 24	7 to 9½	3½	5½
	Poop	3-pdrs	2	5 to 5½	5.6	2¾	3
			92				

SHIPS' NAMES	ORDNANCE On what deck placed	Names of	No. of	Wt of ore of the nature of (cwt.qrs.lbs)	Length (ft. ins)	Shot dia (ins.)	wt (lbs ozs)
THIRD RATES							
Ranelagh (1697)	Gun deck	Demi-cannon	22	54 to 50	9.6	$6\frac{1}{4}$	32
and	Middle deck	Whole culverin	26	49 to 38	9.0	$5\frac{1}{4}$	18
Somerset (1698),	Upper deck	6-pdr	20	26 to 13	7.6	$3\frac{1}{2}$	6
three-deckers	Quarterdeck	3-pdr	4	7	6.0	$2\frac{3}{4}$	3
of 80 guns			72				
Newark (1695),	Gun deck	Demi-cannon	24	50 to 53	9.6	$6\frac{1}{4}$	32
two-decker of	Upper deck	Culverin	32	38 to 43	9.6	$5\frac{1}{4}$	18
80 guns	Quarterdeck & forecastle	Saker	20	17 to 23	8 to $9\frac{1}{2}$	$3\frac{1}{2}$	$5\frac{1}{2}$
	Poop	3-pdr	4	5 to 6	5.6	$2\frac{3}{4}$	3
			80				
Bedford (1698)	Gun deck	24-pdr	22				
and	Gun deck	Culverin	4				
Orford (1698)	Upper deck	Demi-culverin	26				
of 70 guns	Quarterdeck	Saker	12				
	Poop	3 pdr	4				
			68				
Suffolk (1680)	Gun deck	Demi-cannon	22				
of 70 guns	Gun deck	Culverin	4				
	Upper deck	12-pdr	26				
	Quarterdeck & forecastle	Saker	14				
	Poop	3-pdr	4				
			70				
Nassau (1699)	Gun deck	24-pdr	26				
of 70 guns	Upper deck	Demi-culverin	24				
	Quarterdeck & forecastle	Saker	16				
	Poop	Minion	4				
			70				
Yarmouth (1694)	Gun deck	24-pdr	6		10.0		
of 70 guns	Gun deck	24-pdr	20		9.6		
	Upper deck	Demi-culverin	4		10.0		
	Upper deck	Demi-culverin	12		9.6		
	Upper deck	Demi-culverin	10		9.0		
	Forecastle & quarterdeck	Saker	14		10.0		
	Poop	3-pdr	2		6.6		
	Poop	3-pdr	2		6.0		
			70				
FOURTH RATES							
Pembroke (1694)	Gun deck	24-pdr	22				
of 60 guns	Upper deck	Demi-culverin	24				
	Quarterdeck	Saker	10				
	Poop	3-pdr	4				
			60				
Bristol (RB 1693)	Gun deck	Whole cutt	22	36.0.0	9.4	$5\frac{1}{8}$	18
of 50 guns	Upper deck	8-pdr	20	26.0.0	8.4	4	8
	Quarterdeck	Minion	10	11.0.0	7.0	3	4
			52				

SHIPS' NAMES	ORDNANCE On what deck placed	Names of	No. of	Wt of ore of the nature of (cwt.qrs.lbs)	Length (ft. ins)	Shot dia (ins.)	wt (lbs ozs)
Rochester (1693) of 50 guns	Gun deck	12-pdr	18	34.3.0	9.0	$4\frac{4}{10}$	12
	Upper deck	Demi-culverin	20	21.2.0	8.0	4	9
	Quarterdeck	Saker	8	10.0.0	6.0	$3\frac{1}{2}$	$5\frac{1}{4}$
			46				
Weymouth (1693) of 50 guns	Gun deck	12-pdr	18	35 to 33	9.0	$4\frac{1}{2}$	12
	Upper deck	6-pdr	18	22 to 18	8.6	$3\frac{1}{2}$	6
	Quarterdeck	Minion	8	12 to $9\frac{1}{2}$	6.0	$3\frac{1}{4}$	4
			44				
Winchester (1698) of 50 guns	Gun deck	Whole cutt	18	34.1.20	8.9	5	18
	Upper deck	8-pdr	20	23.1.14	8.0	$3\frac{3}{4}$	8
	Quarterdeck	Minion	8	9.2.26	6.4	3	4
			46				
Tiger (RB 1681) of 50 guns	Gun deck	Demi-culverin	18 to 1	30.0.17 19.0.12	10.0 7.0	4	9
	Upper deck	Saker	18	21.2.13 to 16.2.24	8.0 7.6	$3\frac{1}{2}$	5.6
	Quarterdeck	Saker cutt	6	8.3.14 to 8.0.2	5.6	$3\frac{1}{2}$	5.6
			42				

RB=rebuilt

Names	Wt of ore (cwt. qrs. lbs)	Length (ft. ins)	Diam (ins)	Wt. (lbs.ozs)
Cannon-of-7	65.0.0	9.6	7	$48.3\frac{3}{4}$
	60.2.10	9.0	$6\frac{3}{4}$	42.0
	59 to 61	9.0	$6\frac{3}{4}$	42.0
	$70\frac{3}{8}$ to 56	11 to 9		
Demi-cannon	55.0.5	9.6		32.0
	54.1.0	10.6	$6\frac{1}{8}$	32.0
	54.0.0	10.0	$6\frac{1}{8}$	32.0
	54.0.0	9.6	6	30.6
	54 to 50	9.6	$6\frac{1}{4}$	32.0
24-pounder	46.0.19	10.9	$5\frac{5}{8}$	24.0
	49.3.27	10.7	$5\frac{1}{2}$	24.0
	51 to 52	10.0		24.0
	47 to 50	9.6		24.0
	45 to 47 & 48	9.6	$5\frac{1}{2}$	24.0
	$57\frac{1}{8}$ to $37\frac{1}{7}$	from $11\frac{1}{2}$-$9\frac{1}{2}$		
Whole culverin	42.0.0	9.6		
	40.0.0	9.0		
	34.1.20	8.9	5	18.0
	36.0.0	9.4	$5\frac{1}{8}$	18.0
	49 to 38	9.0	$5\frac{1}{4}$	18.0
	40 to 42	9.6		18.0
	53.1.20	9.0		18.0
	47.2.15	11.0	$5\frac{1}{8}$	18.0
	44.3.26	10.0	$5\frac{1}{8}$	18.0
	50.0.0	11.0	$5\frac{1}{8}$	18.0
	48.0.0	10.6	$5\frac{1}{8}$	18.0
	52.0.0	11.6	$5\frac{1}{8}$	18.0
	43.0.0	10.0	$5\frac{1}{8}$	18.0
	45 to 51	11.10	$5\frac{1}{4}$	18.0
12-pounder	32.0.0	9.0	$4\frac{1}{2}$	12.0
	34.3.0	9.0	$4\frac{4}{10}$	12.00
	$36\frac{10}{112}$ to $19\frac{82}{112}$	$9\frac{1}{2}$ to 8		

Names	Wt of ore (cwt.qrs.lbs)	Length (ft.ins)	Diam (ins)	Wt. (lbs.ozs)	Names	Wt of ore (cwt.qrs.lbs)	Length (ft.ins)	Diam (ins)	Wt. (lbs.ozs)
Demi-culverin	21.2.0	8.0	4	9.0	Saker	28 to 16	10.0		5.11
	32.0.17	10.0	4	9.0		16.2.26	7.6	$3\frac{1}{2}$	5.6
	19.0.12	7.0	4	9.0		16.2.4	7.9	$3\frac{1}{2}$	6.0
	34.0.22	9.10	$4\frac{5}{8}$	9.0		16.1.12	7.6	$3\frac{3}{8}$	6.4
	28.2.10	9.10	$4\frac{5}{8}$	9.0	Saker light	16.0.0	7.9	$3\frac{1}{2}$	5.4
	27 to 31	9.0		9.0		16.0.0	7.0		
	33.2.0	10.0		9.0		16 to 15	$8\frac{1}{2}$ to 7	$3\frac{1}{4}$	5.8
	29 to 31	9.6		9.0		10.0.0	6.0	$3\frac{1}{2}$	5.4
	29 to 32	9.0		9.0	Saker cutts	8.3.14	5.6	$3\frac{1}{2}$	5.6
	34.3.5	10.0	$4\frac{1}{4}$	9.0		8.0.2	5.6	$3\frac{1}{2}$	5.6
	14.2.10	6.0	$4\frac{1}{4}$	9.0		8.3.12	6.6	$2\frac{7}{8}$	3.0
	29.0.0	9.0	$4\frac{1}{4}$	9.0		19 to $14\frac{5}{8}$	9 to 8		
	24 to 26	$8\frac{1}{2}$ chase no 2	4	9.0	Minion	11.0.0	7.0	3	4.0
						9.2.26	6.4	3	4.0
8-pounder	26.0.0	8.4	4	8.0		7.0.0	6.0	3	4.0
	23.1.4	8.0	$3\frac{3}{4}$	8.0	3-pounder	10.2.20	6.6		3.0
6-pounder	22 to 18	8.6	$3\frac{1}{2}$	6.0		8.2.22	6.6		3.0
	23 to 13	7.6	$3\frac{1}{2}$	6.0		7.0.0	6.0	$2\frac{3}{4}$	3.0
	14 to 20	9.0		6.0		7.0.0	5.10	$2\frac{3}{4}$	3.0
	26.0.0	9.0	$3\frac{1}{2}$	6.0		6.2.0	6.0	$2\frac{7}{8}$	3.0
	18.0.0	8.0	$3\frac{1}{2}$	6.0		6.0.0	6.0		3.0
Saker	30.0.7	8.6		5.11		6.0.0	5.6	$2\frac{3}{4}$	3.0
	25.0.0	9.0	$3\frac{3}{8}$	5.4		5.0.0	5.0		
	22.0.0	8.6							
	21.2.13	8.0	$3\frac{1}{2}$	5.6					

Appendix VIIIe:

Artillery memorandum, by Captain Robert Lawson, Royal Regiment of Artillery, 1782 (NMM GUN/12)

Lengths, weights and calibres of iron guns used in the Royal Navy

Nature of guns	Length (ft)	Weight (cwt.qrs.lbs)	Calibre of bore (ins)	Windage (ins)	Nature of guns	Length	Weight	Calibre of bore	Windage
42-pdr	$9\frac{1}{2}$	65.0.0	7.03	0.35	9-pdr	8	26.2.0	4.21	0.21
	10	58.0.0				$7\frac{1}{2}$	24.2.0		
32-pdr	$9\frac{1}{2}$	55.0.0	6.42	0.32		7	23.0.0		
	10	52.0.0				9	24.0.0		
24-pdr	$9\frac{1}{2}$	49.0.0	5.83	0.29		$8\frac{1}{2}$	23.0.0		
	9	47.0.0				8	22.0.0		
18-pdr	$9\frac{1}{2}$	42.0.0	5.29	0.26	6-pdr	$7\frac{1}{2}$	20.2.0	3.66	0.18
	9	40.0.0				7	19.0.0		
	$8\frac{1}{2}$	34.0.0				$6\frac{1}{2}$	18.0.0		
12-pdr	9	32.0.0	4.63	0.23		6	12.1.0		
	$8\frac{1}{2}$	31.2.0			4-pdr	$5\frac{1}{2}$	11.1.0	3.21	0.17
	8	28.2.0			3-pdr	$4\frac{1}{2}$	7.1.0	2.91	0.14
	$9\frac{1}{2}$	30.1.0			$\frac{1}{2}$-pdr or swivel	3	1.1.25	1.58	0.06
	9	29.0.0							
	$8\frac{1}{2}$	27.2.0							

Notes

Note: Only titles not given in the Bibliography (in Volume I) are quoted in full.

CHAPTER 1

1. Pepys, *Diary*, 22/7/1664; NRS *Catalogue*, Vol I, p77
2. Bushnell, *The Compleat Shipwright*, 1664
3. CSPD, 16/1/1664–5
4. NRS *Naval Administration*, p204
5. Holland, *Ships of British Oak*, p88
6. BL Addit Mss 9328, f313
7. Deane, *Doctrine of Naval Architecture*, p52
8. PRO Adm 106/3070–1, passim
9. NMM Draught No 645
10. Corbett, *Drake and the Tudor Navy*, Vol I, p349
11. Deane, op cit, p71
12. SNR Occasional Publications No 6, *A Treatise on Shipbuilding and a Treatise on Rigging written about 1625*
13. Deane, op cit, p60–1
14. NRS *Pett*, page xciii
15. Pepys, *Diary*, 19/6/1667
16. *The Double Bottom, or Twin Hulled Ship of Sir William Petty*, ed Marquis of Landsdowne, Roxburghe Club, 1931
17. BL Addit Mss 2754
18. Pepysian Library Sea Mss 2873, f240
19. Pepysian Library Sea Mss 1074
20. See the author's introduction to Deane's *Doctrine of Naval Architecture*, pp22–5, for further explanation
21. John Wallis, *Letter to Sir Robert Murray*, 1684
22. Sutherland, *The Shipbuilder's Assistant*, 1711
23. Baugh, *British Naval Administration in the Age of Walpole*, p253
24. NRS *Naval Administration*, p208
25. Murray, *A Treatise on Shipbuilding and Navigation*, 1750 edition, p145
26. Ibid
27. Rees, *The Cyclopaedia* (article on 'Naval Architecture'), 1819
28. NRS *Barham*, Vol I, p303
29. See Collinge, *Navy Board Officials, 1660–1832*, for lists of officials and general comment
30. See introduction to the Adlard Coles edition of Chapman's *Architectura Navalis Mercatoria*
31. See article by A W Johns in *Transactions of the Institution of Naval Architects*, 1910, pp28–40
32. Sharp, *Memoirs of the Life and Services of Sir William Symonds*, p108n
33. Deane, op cit, p63

CHAPTER 2

1. Pool, *Navy Board Contracts*, passim
2. BL Addit Mss 22183
3. Pepysian Library Sea Mss 2266, f108
4. Holland, op cit, p191
5. For an example, see NRS *Naval Administration*, pp300–1
6. Albion, *Forests and Sea Power*, passim
7. PRO Adm 106/2509, 10/6/1787
8. See the contract for the *Warspite* in Deane's *Doctrine of Naval Architecture*, Appendix, pp116–20
9. Deane, op cit, p54
10. *International Journal of Nautical Archeology*, 7/1, pp29–58, article by Colin Martin on the *Darmouth*
11. See, for example, the contracts for the *Dublin* class in PRO Adm 106/3072

12. PRO Adm 106/3551, 14/10/1715
13. Pool, op cit, p90; PRO Adm 106/2508, 16/11/1773
14. Grey, *Debates in the House of Commons*, Vol IV, p125
15. Admiralty Library Mss 121, 6/10/1710
16. PRO Adm 106/3551, 14/10/1715
17. PRO Adm 106/2508, 7/1/1771
18. Deane, op cit, p58–9
19. PRO Adm 106/3551, 14/10/1715
20. PRO Adm 106/3070–1, passim
21. Seppings, *On a New Principle, & co*, (paper read before the Royal Society, 10/3/1814), p9
22. Ibid, p4
23. Ibid, p8
24. Seppings, *On the Circular Sterns of Ships of War*, 1822, Appendix

CHAPTER 3

1. J H Plumb, *The Growth of Political Stability in England*, p15
2. See, for example, NRS *Catalogue*, Vol IV, pp519–20
3. NRS *Holland's Discourses of the Navy*, pp33–4
4. NRS *Naval Minutes*, p343
5. NRS *Catalogue*, Vol IV, p520
6. NMM POR/B2, 13/4/1679
7. PRO Adm 106/2507, 4/11/1700
8. Quoted in *MM* III, pp20–1
9. NRS *Queen Anne's Navy*, p87
10. PRO Adm 106/2088, 18/8/1796
11. Quoted in full in Bugler, *HMS Victory: Building, Restoration and Repair*, pp248–50
12. See *MM* X, pp183–6, article by L G Carr Laughton
13. PRO Adm 106/2089, 16/7/1801
14. *MM* X, p205

CHAPTER 4

Note: This chapter and the next one are not intended to be exhaustive treatments of a very complex subject, and the reader is referred to James Lees, *The Masting and Rigging of English Ships of War, 1625–1860*, and also to the many contemporary works on rigging which are available in facsimile editions, by writers such as Burney, Deane, Falconer, Fincham, D'Arcy Lever, Rees, Steel and Nares. Most of these are listed in the Bibliography of the first volume.

1. NRS *Catalogue*, Vol IV, p414
2. Falconer, *Dictionary of the Marine*, p190
3. R C Anderson, *Seventeenth Century Rigging*, pp1–2
4. Falconer, op cit, p190
5. Burney, *New Universal Dictionary of the Marine*, p264
6. Ibid
7. Deane, op cit, rigging diagrams, pp92–102
8. PRO Adm 106/2508, 5/7/1779
9. Deane, op cit, p82, is the earliest mention
10. See Albion, op cit, Ch 7; however, Albion's view of the mast crisis requires some modification, according to information supplied to the author by Dr R J B Knight of the National Maritime Museum
11. NRS *Queen Anne's Navy*, p72
12. James Lees, *The Masting and Rigging of English Ships of War, 1625–1860*, 1979, p184
13. NMM Draughts Nos 7729–30

Abbreviations in notes
Addit Mss: British Library Additional Manuscripts
ADM: Admiralty papers in the National Maritime Museum
Adm: Admiralty papers in the Public Record Office
BL: British Library
CSPD: Calendar of State Papers, Domestic
MM: The Mariner's Mirror
NMM: National Maritime Museum
NRS: Navy Records Society (for full titles, see Bibliography in Volume I)
PRO: Public Record Office
SNR: Society for Nautical Research

CHAPTER 5

1. Deane, op cit, p84
2. SNR Occasional Publications No 3, *The Lengths of Masts and Yards, etc, 1640*, p21
3. NMM RUSI/NM/86
4. See K R Gilbert, *The Portsmouth Blockmaking Machinery*, 1965
5. David Steel, *The Elements of Sailmaking, Mastmaking and Rigging*, reprinted 1932, p68
6. NRS *Naval Administration*, p275; Baugh, op cit, p309
7. SNR Occasional Publications No 3, *The Lengths of Masts and Yards, etc, 1640*, pp32-5
8. Steel, op cit, p110
9. Ibid, p109
10. R C Anderson, op cit, p136
11. Rees, op cit, Plate V
12. Edward Hayward, *The Sizes and Lengths of Rigging*, 1656, pp55-7
13. NMM RCE/3
14. PRO Adm 106/2507, 14/2/1727
15. PRO Adm 106/3551, 16/3/1746
16. Lees, op cit, pp115-6
17. Spinney, *Rodney*, p187

CHAPTER 6

1. Burney, op cit, p15
2. Deane, op cit, p106; Burney, op cit, p14
3. Burney, op cit, p64
4. The earliest example of a drumhead capstan is to be found in the prints of the first *Britannia* in Coronelli's *Gli Argonauti*; Deane's *Doctrine of Naval Architecture*, and the well known model of the *Prince* of 1670, both show the older type
5. *MM* 58, pp41-65, article by J H Harland, 'The Early History of the Steering Wheel'
6. PRO Adm 106/3079-80, passim
7. *Model Shipwright*, No 17, p96, article by Robert Gardiner on 'Fittings for Wooden Warships'
8. *MM* 59, pp298-309, article by R J B Knight on 'The Introduction of Copper Sheathing into the Royal Navy, 1779-86'
9. NRS *The Life and Works of Sir Henry Mainwaring*, p203
10. Pamphlet by Robert Ledingham, in British Library, 816 m. 7
11. *Model Shipwright*, No 17, p100
12. Much of the information for this section comes from W E May, *The Boats of Men of War* (NMM Maritime Monographs and Reports No 15), and from *Model Shipwright*, No 19, 'Fittings for Wooden Warships, Part II: Boats'
13. Falconer, op cit, p39
14. PRO Adm 106/2508, 17/9/1771
15. Ibid, 6/10/1771

CHAPTER 7

1. NRS *Queen Anne's Navy*, p364; Burney, op cit, p384
2. Rees, op cit, Plate IV
3. Burney, op cit, p337
4. Falconer, op cit, p143
5. See *Ingrid and Other Studies*, NMM Maritime Monographs and Reports, No 36, pp125-140, article by John Munday, 'Heads and Tails: The Necessary Seating'
6. This section is based on information in NRS *Mainwaring, Boteler, Monson*, etc, but it is not always clear what their descriptions mean, and there are many contradictions.
7. PRO Adm 95/12
8. Ned Ward, *Wooden World Dissected*, p7
9. NRS *Catalogue*, Vol I, pp190-2
10. For the controversy, see *MM* 65, p181
11. NMM Draughts No 4602, *Cumberland*
12. Riksarkivet, Copenhagen, drawing D3579
13. PRO Adm 95/12
14. NRS *Five Naval Journals*, Vol XCI, ed Thursfield, p11
15. Ned Ward, op cit, p88
16. Ibid, p69
17. NRS *Mainwaring*, pp131-2
18. Ibid, p132
19. PRO Adm 106/2508

CHAPTER 8

1. See H C Tomkinson, *Guns and Government – The Ordnance Office under the Later Stuarts*, passim
2. NRS *Dutch War*, Vol I, pp109, 113-4, 119
3. Largely based on 'Fittings for Wooden Warships Part 3: Guns' by Robert Gardiner in *Model Shipwright*, No 20, pp338-53
4. *International Journal of Nautical Archaeology*, 9/4, p341, article by D J Lyon on 'The Goodwins Wreck'
5. 'Fittings for Wooden Warships, Part 3: Guns', loc cit; gun Weights are listed in Falconer, op cit, p66
6. NRS *Dutch War*, Vol III, pp188-9
7. PRO 30/37/8
8. Pepysian Library Sea Mss 2266, ff110-3
9. See Appendix VIII
10. Burney, op cit, pp69, 77
11. See Robertson, *The Evolution of Naval Armament*, Ch VI, for the reasons for the survival of the truck carriage
12. See R F Johnson, *The Royal George*, 1971
13. NMM GUN/12
14. Ibid

INDEX